OFFICE FOR
NATIONAL STATISTICS

Infant Feeding in Asian Families

Early Feeding Practices and Growth

A survey carried out in England by
the Social Survey Division of the Office
for National Statistics on behalf of the
Department of Health

Margaret Thomas and Vivienne Avery

London: The Stationery Office

ISBN 0 11 691693 1

Contents

Foreword

Foreword from the Parliamentary Under Secretary of State for Health (Lords):

This Report is the outcome of a successful collaboration between the Department of Health and the Office for National Statistics in an important and topical area of nutrition. It is the first ever nationally representative study of infant feeding practices among mothers from the Asian communities.

Dietary practices, particularly breastfeeding, are not only fundamentally important for the growth and development of the infant but also lay the foundations for later life. The results from this survey will therefore provide a sound basis for understanding how and why mothers in the

Asian communities adopt their infant feeding practices and for developing future food and health policies appropriate to these groups.

This Report will be of particular relevance to the planners of health care and for nurses, midwives and health visitors and those voluntary organisations who work with mothers in the Asian communities.

I warmly welcome this Report and thank all the respondents who took part.

Julia Cumberledge.

BARONESS CUMBERLEDGE

Acknowledgements

We would like to thank everyone who helped to make this survey a success. A large scale social survey relies on team work and we were supported by colleagues in the Social Survey Division of ONS who carried out the sampling, fieldwork and computing. Our thanks go to Jil Matheson for her support and encouragement, and Hazel Green for her work on the feasibility study. Particular thanks are due to the interviewers and interpreters who showed such commitment to the survey.

We would also like to thank our colleagues at the Department of Health, in particular Ms. V Bahl, Dr. P Clarke, Dr. S Lader, Ms. A Roberts, Mr. R Wenlock for their advice, which was much appreciated; also Dr. T Cole of the Medical Research Council Dunn Nutrition Unit for advising us on the analysis of the measurement data.

The Department of Health is grateful for advice from Ms. L Ahmet, Ms. M Bibi, Ms. V Buxton, Mr. H Dhaliwal, Ms. J Douglas, Dr. M Duggan, Dr. B Mayall, Ms. S Patel, Dr. A Thomas, Ms. M Remtulla, Ms K Shukla, Dr. D Skuse about the design of this study either given individually or through a meeting in July 1993.

Most important of all, we would like to thank the families who participated in the survey, without their co-operation it would not have been possible.

Definitions used in the survey

Ethnicity
Ethnic origin was defined by mothers themselves, when asked by interviewers, using a card, to which ethnic group they considered they belonged (see Appendix A, section 1.1)

Other definitions
A number of terms defined for the infant feeding surveys since 1975 are used throughout this report. The definitions are:

Incidence of breastfeeding – the proportion of babies who were ever breastfed including all babies who were put to the breast at all, even if this was on one occasion only.

Prevalence of breastfeeding – the proportion of all babies who were wholly or partially breastfed at specified ages.

Duration of breastfeeding – the length of time for which breastfeeding continued at all, regardless of when bottles or foods other than milk were introduced.

Notes to tables

The following conventions have been used in the tables:

– No cases

0 Less than 0.5%

[ ] The numbers inside the square brackets are the actual number of observations when the total number of cases, that is the base, is less than 50

The percentages may not add to 100% because of rounding.

The tables exclude respondents for whom information is missing for the items analysed. This means that the number of cases in a category may vary slightly from table to table.

The data shown in all tables have been weighted to take account of sub-sampling Pakistani babies for part of the sampling period (see Appendix A Methodology and Response).

The age of babies at each stage of interviewing is referred to in the tables as 9 weeks (stage 1), 5 months (stage 2), 9 months (stage 3), 15 months (stage 4). These are average ages.

All differences mentioned in the text have been found to be statistically significant at the 95% confidence level.

The data on which diagrams are based are shown in corresponding tables at the end of the same chapter.

Infant Feeding in Asian Families

Introduction

This report presents the findings of a survey of Infant Feeding Practices in Asian families living in England. The survey was carried out by the Social Survey Division of the Office for National Statistics (ONS) for the Department of Health. The Department of Health has commissioned national surveys of infant feeding practices every five years since 1975[1] but the samples have never included sufficient numbers to allow for separate analyses of any ethnic minority groups. This is a survey of babies born to mothers, who defined themselves as being of Bangladeshi, Indian or Pakistani origin, living in England. The survey also includes a sample of babies born to White mothers living in the same geographical areas as the Asian mothers. The White sample is not nationally representative of the White population. Another survey of a sample of babies chosen to be nationally representative has recently been completed and will be published in 1997.[2]

The National Study of Health and Growth showed that at 5 years of age, school children from Asian groups of the Indian subcontinent were shorter than other children.[3] Other small local studies[4,5,6,7] on feeding and weaning practices carried out in England, and anecdotal evidence provided by health professionals working with the Asian community, have suggested that babies born to mothers of Bangladeshi, Indian and Pakistani origin living in England, may not have been achieving their full growth potential and this may be due in part to early feeding practices. The present survey was designed to examine a nationally representative group of infants from these communities to find out how they are being fed and what influences their mothers' choices. It also seeks to establish the patterns of growth and to assess whether Asian babies are growing more slowly in the early months of life and whether this is related to how they are being fed.

The sample for this survey was selected to be representative of all babies born to mothers of Bangladeshi, Indian and Pakistani origin living in England and to provide separate results for each group. The 41 local authority areas selected for the sample covered 95% of the Asian population at the time of the 1991 Census and include areas with the highest density of Asians and those with a lower density. Babies born in the relevant local authorities between 15 August and 11 November 1994, to mothers of Bangladeshi, Indian or Pakistani origin and a sample of babies born to White mothers living in the same areas were included.

For each of the groups in the sample, the survey aimed to:

- establish the feeding practices in families from birth to fifteen months;

- identify the reasons why babies are fed as they are and determine what influences mothers to make their choices about infant feeding;

- identify the sources and quality of information and support provided to mothers;

- examine the growth of babies and relate this to feeding practices.

Information about the feeding practices in this population will enable the development of appropriate educational materials and other support services.

Mothers of the sampled babies were interviewed on four occasions. At first when the baby was aged 6–10 weeks old (October 1994–January 1995) with follow-up interviews at five months (January–March 1995), nine months (May-July 1995) and fifteen months (November 1995–January 1996). Interviews were face-to-face and carried out by trained ONS interviewers with the help of interpreters where appropriate. At each stage, anthropometric measurements of the baby were taken. Details of the questions asked and measurements taken are shown in Appendices C and F.

Interviews were achieved with 86% of eligible respondents at the first interview, with a similar response among the Asian (87%) and the White (85%) samples. Response at subsequent interviews was 94% of eligible respondents at both the second and third interviews and 92% at the fourth interview. This resulted in 71% (2382) of the mothers who were originally eligible to be interviewed being interviewed up to the fourth stage when their baby was about 15 months old. The methodology and response to the survey is described in more detail in Appendix A.

As the first national survey of this kind, it has provided a wealth of information about the feeding practices and circumstances of this population. This report provides an overview of the main results and a detailed description of the methodology.

The Asian children who took part in the survey at fifteen months were followed up in October–November 1996 when they were about two years old. At this stage, a sample of blood was taken from the child to measure iron and vitamin D levels. The results of the blood analysis, which will be reported on separately, will be related to the results of this survey to evaluate the effect of diet on the development of anaemia and on vitamin D status.

Anonymised data from the survey have been deposited with the Data Archive[8] to enable further analysis to be carried out by other researchers. The results of the blood analysis will be deposited later and it will be possible to link them to the main data set.

Notes

1   Martin J. *Infant feeding 1975: attitudes and practices in England and Wales.* HMSO (London 1978).

     Martin J, Monk J. *Infant Feeding 1980.* OPCS (London 1982).

     Martin J, White A. *Infant feeding 1985.* HMSO (London 1988).

     White A, Freeth S, M O'Brien. *Infant Feeding 1990.* HMSO (London 1992).

2   Foster K, Cheesbrough S, Lader D. *Infant Feeding 1995.* HMSO (London 1997).

3   Rona R, Chinn S. *National Study of Health and Growth: social and biological factors associated with height of children from ethnic groups living in England.* Annals of Human Biology, vol.13, 1986, pp13:453-471.

4   Duggan M B, Harbottle L. *The growth and nutritional status of healthy Asian children aged 4-40 months living in Sheffield.* British Journal of Nutrition 1996;76;183-197.

5   Duggan M B, Harbottle L, Noble C. *The weaning diet of healthy Asian children living in Sheffield. 1. The level and composition of the diet in children from 4 to 40 months of age.* Journal of Human Nutrition and Dietetics, vol.5, 1992, pp189-200.

6   Warrington S, Storey D M. *Comparative studies of Asian and Caucasian children. 2. Nutrition, feeding practices and health.* European Journal of Clinical Nutrition, vol.42, 1988, pp69-80.

7   Harris R J, Armstrong D, Ali R, Loynes A. *Nutritional survey of Bangladeshi children aged under 5 years in the London borough of Tower Hamlets.* Archives of Disease in Childhood, vol.58, 1983, pp428-432.

8   For further information about the archived data please contact:

     Data Archive
     University of Essex
     Wivenhoe Park
     Colchester
     Essex CO4 3SQ
     Great Britain

     Tel:[UK]01206 872001
     Fax:[UK]01206 872003   email:sayek@:essex.ac.uk

Summary

- The incidence of breastfeeding was 90% among Bangladeshi, 82% among Indian, 76% among Pakistani and 62% among White mothers. The highest incidence of breastfeeding in all groups was among mothers of first babies.

- Of mothers who started to breastfeed, Pakistani and Bangladeshi mothers stopped breastfeeding sooner than either Indian or White mothers.

- By the time their babies were eight weeks old, of those who started to breastfeed, just over half the Indian and White (52% and 54%), nearly half the Bangladeshi (46%) and just over a third (36%) of the Pakistani mothers were still breastfeeding.

- At four months, of those who started to breastfeed, 39% of White, 34% of Indian, 25% of Bangladeshi and 21% of Pakistani mothers were still breastfeeding.

- The most frequent reasons given at all interviews for having stopped breastfeeding were "insufficient milk" and "the baby would not suck".

- White mothers were more likely than Asian mothers to hold or breastfeed their baby immediately. Mothers who breastfed immediately were much less likely to stop than those who waited more than 24 hours to breastfeed.

- Eighty per cent of Bangladeshi and about three-quarters of other mothers who ever breastfed had their baby beside them all the time in hospital. A high proportion of those whose baby was not always with them said that nurses sometimes fed their baby.

- Mothers who had a caesarean delivery and started breastfeeding were more likely than others to give up.

- By the time mothers who ever breastfed left hospital, White mothers were more likely than Asian mothers to be breastfeeding completely. Pakistani and Bangladeshi mothers were about twice as likely as Indian mothers and three times as likely as White mothers to leave hospital bottle feeding completely.

- Some mothers delayed breastfeeding until they got home.

- Of mothers born outside the UK, about four out of ten Indian and Pakistani and three out of ten Bangladeshi mothers who bottle fed initially or stopped breastfeeding to bottle feed said that they would have fed their baby differently if s(he) had not been born in the UK.

1.1 Introduction

This chapter covers the *incidence* of breastfeeding – the proportion of babies who were ever breastfed including all babies who were ever put to the breast at all, even if this was on one occasion only; and the *prevalence* of breastfeeding up to 15 months – the proportion who were breastfed at each age. The duration of breastfeeding, the factors which influence the length of time a baby is breastfed, and the reasons for stopping breastfeeding are also discussed.

1.2 Incidence of breastfeeding

In 1990[1], the incidence of breastfeeding in England and Wales was 64%. In this survey, the incidence in the White sample (62%) was very similar to 1990. Among Asian mothers, the incidence was much higher – 90% among Bangladeshi, 82% among Indian and 76% among Pakistani mothers.

Figure 1.1

In all ethnic groups, the highest incidence of breastfeeding was among mothers of first babies – 94% among Bangladeshi, 89% among Indian, 80% among Pakistani and 72% among White mothers. Thirty four per cent of Bangladeshi, 35% of Pakistani, 42% of Indian and 48% of White mothers in this sample were first time mothers.

Figure 1.2, Table 1.1, Appendix B Table B3

Figure 1.1

Incidence of breastfeeding by ethnic group

All babies

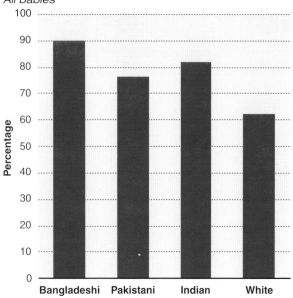

Figure 1.2

Incidence of breastfeeding by birth order and ethnic group

All babies

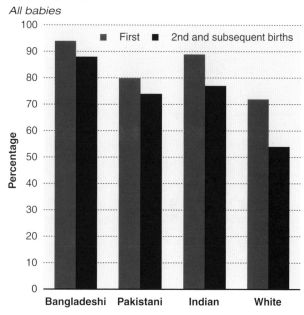

Among Indian mothers, the incidence of breastfeeding was higher among mothers born outside the UK – 84% compared with 77% if she was born in the UK. Among other Asian mothers, there was no significant difference in the incidence of breastfeeding by the mother's country of birth.

Table 1.2

Among White mothers, as in the 1990 survey, the mother's age, level of education and social class were highly associated with her likelihood of breastfeeding, with the highest rates of breastfeeding among mothers with the following characteristics:

- age 30 or older, with a first baby (86% breastfed)

- with a first or later baby and 14 or more years of education – equivalent to completing full-time education at age 18 or older (85% breastfed)

- with a first or later baby and husband/partner in a non-manual occupation (81% breastfed)

Figures 1.3-1.5, Tables 1.3-1.5

Among Asian mothers, the relationship between breastfeeding and these social characteristics was less clear. A logistic regression model[2] was used to identify, for mothers in each ethnic group, the

Figure 1.3

Incidence of breastfeeding by age of mother and ethnic group

All babies

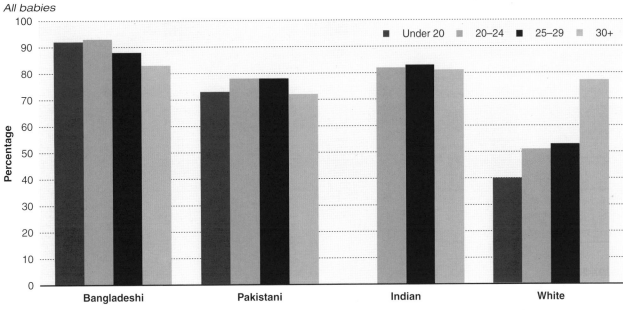

Figure 1.4

Incidence of breastfeeding by mother's full-time education and ethnic group

All babies

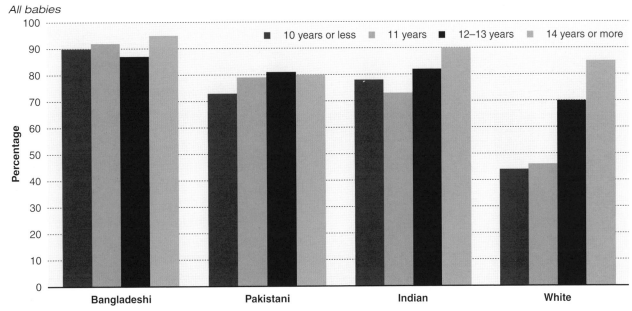

social characteristics which had an effect on the likelihood of her breastfeeding. Whether this was her first baby was also included in the analysis.

The results of the separate effect of each of the mother's characteristics on her likelihood of breastfeeding are shown for Indian and White mothers in Table 1.6. Among Indian mothers, the main characteristics associated with the

incidence of breastfeeding were similar to White mothers. Those most likely to breastfeed were:

Indian

■ mother of a first baby

■ husband/partner in a non-manual occupation

■ born outside the UK

Figure 1.5
Incidence of breastfeeding by social class*
and ethnic group

All babies

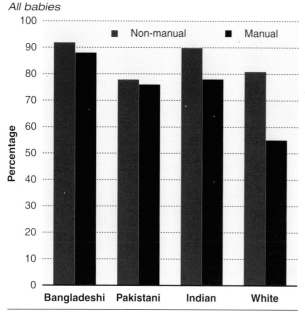

* *Social class defined by the occupation of husband/partner*

White

- mother of a first baby

- aged 30 or older

- fourteen or more years of education

- husband/partner in non-manual occupation

Among Bangladeshi and Pakistani mothers, the analysis showed that there was a greater likelihood of mothers of first babies breastfeeding, but no significant relationship between other social characteristics included in the model and their likelihood of breastfeeding.

Table 1.6

1.3 Prevalence of breastfeeding
The proportion of babies who were ever breastfed is shown above to be considerably higher among Asian than among White babies. Among Indian babies, the proportion who were breastfed at later ages continued to be higher than among White babies and by the time Indian babies were four weeks old, a higher proportion (52%) were breastfed than in any other ethnic group, a trend which continued until babies were nine months old, when all groups had similar rates. Although a high proportion of Pakistani and Bangladeshi mothers breastfed at birth, the

proportion of their babies who continued to be breastfed declined faster than among either Indian or White babies. Figure 1.6 shows the proportion breastfeeding up to eight weeks; the proportion breastfeeding up to 15 months is shown in Table 1.7.

The highest incidence (90%) of breastfeeding was among Bangladeshi mothers but by the time Bangladeshi babies were two weeks old, the prevalence of breastfeeding in this group had declined to a level similar to Indian babies (63% and 62% respectively) but remained higher than among either Pakistani or White babies. By the time Bangladeshi babies were two months old, 27% were breastfed, the same proportion as White babies of the same age.

At birth, 76% of Pakistani mothers were breastfeeding but by the time Pakistani babies were two weeks old, 48% were breastfed, very similar to the proportion (46%) of White babies who were breastfed at the same age, although fewer (62%) White babies were breastfed at birth. The proportion of Pakistani and White babies who were breastfed continued to decline to 37% and 39% respectively at four weeks. At six weeks, fewer (29%) Pakistani babies were breastfed than babies in any other ethnic group.

At two months, the prevalence of breastfeeding among Indian mothers was highest (33%) and the prevalence among Pakistani mothers was lowest (20%). Beyond two months, there was greater similarity in the prevalence of breastfeeding among babies of all ethnic groups, although prevalence remained slightly lower among Pakistani babies until they were about nine months old when all groups had similar rates.

Figure 1.6, Table 1.7

1.4 Duration of breastfeeding
The prevalence of breastfeeding at different ages indicates that mothers in some ethnic groups stopped breastfeeding sooner than others. Looking only at those who began breastfeeding, Pakistani mothers were the most likely to stop in the first few weeks. Twenty eight per cent of Pakistani mothers stopped breastfeeding before their baby was two weeks old, over a half (56%)

Figure 1.6
Prevalence of breastfeeding up to 8 weeks by ethnic group

All babies

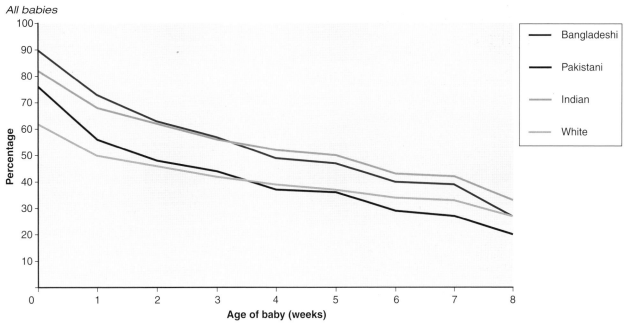

Figure 1.7
Percentage of mothers who stopped breastfeeding by ages up to 8 weeks

Breastfed initially and interviewed on four occasions*

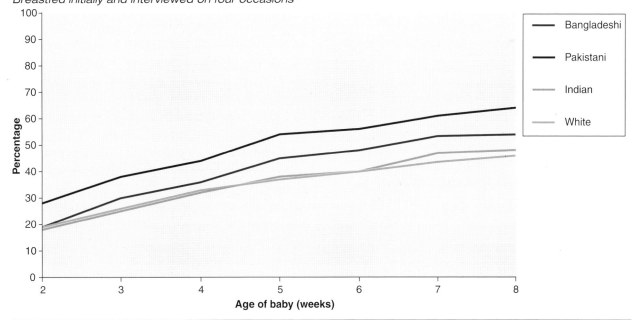

* Interviewed at 9 weeks, 5 months, 9 months and 15 months.

had stopped by the time the baby was six weeks old and about two thirds (64%) had stopped by the time the baby was eight weeks old.

Figure 1.7, Table 1.9

Bangladeshi mothers did not stop breastfeeding as promptly as Pakistani mothers. Nineteen per cent of Bangladeshi mothers stopped

breastfeeding before the baby was two weeks old, nearly half (48%) had stopped by the time the baby was six weeks old and just over a half (54%) by the time the baby was eight weeks old. When the baby was four months old, three quarters of Bangladeshi mothers had stopped breastfeeding.

Indian and White mothers were likely to breastfeed longer than other mothers. Eighteen per cent of Indian and 19% of White mothers stopped breastfeeding before the baby was two weeks old; 40% of Indian and White mothers had stopped by the time the baby was six weeks old; nearly a half (48% of Indian and 46% of White mothers) had stopped before the baby was eight weeks old. At four months, about two thirds (66% of Indian and 61% of White mothers) had stopped breastfeeding compared with the much higher proportions of Bangladeshi (75%) and Pakistani (79%) mothers who had stopped breastfeeding by the same age.

Figure 1.7, Table 1.9

While in all groups, first-time mothers were the most likely to start breastfeeding, both Indian and White mothers were more likely to stop breastfeeding earlier if this was their first than if it was a second or later baby. By the time their baby was six weeks old, 44% of White mothers and 43% of Indian mothers with a first baby had stopped breastfeeding compared with 35% of White and 38% of Indian mothers of second or later babies who had stopped. Among White mothers, the difference in duration of breastfeeding first and later babies continued, but among Indian mothers there was little difference beyond 6 weeks. Among Bangladeshi and Pakistani mothers there was no significant difference at any age in the duration of breastfeeding first and later babies.

Table 1.10

1.5 Influences on the duration of breastfeeding

1.5.1 Length of time in hospital

Nearly all (99%) births were in hospital. The period during and immediately following the birth can affect whether breastfeeding gets off to a good start. The trend for spending less time in hospital has continued. In 1990, nearly two fifths of mothers were in hospital for less than 48 hours. In this survey, 56% of White and Bangladeshi, 53% of Pakistani and 47% of Indian mothers spent 48 hours or less in hospital.

Table 1.11

1.5.2 Delays in starting breastfeeding

Previous surveys[1] have shown that mothers who breastfed in the first few hours after the birth were more likely to continue than those who started breastfeeding later. White mothers were more likely than Asian mothers in general to either hold or breastfeed their baby immediately, although the experience of mothers in each of the Asian groups differed. About two-thirds (67%) of White mothers, 58% of Indian, 46% of Pakistani and 32% of Bangladeshi mothers held their baby immediately. There was no significant difference in the proportion of White mothers who held their baby immediately and subsequently breast or bottle fed but Asian mothers who waited more than 12 hours before they held their baby were about twice as likely to bottle feed.

Figure 1.8, Table 1.12

Of those who ever breastfed, White mothers were more likely than Asian mothers to have started to breastfeed immediately or within an hour of birth (60% of White, 35% of Indian, 21% of Pakistani and 21% of Bangladeshi mothers). Over eight out of ten mothers in all groups who started breastfeeding immediately or within an hour were likely to still be breastfeeding at two weeks. Those who delayed more than 24 hours were the most likely to have stopped by two weeks (38% of Pakistani, 32% of Indian, 22% of Bangladeshi).

Figure 1.9, Tables 1.13-1.14

1.5.3 Complications affecting mother and baby

Previous infant feeding surveys[1] showed that a caesarean was the type of delivery most associated with breastfeeding problems. In this survey, 18% of Indian, 16% of White, 13% of Pakistani and 12% of Bangladeshi mothers reported having a caesarean delivery. Only Pakistani mothers were significantly less likely than other mothers not to breastfeed initially if they had a caesarean delivery. Among mothers who started breastfeeding, those who had a caesarean delivery were more likely than others to give up. Thirty five per cent of Pakistani, 33% of Bangladeshi, 27% of White and 23% of Indian mothers had stopped breastfeeding before the baby was two weeks old if the delivery was a caesarean.

Tables 1.15-1.17

Figure 1.8
Length of time until mothers first held their baby by ethnic group

All mothers

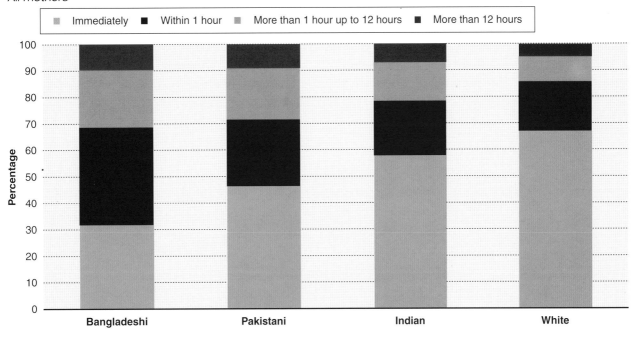

Figure 1.9
Length of time until baby was put to breast by ethnic group

All breastfeeding mothers

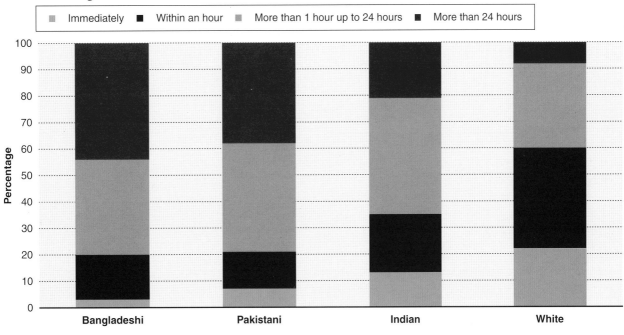

Early contact could be affected if the baby was in special care. The same proportion (14%) of babies in all groups were in special care, including being put under a lamp for jaundice. Only Pakistani mothers were less likely than other mothers of 'special care' babies to breastfeed initially. Having started to breastfeed, mothers with babies who had received special care were no more likely than others to stop breastfeeding before the baby was two weeks old.

Tables 1.18-1.20

1.5.4 Feeding schedule

Just over three quarters of all Bangladeshi mothers, 74% of all Indian, 71% of all Pakistani and 69% of all White mothers had their baby beside them all the time in hospital (table not shown). Mothers in all groups were more likely to have ever breastfeed if their baby was always beside them.

Table 1.21

Eighty per cent of Bangladeshi mothers who ever breastfed and about three quarters of all other breastfeeding mothers had their baby beside them all the time in hospital. Mothers who had their baby always beside them were more likely than others to feed on demand. Even so, 38% of Bangladeshi, 26% of Pakistani, 19% of Indian and 5% of White mothers fed their baby at set times rather than on demand.

Tables 1.22-1.24

Of those breastfeeding mothers who said that their baby was not with them all the time, a high proportion (89% of Pakistani, 86% of Bangladeshi, 71% of Indian and 64% of White mothers) said that nurses sometimes fed their baby. Nearly all these babies were given infant formula. Nurses were more likely to give expressed milk if the baby was White (19%) or Indian (14%) than if s(he) was Bangladeshi (9%) or Pakistani (6%).

Table 1.22

1.5.5 Establishing breastfeeding in hospital

By the time breastfeeding mothers left hospital, 78% of White, 56% of Indian, 41% of Pakistani and 21% of Bangladeshi mothers were breastfeeding completely. Some mothers, Bangladeshi mothers in particular, left hospital both breast and bottle feeding – Bangladeshi (50%), Indian (29%), Pakistani (28%), White (12%). Other mothers who ever breastfed left hospital bottle feeding completely – Pakistani (30%), Bangladeshi (28%), Indian (15%), White (10%).

Figure 1.10, Table 1.25

The reason some mothers left hospital bottle feeding completely may not have been because they had stopped breastfeeding but because they delayed breastfeeding until they got home. A question was asked about this at the third interview. By then, babies were on average nine months old and the answers which are based on the mother remembering an event which happened some time ago. Nevertheless the data give an indication of what happened. If the baby was born in hospital, mothers who breastfed but delayed more than 24 hours before starting to breastfeed were asked whether they first breastfed before or after they left hospital. Of these mothers, 54% of Pakistani, 44% of Bangladeshi, 26% of Indian mothers waited to

Figure 1.10
Method of feeding when mothers left hospital by ethnic group

All breastfeeding mothers

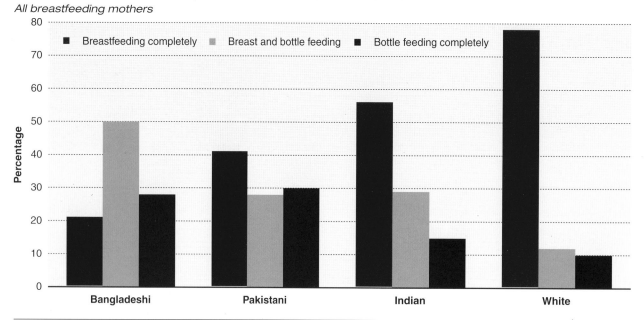

breastfeed until after they left hospital. The number of White mothers who delayed more than 24 hours before starting to breastfeed is too small to comment on. **Table 1.26**

For some Asian mothers it is customary not to feed the baby colostrum but to wait until the mature milk is through. Very few mentioned directly that they delayed breastfeeding for this reason. The reasons most frequently given for the delay were:

- did not have enough milk – Bangladeshi (41%), Indian (35%), Pakistani (21%)

- not feeling relaxed in hospital – Pakistani (22%), Bangladeshi (18%), Indian (18%)

- didn't want to breastfeed in public – Pakistani and Indian (12%), Bangladeshi (9%)

1.5.6 Cultural influences

Of mothers who were born outside the UK, about four out of ten Indian and Pakistani and three out of ten Bangladeshi mothers, who had never breastfed or had stopped breastfeeding by the time of the first interview said that they would have fed their baby differently if s(he) had been born in the mother's country of birth. Of those who stopped breastfeeding, about eight out of ten reported that, in their country of birth, they would have breastfed entirely and nearly two out of ten would have breastfed longer.

Figure 1.11, Table 1.27

1.6 Reasons for stopping breastfeeding

1.6.1 Reasons for stopping breastfeeding by the first interview

At the first interview when babies were about 6-10 weeks old, the reason most frequently given for having stopped breastfeeding was insufficient milk, mentioned by 43% of Pakistani, 39% of Indian, 36% of Bangladeshi and 32% of White mothers. Also mentioned frequently, particularly by Asian mothers (37% of Bangladeshi, 30% of Pakistani, 27% of Indian, 18% of White mothers) was that the baby would not suck. Painful breasts or nipples were mentioned by 25% of White mothers but by fewer Asian mothers – Pakistani

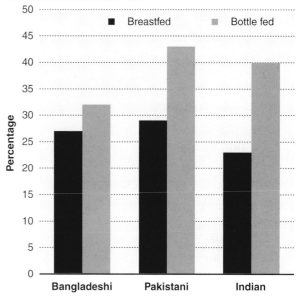

Figure 1.11
Percentage of mothers who would have fed baby differently in their country of birth by whether breast or bottle fed and ethnic group

Mothers born outside UK

(15%), Indian (14%), Bangladeshi (12%). More White and Indian mothers (15% and 14%) than either Pakistani or Bangladeshi mothers (8% and 6%) stopped breastfeeding because it took too long. Just over one in ten of all mothers stopped breastfeeding because they were ill.

Table 1.28

1.6.2 Reasons for stopping breastfeeding by the second interview

At the second interview, when babies were on average five months old, insufficient milk was again the reason most frequently given for having stopped breastfeeding, around a half of Asian mothers – Bangladeshi (58%), Pakistani (54%), Indian (48%) and just over a third (35%) of White mothers had stopped for this reason since the previous interview. About a third of Bangladeshi but fewer other mothers – Pakistani (20%), Indian (13%), White (11%) stopped because the baby would not suck. Indian and White mothers were those most likely to have returned to work by this interview (see Appendix B Table B16). This is reflected in the higher proportion of Indian and White mothers (14% and 15% respectively) who gave their return to work as the reason for having stopped breastfeeding. This reason was given by only 1%

of Bangladeshi and 2% of Pakistani mothers. White mothers were twice as likely as Asian mothers to have stopped because they were ill (15% compared with about 7%). Eleven per cent of White, 8% of Indian and Pakistani and 4% of Bangladeshi mothers stopped because they had breastfed for as long as they intended.

Table 1.29

1.6.3 Reasons for stopping breastfeeding by the third interview

At the third interview when babies were on average nine months old, the reasons most frequently given for having stopped breastfeeding since the last interview, were again, insufficient milk and the baby would not suck. At this interview, both these reasons were given by more Bangladeshi than other mothers (38% mentioned insufficient milk compared with 32% of Indian, 29% of Pakistani and 20% of White mothers; 35% said that the baby would not suck compared with 24% of Pakistani, 14% of Indian and 20% of White mothers). Again, Indian and White mothers were far more likely than others to have stopped breastfeeding because they had returned to work (14% and 11% respectively) compared with only 2% of Pakistani mothers and no Bangladeshi mothers. About a quarter of White mothers, 16% of Indian, 8% of Pakistani and 7% of Bangladeshi mothers said that they had breastfed for as long as they intended. White mothers stopped because their baby was biting or teething (11%); Indian mothers stopped because their baby was still hungry (18%); Pakistani mothers stopped because they were ill (14%).

Table 1.30

1.6.4 Reasons for stopping breastfeeding by the fourth interview

The reasons for stopping breastfeeding between the third and fourth interview are not shown because the number of mothers who stopped in this period is too few to comment on.

Notes

1   White A, Freeth S, O'Brien M. *Infant Feeding 1990.* HMSO (London 1992).

2   Logistic regression was used to identify the characteristics of a mother associated with breastfeeding. The results of the analysis are shown in Table 1.6 for Indian and White mothers. Bangladeshi and Pakistani mothers are not shown in the table because the characteristics included in the model were not significant in predicting the likelihood of a mother breastfeeding her baby.

The dependent variable in this model was 'whether the baby was ever breastfed – Yes or No'. The characteristics in the first column of Table 1.6 are the independent variables used in the model. For each category of an independent variable, the logistic procedure produces a coefficient which represents the factor by which the odds of a mother breastfeeding differ from the reference group. These factors, or odds ratios, are shown in the column headed 'Multiplying factors'. The reference group has a multiplying factor of 1.00. The choice of the reference group is arbitrary. In this model, the reference group has been chosen as the group least likely to breastfeed.

The multiplying factors can be used to calculate the odds of a mother breastfeeding. To do this, the baseline odds shown at the top of the table are multiplied by the appropriate factors. For example, the odds for an Indian mother, not born in the UK, with a husband/partner in a non-manual occupation, and the mother of a first baby would be: 1.186 x 1.55 x 2.04 x 2.26 = 8.48. The odds of a mother with these characteristics ever breastfeeding their baby would be 8.48/1. This can be translated into percentage terms by dividing the odds by the odds plus one: [8.48/(8.48+1)] x 100 = 89%. Thus the model would predict that 89% of Indian mothers with these characteristics would have ever breastfed their baby.

Table 1.1
Incidence of breastfeeding by birth order and ethnic group

All mothers

Birth order	Ethnic group			
	Bangladeshi	Pakistani	Indian	White
				Percentage who breastfed initially
First birth	94	80	89	72
Second birth	91	77	80	53
Third birth	85	80	75	50
Fourth or later birth	87	66	68	[23]
Second and subsequent birth	88	74	77	54
All	90	76	82	62
Base = 100%				
First birth	*209*	*251*	*391*	*295*
Second birth	*140*	*206*	*301*	*194*
Third birth	*93*	*115*	*160*	*93*
Fourth or later birth	*165*	*155*	*78*	*35*
Second and subsequent birth	*401*	*480*	*543*	*324*
All	*610*	*731*	*934*	*619*

Table 1.2
Incidence of breastfeeding by mother's country of birth and ethnic group

All mothers

	Ethnic group						
	Bangladeshi		Pakistani		Indian		White
	Born UK	Born elsewhere	Born UK	Born elsewhere	Born UK	Born elsewhere	Born UK
	%	%	%	%	%	%	%
Percentage who breastfed initially	[41]	90	80	75	77	84	62
Base = 100%	*47*	*563*	*222*	*509*	*228*	*706*	*592*

Table 1.3

Incidence of breastfeeding by age of mother and ethnic group

All mothers

Mother's age	Ethnic group			
	Bangladeshi	Pakistani	Indian	White
	%	%	%	%
				Percentage who breastfed initially
All mothers				
Under 20	92	73	[13]	[14]
20 - 24	93	78	82	51
25 - 29	88	78	83	53
30 +	83	72	81	77
All	90	76	82	62
Mothers of first babies				
Under 20	92	[27]	[12]	[12]
20 - 24	96	83	88	62
25 - 29	[15]	[36]	91	73
30 +	0	[11]	90	86
All	94	80	89	72
Base = 100%				
All mothers				
Under 20	*63*	*52*	*16*	*35*
20 - 24	*290*	*300*	*255*	*119*
25 - 29	*126*	*222*	*359*	*187*
30 +	*131*	*157*	*304*	*278*
All	*610*	*730*	*934*	*619*
Mothers of first babies				
Under 20	*59*	*39*	*15*	*31*
20 - 24	*133*	*153*	*179*	*64*
25 - 29	*17*	*45*	*140*	*93*
30 +	*0*	*14*	*57*	*107*
All	*209*	*251*	*391*	*295*

Table 1.4

Incidence of breastfeeding by mother's full-time education and ethnic group

All mothers

Number of years of full time education	Ethnic group			
	Bangladeshi	Pakistani	Indian	White
	%	%	%	%
				Percentage who breastfed initially
10 years or less	90	73	78	[20]
11 years	92	79	73	46
12 - 13 years	87	81	82	70
14 years or more	[29]	80	90	85
All	90	76	82	62
Base = 100%				
10 years or less	*329*	*310*	*147*	*45*
11 years	*114*	*130*	*193*	*234*
12 - 13 years	*119*	*139*	*251*	*187*
14 years or more	*40*	*138*	*332*	*151*
All	*602*	*717*	*923*	*617*

Table 1.5
Incidence of breastfeeding by social class and ethnic group*

All mothers

Social class of husband/partner	Ethnic group			
	Bangladeshi	Pakistani	Indian	White
	%	%	%	%
				Percentage who breastfed initially
Non-manual				
Professional and managerial	[35]	83	89	83
Skilled non-manual	[34]	73	91	76
All non-manual	92	78	90	81
Manual				
Skilled manual	88	76	76	56
Partly skilled manual	91	80	79	55
Unskilled	[19]	[27]	[24]	[12]
All manual	88	76	78	55
All [†]	90	76	82	62
Base = 100%				
Non-manual				
Professional and managerial	*38*	*88*	*262*	*178*
Skilled non-manual	*37*	*75*	*128*	*54*
All non-manual	*75*	*163*	*390*	*232*
Manual				
Skilled manual	*236*	*211*	*271*	*199*
Partly skilled manual	*173*	*163*	*179*	*67*
Unskilled	*28*	*46*	*29*	*25*
All manual	*437*	*420*	*479*	*291*
All [†]	*610*	*731*	*934*	*619*

* Social class defined by the occupation of husband/partner.

[†] Includes cases where social class could not be determined.

Table 1.6
Odds of mother ever breastfeeding her baby by ethnic group*

	Indian	White
Baseline odds	1.186	0.308
Characteristics	**Multiplying factors**	
First baby	2.26	2.88
Mother's age	ns	
30 or over		3.90
25-29		[1.20]
20-24		[1.58]
Under 20		1.00
Mother's education		
14 years or more	[1.69]	2.67
12-13 years	[1.21]	[1.97]
11 years	[0.74]	[0.72]
10 years or less	1.00	1.00
Social class		
Non-manual	2.04	2.48
Not described	0.47	[0.59]
Manual	1.00	1.00
Country of birth		
Born outside UK	1.55	ns

Factors in square brackets were not significant at the 95% level.

* Bangladeshi and Pakistani mothers are not shown in this table because these social characteristics were not significant in predicting the odds of a mother breastfeeding her baby.

ns These variables were not significant in predicting the odds of a mother breastfeeding her baby.

Table 1.7
Prevalence of breastfeeding up to 15 months by ethnic group

All babies

| | Ethnic group | | | |
| | Bangladeshi | Pakistani | Indian | White |
	%	%	%	%
Birth	90	76	82	62
1 week	73	56	68	50
2 weeks	63	48	62	46
4 weeks	49	37	52	39
6 weeks	40	29	43	34
2 months	27	20	33	27
4 months	21	15	25	21
6 months	14	10	18	15
9 months	9	8	11	8
12 months	6	5	7	5
15 months	6	4	6	3
Base = 100%	*610*	*731*	*934*	*619*

Table 1.8
Prevalence of breastfeeding up to 15 months by birth order and ethnic group

All babies

| | Ethnic group | | | |
| | Bangladeshi | Pakistani | Indian | White |
	%	%	%	%
First births:				
Birth	94	80	89	72
1 week	77	59	72	56
2 weeks	65	50	66	50
4 weeks	49	38	56	41
6 weeks	40	29	47	36
2 months	27	17	36	26
4 months	20	12	27	21
6 months	12	9	19	14
9 months	8	7	11	6
12 months	4	6	6	4
15 months	2	5	5	2
Later births:				
Birth	88	74	77	54
1 week	72	54	64	46
2 weeks	62	47	60	42
4 weeks	49	37	49	36
6 weeks	39	30	40	33
2 months	28	21	31	28
4 months	21	16	24	21
6 months	15	11	18	16
9 months	9	8	11	10
12 months	8	5	7	6
15 months	8	4	7	4
Base = 100%				
First births	*209*	*250*	*391*	*295*
Subsequent births	*401*	*480*	*543*	*324*

Table 1.9
Duration of breastfeeding for those who were breastfed initially by ethnic group

Breastfed initially and included at all stages

Ethnic group			
Bangladeshi	Pakistani	Indian	White
%	%	%	%
			Percentage stopping breastfeeding

Stopped breastfeeding before baby was aged:	Bangladeshi	Pakistani	Indian	White
2 weeks	19	28	18	19
4 weeks	36	44	32	33
6 weeks	48	56	40	40
8 weeks	54	64	48	46
4 months	75	79	66	61
6 months	81	83	72	68
9 months	86	87	83	82
12 months	91	90	88	90
15 months	92	93	92	94
Base = 100%	*423*	*447*	*610*	*347*

Table 1.10
Duration of breastfeeding for those who were breastfed initially by birth order and ethnic group

Breastfed initially and included at all stages

Ethnic group			
Bangladeshi	Pakistani	Indian	White
%	%	%	%
			Percentage stopping breastfeeding

Stopped breastfeeding before baby was aged:	Bangladeshi	Pakistani	Indian	White
First births:				
2 weeks	16	29	20	21
4 weeks	35	44	34	35
6 weeks	47	60	43	44
8 weeks	55	65	50	51
4 months	78	83	68	67
6 months	83	86	75	73
9 months	86	89	84	86
12 months	92	89	90	93
15 months	97	92	93	96
Later births:				
2 weeks	20	28	16	17
4 weeks	36	44	29	30
6 weeks	49	55	38	35
8 weeks	54	64	47	40
4 months	74	77	64	55
6 months	79	81	70	62
9 months	86	86	82	78
12 months	90	91	87	87
15 months	90	94	90	92
Base = 100%				
First births	*152*	*158*	*275*	*187*
Later births	*271*	*288*	*335*	*160*

Table 1.11

Length of time mothers stayed in hospital by ethnic group

All mothers, hospital birth

Length of time in hospital	Ethnic group			
	Bangladeshi	Pakistani	Indian	White
	%	%	%	%
2 days or less	56	53	47	56
3-5 days	31	34	37	32
6-7 days	9	10	11	7
8-10 days	3	3	3	2
11-14 days	1	0	3	2
Base = 100%	*604*	*721*	*929*	*610*

Table 1.12

Length of time until mothers first held their baby by whether they breast or bottle fed and ethnic group

All mothers

Mother held baby:	Ethnic group							
	Bangladeshi		Pakistani		Indian		White	
	Breast	Bottle	Breast	Bottle	Breast	Bottle	Breast	Bottle
	%	%	%	%	%	%	%	%
Immediately	32	31	48	42	59	52	68	65
Within 1 hour	37	33	27	19	22	15	18	19
More than 1 hour up to 12 hours	22	20	18	23	13	21	8	12
More than 12 hours	9	16	7	16	6	12	5	4
Base = 100%	*545*	*61*	*558*	*170*	*765*	*168*	*387*	*232*

Table 1.13

Length of time until baby was put to breast by ethnic group

All breastfeeding mothers

Baby put to breast:	Ethnic group			
	Bangladeshi	Pakistani	Indian	White
	%	%	%	%
Immediately	4	7	13	22
Within an hour	17	14	22	38
More than 1 hour up to 4 hours later	19	18	22	21
More than 4 hours up to 12 hours later	11	16	16	9
More than 12 hours up to 24 hours later	7	7	6	3
More than 24 hours	44	38	21	8
Base = 100%	*544*	*558*	*764*	*387*

Table 1.14

Proportion of mothers who stopped breastfeeding before the baby was two weeks old by length of time until baby was put to breast and ethnic group

All breastfeeding mothers

Baby put to breast:	Ethnic group			
	Bangladeshi	Pakistani	Indian	White
				Percentage who stopped breastfeeding within two weeks
Immediately / within an hour	13	15	13	15
More than 1 hour up to 4 hours later	17	24	11	24
More than 4 hours up to 12 hours later	17	22	14	[7]
More than 12 hours up to 24 hours later	[6]	[8]	[10]	[3]
More than 24 hours	22	38	32	[11]
Base = 100%				
Immediately / within an hour	*110*	*119*	*268*	*231*
More than 1 hour up to 4 hours later	*102*	*103*	*170*	*80*
More than 4 hours up to 12 hours later	*59*	*86*	*120*	*35*
More than 12 hours up to 24 hours later	*36*	*37*	*48*	*11*
More than 24 hours	*237*	*213*	*158*	*30*

Table 1.15

Type of delivery by ethnic group

All mothers

Type of delivery	Ethnic group			
	Bangladeshi	Pakistani	Indian	White
	%	%	%	%
Normal	82	80	72	74
Caesarean	12	13	18	16
Forceps	4	5	7	7
Vacuum extraction	2	2	4	4
Base = 100%	*607*	*728*	*934*	*619*

Table 1.16

Incidence of breastfeeding by type of delivery and ethnic group

All mothers

Type of delivery	Ethnic group			
	Bangladeshi	Pakistani	Indian	White
				Percentage who breastfed initially
Caesarean	83	66	81	63
Other delivery	91	78	82	62
All	90	7	82	62
Base = 100%				
Caesarean	*72*	*96*	*164*	*98*
Other delivery	*535*	*631*	*770*	*521*
All	*607*	*728*	*934*	*619*

Table 1.17

Percentage of mothers who stopped breastfeeding within two weeks by type of delivery and ethnic group

All breastfeeding mothers

Type of delivery	Ethnic group			
	Bangladeshi	Pakistani	Indian	White
				Percentage stopping breastfeeding within two weeks
Caesarean	33	35	23	27
Other delivery	16	26	16	18
All	18	27	18	19
Base = 100%				
Caesarean	*60*	*63*	*133*	*62*
Other delivery	*485*	*495*	*633*	*325*
All	*545*	*558*	*766*	*387*

Table 1.18

Whether received special care by ethnic group

All babies

	Ethnic group			
	Bangladeshi	Pakistani	Indian	White
	%	%	%	%
Special care *	14	14	14	14
No special care	87	87	87	87
Base = 100%	*603*	*728*	*933*	*619*

Adds to more than 100 because some babies were put into special care and under a lamp for jaundice.

*   Includes babies put under a special lamp for jaundice.

Table 1.19

Incidence of breastfeeding by whether received special care and ethnic group

All babies

	Ethnic group			
	Bangladeshi	Pakistani	Indian	White
				Percentage who breastfed initially
Special care*	88	66	80	63
No special care	90	78	82	62
All	90	76	82	62
Base = 100%				
Special care	*83*	*98*	*126*	*87*
No special care	*523*	*361*	*814*	*539*
All	*603*	*728*	*933*	*619*

The bases for the sub-groups add to more than the total because some babies were put into special care and put under a lamp for jaundice.

*   Includes babies put under a special lamp for jaundice.

Table 1.20

Proportion of mothers who stopped breastfeeding before the baby was two weeks old by whether received special care and ethnic group

All breastfed babies

	Ethnic group			
	Bangladeshi	Pakistani	Indian	White
			Percentage stopping breastfeeding within two weeks	
Special care*	19	31	17	20
No special care	18	27	18	19
Base = 100%				
Special care	*73*	*65*	*101*	*55*
No special care	*471*	*494*	*669*	*336*

*   Includes babies put under a special lamp for jaundice

Table 1.21

Proportion who ever breastfed by whether the baby was always beside the mother in hospital and ethnic group

Baby always beside mother	Ethnic group			
	Bangladeshi	Pakistani	Indian	White
				Proportion who ever breastfed
Yes	91	80	84	67
No	85	69	76	52
Base 100%				
Baby beside mother	*474*	*514*	*691*	*419*
Baby not beside mother	*130*	*208*	*238*	*192*

Table 1.22

Contact between breastfeeding mothers and their babies in hospital by ethnic group

Breastfeeding mothers

Contact in hospital	Ethnic group			
	Bangladeshi	Pakistani	Indian	White
	%	%	%	%
Baby always beside mother	80	74	76	74
Baby away sometimes				
Mother always fed	14	11	29	36
Nurses sometimes fed	86	89	71	64
Nurses sometimes fed				
Expressed breast milk	9	6	14	19
Other baby milk	92	96	93	89
Dextrose or glucose	2	2	4	–
Water	3	–	1	2
Base = 100%				
Baby always beside mother	*542*	*553*	*764*	*382*
Baby away sometimes	*111*	*142*	*181*	*100*
Nurses sometimes fed	*96*	*126*	*126*	*63*

Table 1.23

Feeding schedule followed by breastfeeding mothers in hospital by ethnic group

Breastfeeding mothers

Feeding schedule	Ethnic group							
	Bangladeshi		Pakistani		Indian		White	
	Baby always beside mother		Baby always beside mother		Baby always beside mother		Baby always beside mother	
	Yes	No	Yes	No	Yes	No	Yes	No
	%	%	%	%	%	%	%	%
Set time	38	46	26	35	19	28	5	18
On demand	57	47	72	63	76	70	88	77
Other arrangement	1	6	0	1	0	3	1	3
In hospital only few hours	4	1	2	1	4	–	6	2
Base = 100%	*430*	*110*	*410*	*144*	*582*	*181*	*282*	*100*

Table 1.24

Proportion of mothers who stopped breastfeeding within two weeks by hospital feeding schedule and ethnic group

Breastfeeding mothers, hospital birth

Feeding schedule	Ethnic group			
	Bangladeshi	Pakistani	Indian	White
			Percentage stopping breastfeeding within two weeks	
Set times	22	33	18	[15]
More flexible arrangements	15	25	17	17
Base = 100%				
Set times	*214*	*157*	*163*	*33*
More flexible arrangements	*310*	*386*	*578*	*331*

Table 1.25

Method of feeding when mothers left hospital by ethnic group

All breastfeeding mothers

	Ethnic group			
	Bangladeshi	Pakistani	Indian	White
	%	%	%	%
Breastfeeding completely	21	41	56	78
Breast and bottle feeding	50	28	29	12
Bottle feeding completely	28	30	15	10
Base = 100%	*541*	*553*	*764*	*382*

Table 1.26
When started to breastfeed if breastfeeding was delayed 24 hours or more by ethnic group*

Hospital birth, delayed breastfeeding for 24 hours or more

| | Ethnic group | | | |
	Bangladeshi	Pakistani	Indian	White
	%	%	%	%
Before left hospital	56	46	74	[25]
After left hospital	44	54	26	[3]
Base = 100%	200	181	132	28

* This question was not asked until the third interview so the results should be used with caution.

Table 1.27
Whether mother would have fed baby differently in her country of birth by current method of feeding at stage 1 and ethnic group

Mothers born outside UK

Would have fed differently	Ethnic group								
	Bangladeshi			Pakistani			Indian		
	Breast now	Bottle breast stopped	Bottle breast never	Breast now	Bottle breast stopped	Bottle breast never	Breast now	Bottle breast stopped	Bottle breast never
	%	%	%	%	%	%	%	%	%
Yes	22	31	32	14	39	43	10	41	40
No	78	69	68	86	61	57	90	59	60
Base = 100%	219	265	54	145	217	114	313	238	102

Table 1.28
Reasons given at first interview (baby 6-10 weeks old) for having stopped breastfeeding by ethnic group

All mothers who had stopped breastfeeding by first interview

| Reasons for stopping breastfeeding | Ethnic group | | | |
	Bangladeshi	Pakistani	Indian	White
	%	%	%	%
Insufficient milk	36	43	39	32
Baby would not suck	37	30	27	18
Breast or nipples painful / other problems	12	15	14	25
Mother was ill	12	12	14	12
Breastfeeding took too long	6	8	14	15
Baby was ill	7	8	6	4
Did not like breastfeeding	10	5	5	8
Baby still hungry	1	3	3	7
Baby could not be fed by others	0	2	4	4
Returned to work	1	1	4	3
Baby losing / not gaining weight	0	1	1	4
Lack of privacy	0	1	1	1
Other	5	5	7	10
Base = 100%	304	356	379	201

Percentages do not add to 100 as some mothers gave more than one reason.

Table 1.29

Reasons given at second interview (babies on average 5 months old) for having stopped breastfeeding by ethnic group

All mothers breastfeeding at first interview but stopped by second interview

Reasons for stopping breastfeeding	Ethnic group			
	Bangladeshi	Pakistani	Indian	White
	%	%	%	%
Insufficient milk	58	54	48	35
Baby would not suck	32	20	13	11
Returned to work	1	2	14	15
Breastfeeding took too long	7	5	9	9
Breastfed for as long as was intended	4	8	8	11
Mother was ill	5	9	8	15
Baby was ill	2	6	3	4
Inconvenient / no place to feed	–	4	8	6
Baby could not be fed by others	–	2	4	2
Breast or nipples painful / other problems	4	1	2	–
Baby losing / not gaining weight	–	2	1	2
Baby still hungry	–	2	1	2
Other	1	7	8	11
Base = 100%	*98*	*79*	*132*	*54*

Percentages do not add to 100 as some mothers gave more than one reason.

Table 1.30

Reasons given at third interview (babies on average 9 months old) for having stopped breastfeeding by ethnic group

All mothers breastfeeding at second interview but stopped by third interview

Reasons for stopping breastfeeding	Ethnic group			
	Bangladeshi	Pakistani	Indian	White
	%	%	%	%
Insufficient milk	38	29	32	20
Baby would not suck	35	24	14	20
Breastfed for as long as intended	7	8	16	24
Baby still hungry	6	5	18	9
Breastfeeding took too long	9	9	9	11
Mother was ill	7	14	6	10
Baby was ill	6	7	2	2
Returned to work	–	2	14	11
Baby biting / teething	–	2	5	11
Inconvenient / no place to feed	3	–	6	6
Pregnant	2	4	3	2
Baby could not be fed by others	–	5	3	1
Baby losing / not gaining weight	–	7	1	2
Other	2	5	2	3
Base = 100%	*68*	*63*	*133*	*89*

Percentages do not add to 100 as some mothers gave more than one reason.

2   Choice of feeding method

Summary

- The majority of mothers decided before the birth how they would feed their baby. Seventy three per cent of Indian, 68% of Pakistani and 61% of White mothers planned to breastfeed exclusively. Bangladeshi mothers were less likely to plan to breastfeed exclusively (48%) but a further 26% planned to both breast and bottle feed.

- Of those who planned to breastfeed, over 90% of mothers in each group carried out their intentions.

- Mothers in all ethnic groups were more likely to plan to breastfeed if this was their first baby.

- Mothers with a second or later baby were more likely to plan to breastfeed if they had breastfed a previous child.

- Mothers were more likely to plan to breastfeed if most of the other mothers they knew breastfed.

- About a quarter of all White mothers and Asian mothers born in the UK said that they themselves were breastfed entirely. The proportion of Asian mothers born elsewhere who were breastfed entirely was much higher (about three quarters).

- White and Indian mothers were most likely to plan to breastfeed if they themselves were breastfed.

- Among those intending to breastfeed, the reason given for this choice by more than eight out of ten in all ethnic groups was that they thought it best for the baby.

- The convenience of bottle feeding was frequently mentioned by all mothers planning to bottle feed.

- Bangladeshi mothers were the most concerned about having sufficient milk. One in five gave this as a reason for planning to give a bottle as well as breastfeed.

2.1 Introduction

This chapter covers the plans made by mothers to feed their new baby, whether they carried out their intentions, and the factors which influenced the way they planned to feed their baby. The reasons for their choice of feeding method are discussed.

2.2 Planned method of feeding

All but 4% of Indian and White, 7% of Pakistani and 10% of Bangladeshi mothers decided before the birth how they would feed their baby. Indian and Pakistani mothers were most likely to plan to breastfeed (73% and 68% respectively). Of White mothers, 61% planned to breastfeed and a much higher proportion (33%) than any other group planned to bottle feed. In comparison, just under a half (48%) of Bangladeshi mothers planned to breastfeed but about another quarter (26%) planned to both breast and bottle feed. Only 2% of White, 6% of Pakistani and 7% of Indian mothers planned to use both methods of feeding.   **Figure 2.1, Table 2.1**

Table 2.2 suggests that mothers in all ethnic groups, and Indian mothers in particular, were more likely to plan to breastfeed entirely if this was their first baby, although it should be noted that the difference in intentions to breastfeed between first time and other Bangladeshi and

Pakistani mothers was not statistically significant. The proportion of Indian and White mothers who planned to bottle feed was considerably higher among those with a second or later baby than among first time mothers (second or later baby – White 40%, Indian 22%; first baby – White 26%, Indian 8%).   **Table 2.2**

Pakistani mothers were more likely to plan to breastfeed if they were born in the UK (75%) than elsewhere (65%). In contrast, Indian mothers born in the UK were less likely (68%) to plan to breastfeed than those born elsewhere (75%). Too few Bangladeshi mothers were born in the UK to compare their feeding plans with those born in Bangladesh.   **Figure 2.2, Table 2.3**

2.3 Carrying out intentions

Over 90% of mothers who planned to breastfeed actually did so. Of those who planned to bottle feed entirely, nearly two thirds (62%) of Bangladeshi, nearly a third (31%) of Pakistani and about a fifth (21%) of Indian mothers changed their mind and went on to breastfeed their baby, at least some of the time. Only 7% of White mothers who planned to bottle feed entirely ever breastfed their baby.   **Table 2.4**

Figure 2.1

Intended method of feeding by ethnic group

All mothers

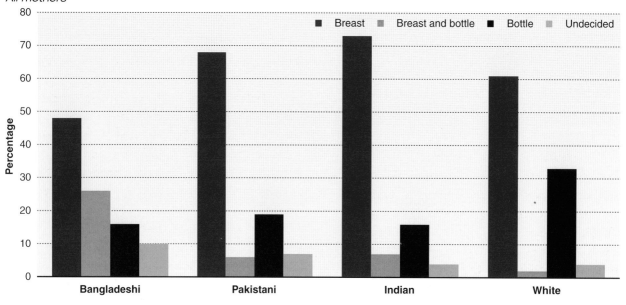

Figure 2.2
Intended method of feeding by mother's country of birth and ethnic group

All mothers

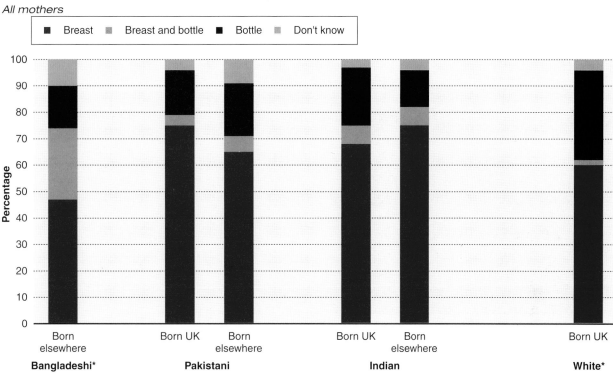

* Bangladeshi mothers born in the UK and White mothers born elsewhere are not shown because the sample sizes are small

2.4 Influences on choice of feeding method

Previous infant feeding surveys show that the way a mother plans to feed her baby is not only associated with birth order but also with her previous experience of breastfeeding, how her friends feed their babies and how the mother herself was fed[1]. These factors again showed an association with feeding practices in this study. Among all groups, those most likely to plan to breastfeed were those with previous experience of breastfeeding and those who knew other mothers who breastfed. Among Indian and White mothers, those who were themselves breastfed were most likely to breastfeed their own babies.

2.4.1 Previous experience

Asian mothers were more likely than White mothers to have breastfed at least one of their previous children – Bangladeshi (83%), Indian (80%), Pakistani (72%), White (65%). Among those with a second or later baby, about seven out of ten Pakistani, Indian and White mothers and nearly a half of Bangladeshi mothers who breastfed a previous child, planned to breastfeed

entirely again. In comparison, mothers who did not breastfeed any of their previous children were less likely to plan to breastfeed this baby – 51% of Pakistani, 42% of Indian, 36% of Bangladeshi and 20% of White mothers. Bangladeshi mothers were more likely to plan to both breast and bottle feed if they had previous experience of breastfeeding than if they had none (30% compared with 19%).

Figure 2.3, Table 2.5

2.4.2 Influence of friends

Nine out of ten White but fewer (three quarters) Asian mothers said that they knew other mothers with babies. Of those who knew others with babies, Indian and White mothers were more likely (28% and 22% respectively) than Pakistani and Bangladeshi mothers (16% and 12% respectively) to know other mothers who breastfed entirely. Bangladeshi mothers were the most likely (44%) to know other mothers who both breast and bottle fed.

Of those who said that most of the other mothers they knew breastfed entirely, 88% of Indian, 84% of White, 82% of Pakistani but fewer (69%)

Figure 2.3

Percentage of mothers intending to breastfeed by previous experience of breastfeeding and ethnic group

Mothers of second or later babies

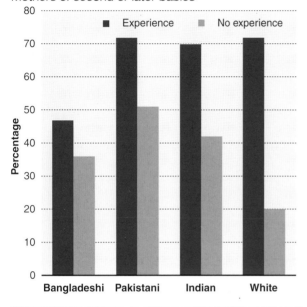

Bangladeshi mothers planned to breastfeed. Nineteen per cent of Bangladeshi mothers who knew others who breastfed entirely planned to both breast and bottle feed. Those who knew other mothers who bottle fed entirely were less likely to plan to breastfeed – 65% of Indian, 50% of White, 68% of Pakistani and 46% of bottle feeding Bangladeshi mothers planned to breastfeed. About a fifth of Bangladeshi mothers

with bottle feeding friends planned to both breast and bottle feed.

Of those whose friends or relatives were evenly divided between breast and bottle feeding, around two thirds of Indian, White and Pakistani and nearly a half the Bangladeshi mothers planned to breastfeed entirely.

Figure 2.4, Tables 2.6-2.8

2.4.3 Influence of mother

About three quarters of all Asian mothers who were born outside the UK said that they themselves were breastfed. Of Asian mothers born in the UK, the proportion who were breastfed was very similar (about a quarter) to the proportion of White mothers who were themselves breastfed.

The way mothers were themselves fed was associated with the way they planned to feed their baby, although the association was stronger among White than Asian mothers. Of those who were themselves breastfed entirely, 81% of White, 76% of Indian, 69% of Pakistani and 49% of Bangladeshi mothers planned to breastfeed. About a quarter of Bangladeshi mothers who were themselves breastfed planned to both breast and bottle feed. Those who said that they themselves were bottle fed entirely were less

Figure 2.4

How mother's friends fed their babies by ethnic group

All mothers

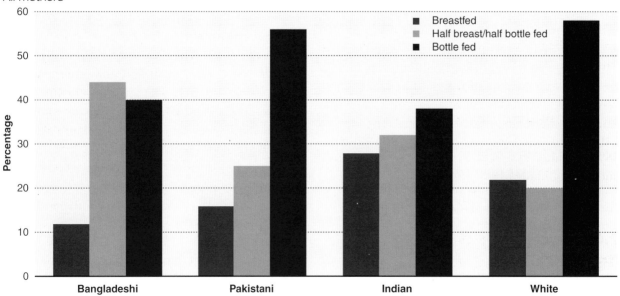

likely to plan to breastfeed – 68% of Indian, 64% of Pakistani and 47% of White mothers.

Table 2.9-2.10

2.5 Reasons for planning to breastfeed

More than eight out of ten mothers in all groups who planned to breastfeed said it was because they thought it best for the baby. Other reasons for planning to breastfeed, frequently mentioned in all groups, were that breastfeeding was natural or that it forged a closer bond between mother and baby. Indian and Pakistani mothers were more likely than other mothers to breastfeed because they thought it was natural (23% and 19% respectively compared with 14% of Bangladeshi and White mothers). White and Indian mothers were more likely than others to plan to breastfeed because they thought it forged a closer bond between mother and baby (18% and 15% respectively compared with 9% of Bangladeshi and 7% of Pakistani mothers).

The convenience of breastfeeding was mentioned by a higher proportion of White (35%) than Asian mothers – Pakistani (19%), Indian (18%), Bangladeshi(10%). White mothers were also more likely than Asian mothers to plan to breastfeed because it was cheaper than bottle feeding – mentioned by 15% of White but by only 4% of Indian, 2% of Pakistani and 1% of Bangladeshi mothers.

Among White mothers, the economy of breastfeeding was more likely to be mentioned by first time mothers and the convenience of breastfeeding by mothers with a second or later baby.

Among mothers of second or later babies, their previous experience of breastfeeding was given as a reason for choosing to breastfeed this baby by 38% of White, 24% of Indian, 16% of Pakistani and 12% of Bangladeshi mothers.

Tables 2.11-2.12

2.6 Reasons for planning to bottle feed

The convenience of bottle feeding was mentioned frequently as a reason for planning

this method (by nearly one in five of all Asian mothers and about a quarter of all White mothers). Mothers of second and later babies most frequently based their plans to bottle feed on their previous experience – mentioned by 45% of Pakistani and White, 40% of Indian and 36% of Bangladeshi mothers.

The advantage of bottle feeding because other people can feed the baby was frequently mentioned by all first time mothers – Indian (24%), Pakistani (20%), White (19%), Bangladeshi (17%) and also by 19% of Indian and 15% of White mothers with a second or later baby. Indian mothers were the most likely (14%) to plan to bottle feed because they expected to return to work soon.

White mothers, especially if this was their first baby, were the most likely to plan to bottle feed because they disliked the idea of breastfeeding. Among first time mothers who planned to bottle feed, nearly two thirds (63%) of White mothers gave this reason compared with only 19% of Pakistani, 12% of Bangladeshi and 9% of Indian mothers. White and Pakistani mothers with a first baby were about twice as likely as those with a second or later baby to plan to bottle feed because they disliked the idea of breastfeeding.

Of all mothers, Bangladeshi mothers were the most concerned about having sufficient milk. Fourteen per cent planned to bottle feed for this reason compared with 5% of Pakistani, 4% of Indian and less than 1% of White mothers. One in five Bangladeshi mothers planned to give a bottle in addition to breastfeeding because they did not expect to have sufficient milk (table not shown).

Tables 2.13-2.14

Notes

1 White A, Freeth S, O'Brien M. *Infant Feeding 1990.* HMSO (London 1992).

Table 2.1

Intended method of feeding by ethnic group

All mothers

Intended method of feeding	Ethnic group			
	Bangladeshi	Pakistani	Indian	White
	%	%	%	%
Breast	48	68	73	61
Breast and bottle	26	6	7	2
Bottle	16	19	16	33
Undecided	10	7	4	4
Base = 100%	*609*	*728*	*934*	*619*

Table 2.2

Intended method of feeding by birth order and ethnic group

All mothers

Intended method of feeding	Ethnic group							
	Bangladeshi		Pakistani		Indian		White	
	First baby	Later baby	First baby	Later baby	First baby	Later baby	First baby	Later baby
	%	%	%	%	%	%	%	%
Breast	53	46	72	66	84	65	69	54
Breast and bottle	21	28	5	6	5	8	1	3
Bottle	14	17	17	20	8	22	26	40
Undecided	12	9	7	7	2	5	4	3
Base = 100%	*209*	*400*	*250*	*479*	*391*	*543*	*295*	*324*

Table 2.3

Intended method of feeding by country of birth and ethnic group

All mothers

Intended method of feeding	Ethnic group						White
	Bangladeshi		Pakistani		Indian		
	Born UK	Born elsewhere	Born UK	Born elsewhere	Born UK	Born elsewhere	Born UK
	%	%	%	%	%	%	%
Breast	[30]	47	75	65	68	75	60
Breast and bottle	[6]	27	4	6	7	7	2
Bottle	[10]	16	17	20	22	14	34
Undecided	[1]	11	4	9	3	4	4
Base = 100%	*47*	*562*	*220*	*508*	*228*	*706*	*592*

Table 2.4
Mother's actual method of feeding by how she intended to feed her baby and ethnic group

All mothers

Actual method	Planned method							
	Bangladeshi		Pakistani		Indian		White	
	Breast *	Bottle	Breast *	Bottle	Breast *	Bottle	Breast *	Bottle
	%	%	%	%	%	%	%	%
Breast †	95	62	90	31	95	21	92	7
Bottle	5	38	11	69	5	79	8	93
Base = 100%	*449*	*97*	*538*	*139*	*747*	*150*	*391*	*205*

*   Includes those who planned to both breast and bottle feed.

†   Includes all babies who were ever put to the breast even if they were also bottle fed.

Table 2.5
Intended method of feeding by mother's previous experience of breastfeeding and ethnic group

Mothers of later babies

Intended method of feeding	Experience of breastfeeding							
	Bangladeshi		Pakistani		Indian		White	
	Yes	No	Yes	No	Yes	No	Yes	No
	%	%	%	%	%	%	%	%
Breast	47	36	72	51	70	42	72	20
Breast and bottle	30	19	7	4	9	6	3	3
Bottle	12	40	14	36	17	41	22	74
Undecided	10	4	6	9	4	11	3	4
Base = 100%	*331*	*67*	*341*	*134*	*430*	*109*	*210*	*112*
% with experience of breastfeeding	83		72		80		65	
Base = 100%	*398*		*475*		*539*		*322*	

Table 2.6
Whether mother knows any other mothers with babies by ethnic group

All mothers

Knows other mothers with babies	Ethnic group			
	Bangladeshi	Pakistani	Indian	White
	%	%	%	%
Yes	74	76	76	92
No	26	24	24	8
Base = 100%	*608*	*730*	*934*	*619*

Table 2.7

How mother's friends fed their babies by ethnic group

All mothers who knew others with babies

Mother's friends:	Ethnic group			
	Bangladeshi	Pakistani	Indian	White
	%	%	%	%
Breastfed	12	16	28	22
Half breast / half bottle fed	44	25	32	20
Bottle fed	40	56	38	58
Don't know	5	2	2	1
Base = 100%	*453*	*553*	*710*	*569*

Table 2.8

Intended method of feeding by how most of mother's friends fed their babies and ethnic group

All mothers

Intended method of feeding	Mother's friends' methods of feeding											
	Bangladeshi			Pakistani			Indian			White		
	Breast fed	Half breast / half bottle	Bottle fed	Breast fed	Half breast / half bottle	Bottle fed	Breast fed	Half breast / half bottle	Bottle fed	Breast fed	Half breast / half bottle	Bottle fed
	%	%	%	%	%	%	%	%	%	%	%	%
Breast	69	48	46	82	67	68	88	72	65	84	68	50
Breast and bottle	19	35	21	4	10	5	5	10	7	2	4	2
Bottle	8	8	23	11	19	21	6	13	25	11	25	43
Undecided	4	8	10	3	4	6	1	5	3	2	3	5
Base = 100%	*52*	*199*	*179*	*91*	*139*	*309*	*200*	*225*	*273*	*126*	*111*	*327*

Table 2.9

How mother herself was fed by country of birth and ethnic group

All mothers

How mother was fed	Ethnic group						
	Bangladeshi		Pakistani		Indian		White
	Born UK	Born elsewhere	Born UK	Born elsewhere	Born UK	Born elsewhere	All
	%	%	%	%	%	%	%
Breast	[15]	72	27	75	24	77	24
Breast and bottle	[15]	16	25	8	20	8	18
Bottle	[13]	6	40	9	42	6	50
Don't know	[4]	6	8	8	14	9	8
Base = 100%	*47*	*561*	*220*	*509*	*228*	*705*	*619*

Table 2.10

Intended method of feeding her baby by how mother herself was fed and ethnic group

All mothers

Intended method of feeding	How mother was fed											
	Bangladeshi			Pakistani			Indian			White		
	Breast fed	Half breast / half bottle	Bottle fed	Breast fed	Half breast / half bottle	Bottle fed	Breast fed	Half breast / half bottle	Bottle fed	Breast fed	Half breast / half bottle	Bottle fed
	%	%	%	%	%	%	%	%	%	%	%	%
Breast	49	49	[20]	69	70	64	76	76	68	81	81	47
Breast and bottle	26	32	[8]	4	11	6	7	6	8	1	4	2
Bottle	15	9	[18]	19	15	23	14	16	21	16	13	47
Undecided	10	11	[3]	8	4	7	3	1	4	2	3	5
Base = 100%	419	104	49	441	98	134	600	98	140	150	110	311

Table 2.11

Reasons for planning to breastfeed: **all** babies by ethnic group

*All mothers who planned to breastfeed **

Reasons for planning to breastfeed	Ethnic group			
	Bangladeshi	Pakistani	Indian	White
	%	%	%	%
Best for baby	85	86	88	82
Previous experience	8	11	13	19
Natural	14	19	23	14
Convenient	10	19	18	35
Bond between mother and baby	9	7	15	18
Best for mother	6	11	9	7
Cheaper	1	2	4	15
Builds up immunity	0	1	3	5
Tradition / culture	1	3	2	0
Advice from family / friends / others	2	2	2	2
No particular reason	2	2	1	1
Other	2	4	4	6
Base = 100%	447	537	746	391

Percentages do not add to 100 as some mothers gave more than one reason.

* Includes mothers who planned to both breast and bottle feed.

Table 2.12

Reasons for planning to breastfeed: **first and later** babies by ethnic group

*All mothers of first and later babies who planned to breastfeed **

Reasons for planning to breastfeed	First babies				Later babies			
	Ethnic group				Ethnic group			
	Bangladeshi	Pakistani	Indian	White	Bangladeshi	Pakistani	Indian	White
	%	%	%	%	%	%	%	%
Best for baby	86	91	90	91	84	84	85	72
Previous experience	–	–	–	–	12	16	24	38
Natural	19	23	26	16	12	17	21	12
Convenient	9	14	17	32	10	23	18	40
Bond between mother and baby	13	9	19	21	7	6	11	16
Best for mother	8	8	10	7	5	13	9	6
Cheaper	1	2	3	20	0	2	4	9
Builds up immunity	1	1	3	5	0	1	3	4
Tradition / culture	3	3	2	0	1	3	1	0
Advice from family / friends / others	2	3	3	4	2	1	1	0
No particular reason	1	2	1	1	2	2	2	2
Other	2	3	4	3	3	4	3	9
Base = 100%	154	190	349	206	293	347	397	185

Percentages do not add to 100 as some mothers gave more than one reason.

* Includes mothers who planned to both breast and bottle feed.

Table 2.13

Reasons for planning to bottle feed: **all** babies by ethnic group

*All mothers who planned to bottle feed ***

Reasons for planning to bottle feed	Ethnic group			
	Bangladeshi	Pakistani	Indian	White
	%	%	%	%
Previous experience	26	32	30	30
Convenient	18	19	18	24
Others can feed baby	7	12	20	17
Disliked idea of breastfeeding	9	11	12	44
Embarrassed to breastfeed	6	8	7	8
Can see how much baby had	8	6	5	6
Medical reasons	9	8	8	3
May not have enough milk	14	5	4	0
Top up breastfeeds	2	2	0	0
Expect to return to work soon	2	1	14	5
Breastfeeding difficult with twins/triplets	0	2	5	2
No particular reason	9	9	6	3
Other	11	8	9	6
Base = 100%	*252*	*181*	*216*	*217*

Percentages do not add to 100 as some mothers gave more than one reason.

* Includes mothers who planned to both breast and bottle feed.

Table 2.14

Reasons for planning to bottle feed: **first and later** babies by ethnic group

*All mothers of first and later babies who planned to bottle feed ***

Reasons for planning to bottle feed	First babies				Later babies			
	Ethnic group				Ethnic group			
	Bangladeshi	Pakistani	Indian	White	Bangladeshi	Pakistani	Indian	White
	%	%	%	%	%	%	%	%
Previous experience	–	–	–	–	36	45	40	45
Convenient	21	18	22	22	17	20	17	25
Others can feed baby	17	20	24	19	3	9	19	15
Disliked idea of breastfeeding	12	19	9	63	7	8	13	33
Embarrassed to breastfeed	7	17	9	13	6	4	6	6
Can see how much baby had	6	10	7	4	9	4	4	8
Medical reasons	4	10	7	2	11	8	9	4
May not have enough milk	12	0	2	0	14	8	4	0
Top up breastfeeds	3	2	0	0	1	2	1	0
Expect to return to work soon	3	1	26	6	1	2	10	4
Breastfeeding difficult with twins/triplets	0	0	6	2	0	2	4	1
No particular reason	15	14	15	4	7	7	4	3
Other	15	10	8	6	9	6	9	6
Base = 100%	*72*	*54*	*54*	*79*	*180*	*127*	*162*	*138*

Percentages do not add to 100 as some mothers gave more than one reason.

* Includes mothers who planned to both breast and bottle feed.

3   Bottle feeding

Summary

- Ten per cent of Bangladeshi, 24% of Pakistani, 18% of Indian and 38% of White babies were only ever bottle fed.

- When babies were on average nine weeks old, 95% of Bangladeshi, 91% of Pakistani, 83% of White and 81% of Indian babies were bottle fed at least some of the time.

- By fifteen months, at least nine out of ten children in each of the Asian groups and three quarters of White children were still bottle fed.

- Asian babies who were bottle fed were more likely than White babies to be given whey dominant formula.

- White babies were much more likely to be given a whey than a casein dominant formula if they were simultaneously breast and bottle fed than if they were only bottle fed. The difference was less significant among Indian and Pakistani babies and not at all significant among Bangladeshi babies.

- By nine months, follow-on milk was given as the main milk to more White and Indian than Pakistani and Bangladeshi babies. At this age, cow's milk was more likely to be given to Pakistani and Bangladeshi babies than to Indian and White babies.

- By fifteen months, the main milk given to the great majority of children in each group was cow's milk. Nearly all were given whole milk.

- Bangladeshi mothers were the most likely to have added something to the milk in their baby's bottle at both nine and fifteen months. Rusks were the most common addition at nine months among all Asian groups and continued to be added most often at 15 months by Bangladeshi mothers.

- Mothers most frequently chose to buy the brand of formula which was recommended by health professionals, family or friends.

- Sterilising tablets and fluid were used to sterilise bottles by nearly all Bangladeshi and Pakistani mothers but less frequently by Indian and White mothers. White and Indian mothers were more likely than others to use a bottle steamer.

- The majority of White but many fewer Asian mothers made up more than one bottle at a time. Of those who made up more than one bottle at a time, nearly all White but fewer Asian mothers stored them in a refrigerator.

- A higher proportion of Bangladeshi and Pakistani than Indian and White mothers said they received tokens for free milk. This reflects the proportion of each group who were eligible for milk tokens because they were receiving income support.

3.1 Introduction

This chapter examines the prevalence of bottle feeding and the type and quantity of non-human milk given to babies at each age. The reasons for choosing a brand of formula, the methods used by mothers to sterilise and store bottles and the help received with the cost of milk are also discussed.

3.2 Prevalence of bottle feeding

Ten per cent of Bangladeshi, 24% of Pakistani, 18% of Indian and 38% of White babies were only ever bottle fed (Figure 1.1). By the first interview, when babies were on average nine weeks old, the majority were bottle fed at least some of the time. Bangladeshi and Pakistani babies were more likely to be bottle fed than Indian or White babies – 95% of Bangladeshi and 91% of Pakistani compared with 83% of White and 81% of Indian babies. By five months, the proportion of White and Indian babies who were bottle fed had increased slightly to 88% and 87% respectively. At nine months, about 95% of all babies were bottle fed and at fifteen months at least nine out of ten children in each of the Asian groups and three quarters of White children were still bottle fed. Figure 3.1, Table 3.1

White children were more likely than Asian children to be drinking milk from a cup, glass or beaker at fifteen months, even if only occasionally – 67% of White children compared with 50% of Indian, 41% of Pakistani and 26% of Bangladeshi children. Of those who were given milk in a cup at fifteen months, White children were given cups of milk more frequently than Asian children. Seventy four per cent of White children were given at least one cup of milk a day compared with 61% of Pakistani, 58% of Indian and 51% of Bangladeshi children. Ten per cent of White children and 3% of Pakistani, 2% of Indian and 1% of Bangladeshi children were given as many as four or more cups of milk a day. Table 3.2

3.3 Type of non-human milk given at each stage

Information about the type of non-human milk given to babies who were bottle fed was collected at all four stages. Most infant formulas can be classified as whey or casein dominant. Whey dominant infant formulas have a whey:casein ratio which is closer to that in human milk whereas casein formulas have a whey:casein ratio which is closer to that in cow's milk. There are also infant formulas based on soya protein.

Figure 3.1

Proportion of mothers giving milk from a bottle at each stage by ethnic group

All mothers

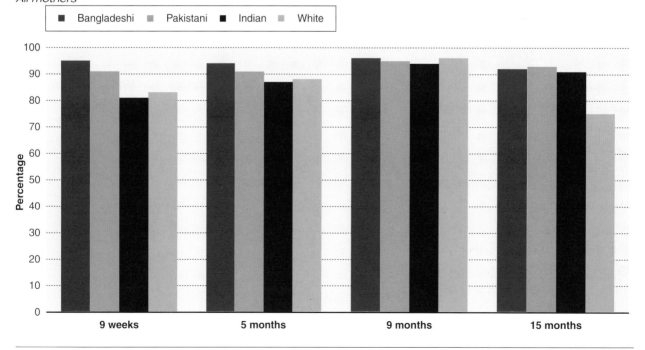

Among all groups, 3% or fewer babies at any stage were given soya based formula. For older babies, there are follow-on milks which are intended to provide the milk drink element in more diversified diets.

Among babies who were bottle fed, the type of infant formula given to them varied considerably between Asian and White babies. At about nine weeks old, 90% of Bangladeshi, 83% of Indian and 82% of Pakistani babies but only 48% of White babies were given whey dominant formula. Forty seven per cent of White babies were given casein dominant formula.

At five months, the proportion given a whey dominant formula had decreased among all ethnic groups to 76% of Bangladeshi, 68% of Indian, 65% of Pakistani and 41% of White babies. Conversely, the proportion given a casein dominant formula increased to 20% of Bangladeshi, 25% of Indian, 28% of Pakistani and 51% of White babies. Very few were given any other type of non-human milk.

By nine months, 52% of White, 44% of Indian, 39% of Pakistani and 35% of Bangladeshi babies who were given milk from a bottle or cup were no longer given whey or casein dominant formula as their main milk but had been introduced to other types of milk. Cow's milk was the main milk given to Pakistani and Bangladeshi babies (31% and 28% respectively) and to slightly fewer Indian (24%) and White (22%) babies. Twenty five per cent of White and 16% of Indian babies were given follow-on milk. Follow-on milk was given to only 5% of Pakistani and 3% of Bangladeshi babies.

By fifteen months, of those who were given milk in either a bottle or cup, the main milk given to the great majority of children in each group was cow's milk. Nearly all were given whole milk but 5% in each group were given either semi-skimmed or skimmed milk. **Figure 3.2, Table 3.3**

3.4 Type of non-human milk given to babies bottle fed exclusively and those who were also breastfed

As in the 1990 survey of infant feeding, White babies were much more likely to be given a whey than a casein dominant formula if they were simultaneously breast and bottle fed (79% were given a whey dominant formula at nine weeks, 74% at five months) than if they were only bottle fed (42% were given a whey dominant formula at nine weeks, 38% at five months).

Among Pakistani and Indian babies, the difference was only slight at nine weeks, but more significant at five months when about eight out of ten who were both breast and bottle fed were given a whey dominant formula compared with about two thirds who were only bottle fed. Bangladeshi babies who were only bottle fed were just as likely to be given a whey dominant formula as those who were both breast and bottle fed at both nine weeks and five months. **Table 3.4**

3.5 Reasons for choosing brand of formula

At the third interview, when babies were about nine months old, mothers were asked how they chose which brand of formula to buy. The reason mentioned most frequently by all groups was that they bought the brand recommended by health professionals, family or friends. Bangladeshi and Pakistani mothers were particularly likely to choose a brand recommended by health professionals (43% and 42% respectively compared with 33% of Indian and 30% of White mothers). Indian mothers were more likely than other mothers to choose a brand recommended by family or friends (30% of Indian compared with 26% of Pakistani, 21% of Bangladeshi and 18% of White mothers). The brand chosen by about one in five mothers in all ethnic groups was based on their previous experience. Some mothers chose a brand because their baby liked it or it suited the baby – mentioned by about one in ten White and Bangladeshi, 8% of Indian and 4% of Pakistani mothers. White mothers were the most likely to be influenced by advertising or having tried a free sample (7%) or to choose a brand because it was well known (5%). Bangladeshi mothers were more likely than others to choose a brand for religious or dietary reasons (6%). **Table 3.5**

Figure 3.2
Main type of non-human milk given at each stage by ethnic group
All bottle fed babies

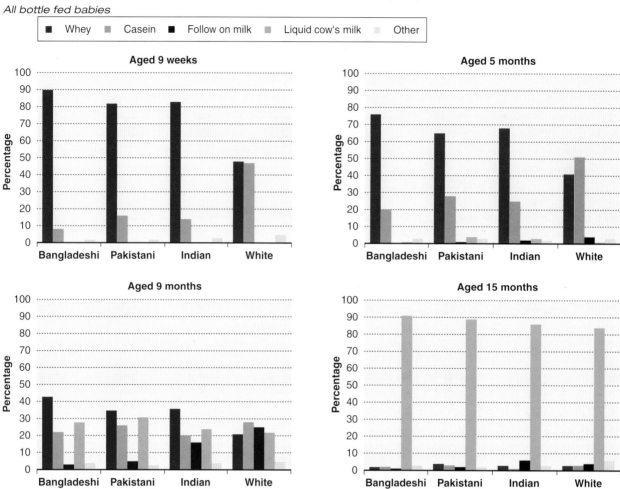

3.6 Liquid cow's milk

3.6.1 Use of liquid cow's milk at each stage

When babies were about five months old, very few were ever given liquid cow's milk – only 1% of all White and Bangladeshi, 3% of all Indian and 4% of all Pakistani babies.

By nine months, the proportion of all babies who were given liquid cow's milk had increased to a half of all White babies, about four out of ten Indian and Pakistani and about a third of Bangladeshi babies. The proportion for whom liquid cow's milk was the main milk if they were bottle fed was slightly higher among Asian than White babies (30% of Pakistani, 27% of Bangladeshi, 23% of Indian compared with 20% of White babies). White babies were much more likely than other babies to be given cow's milk in addition to infant formula if they were bottle fed (nearly a third of all White babies compared with 17% of Indian, 12% of Pakistani and 7% of all Bangladeshi babies).

At fifteen months, about 95% of children in all groups were given cow's milk either as a drink or mixed with food. Children in the Asian groups continued to be slightly more likely than White children to be given cow's milk as their main milk (86% of Pakistani and Bangladeshi, 85% of Indian and 79% of White children). White children were at least twice as likely as Asian children to have been given cow's milk as a second milk (13% of White, 7% of Indian, 4% of Pakistani, 3% of Bangladeshi). At fifteen months, cow's milk was also used to mix food for about three quarters of all White (78%), Pakistani (73%) and Indian (72%) children and just over a half of all Bangladeshi (54%) children.

Of those who were given cow's milk, nearly all were given whole milk. The group most likely to be given semi-skimmed milk were the White children who were bottle fed and given cow's milk in addition to infant formula – 5% of all White children at nine months and 6% of all White children at fifteen months. At any age, 1% or less in any group were given skimmed milk.

Table 3.6

3.6.2 Age introduced to liquid cow's milk

At the third interview when babies were about nine months old, mothers who gave their baby cow's milk most of the time were asked how old their baby was when they started giving this type of milk. On average, babies in all ethnic groups were about the same age, seven months, when they were first introduced to cow's milk, although White children were introduced slightly earlier than Bangladeshi children (7.1 and 7.5 months respectively).

Figure 3.3

3.7 Quantity of milk given

At both the second and third interviews when babies were about five and nine months old, mothers were asked how many bottles of milk

they gave their baby each day and how many fluid ounces of milk the baby drank at each feed.

At five months, White babies who were entirely bottle fed usually drank on average 28 fluid ounces of milk a day compared with Pakistani and Indian babies who drank on average 25 fluid ounces and Bangladeshi babies who drank on average 19 fluid ounces. Babies who were both breast and bottle fed at five months drank similar amounts in all groups (12 to 14 ounces of milk a day).

At nine months, Pakistani, Indian and White babies who were entirely bottle fed were given similar amounts of milk (23, 22 and 20 fluid ounces respectively). Bangladeshi babies drank slightly less (17 fluid ounces). The number who were both breast and bottle fed at nine months was too few to show the amount they drank.

Table 3.7

3.8 Additives to milk

When babies were on average nine weeks old, very few mothers added anything such as solid food or sugar to the milk in their baby's bottle. By nine months, Bangladeshi mothers were the most likely to have added something to the milk (22% compared with 12% of Pakistani, 9% of

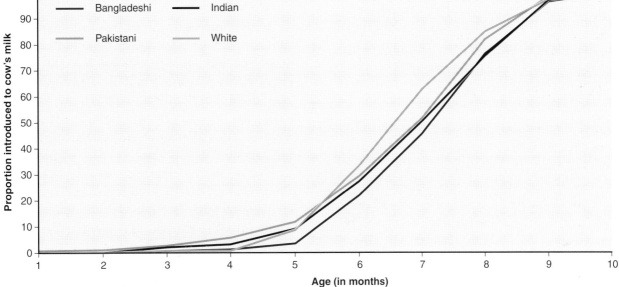

Figure 3.3
Proportion of babies introduced to cow's milk up to 10 months* by ethnic group

Y-axis: Proportion introduced to cow's milk
X-axis: Age (in months)

Legend: Bangladeshi, Indian, Pakistani, White

* Based on babies given cow's milk most of the time at the third interview (9 months)

Indian and 8% of White mothers). At fifteen months, Bangladeshi mothers were still most likely to have added something to their baby's milk (about a third compared with about a quarter of Pakistani and a fifth of all other mothers).   Table 3.8

At nine months, rusks were the most common addition to the baby's bottle in all Asian groups (added by 11% of Bangladeshi, 5% of Pakistani and 4% of Indian bottle feeding mothers). Bangladeshi mothers were the most likely to add baby rice or cereal (8%). White mothers were the most likely to add milk shakes or other milk drinks (4%).

At fifteen months, Bangladeshi mothers continued to be the most likely to add rusks to their baby's bottle (23% compared with 7% of Pakistani, 4% of Indian and 1% of White mothers). The proportion of Pakistani mothers who added sugar to the bottle had increased to 10% compared with 5% or less in other groups. White mothers continued to be the most likely to give milk shakes or other milk drinks (13%).

                                        Table 3.9

3.9 Hygiene practices

Mothers who bottle fed their babies at either the first or second stage of the survey were asked how they usually sterilised the bottles. Sterilising tablets or fluid were used by nearly all Bangladeshi and Pakistani mothers (94% and 90% respectively) but less frequently by Indian and White mothers (73% and 53% respectively). Thirty eight per cent of White and 19% of Indian mothers used a bottle steamer. Five per cent of White and 2% of Indian mothers used a microwave. Bottle steamers and microwaves were used by very few Bangladeshi and Pakistani mothers.   Table 3.10

Nearly all mothers usually made up the bottles themselves. Seven per cent of White but very few other mothers said that their husband or partner usually made up the bottles.   Table 3.11

The majority (84%) of White mothers but many fewer Asian mothers (21% of Indian, 13% of Pakistani, 9% of Bangladeshi) usually made up more than one bottle at a time.   Table 3.12

Of those who did make up more than one bottle at a time, nearly all (95%) White mothers stored the bottles in the fridge. Although they were just as likely as White mothers to have the use of a refrigerator (see Appendix B), fewer Asian mothers made up more than one bottle at a time and of those who did, fewer stored the bottles in the fridge (84% of Indian, 72% of Pakistani and 66% of Bangladeshi). Of those who made up more than one bottle at a time, Bangladeshi and Pakistani mothers were most likely to leave them on the kitchen work surface or in a cool place (22% and 16% respectively); and Bangladeshi mothers were the most likely to leave the made up bottles in the bedroom to use at night (6%). The great majority of mothers did not keep unused feeds for later.   Tables 3.12-3.14

3.10 Help with the cost of milk

Families receiving income support[1] are entitled to tokens available from early pregnancy to when the child is five years old, which may be exchanged for free liquid cow's milk. During the first year, the tokens may instead be exchanged for free infant formula. Breastfeeding mothers may take the entitlement in the form of liquid cow's milk to drink themselves. At stage 1, 49% of Bangladeshi, 40% of Pakistani, 21% of Indian and 23% of White mothers said that they or their husband had drawn income support in the last 14 days. Similar proportions reported receiving income support at later interviews.

                        Appendix B Table B21

At the first interview, 45% of Bangladeshi, 39% of Pakistani, 24% of White and 19% of Indian mothers said that they were receiving tokens for free milk. By the second and third interviews, the proportion of Bangladeshi mothers who said they were receiving tokens for free milk had risen to 50%. The proportions of other mothers receiving tokens remained unchanged at later stages.

                                        Table 3.15

Nearly all those eligible for tokens for free milk, because they were in receipt of income support, said they received them, but of those who were eligible, Asian mothers were less likely than White mothers to say they received them. At aged nine weeks, 83% of Indian, 85% of Bangladeshi, 87% of

Pakistani mothers and 93% of White mothers who said they were in receipt of income support also said they received their tokens. By nine months, the proportion of Bangladeshi and Pakistani mothers in families receiving Income Support who said they received milk tokens had increased to 93% and 95% respectively. By nine months, the proportion of Indian mothers who said they received milk tokens had increased to 88%.

These data should be interpreted with caution, because as Table 3.16 shows, some mothers gave inconsistent answers. This may be because they did not understand the question or they were unclear whether they or their husband received income support or whether they received tokens for free milk. For example, among Bangladeshi mothers, 2% who said they received Income Support said that their milk tokens were for reduced price milk whereas they were entitled to free milk. A further inconsistency is that of those who said that they did not receive income support, 6% of Bangladeshi mothers said they received tokens for free milk and a further 6% said they received tokens for reduced price milk. At the time of the survey families receiving Family Credit could buy infant formula for a baby under one year at reduced price from maternity and child health clinics and welfare food distribution centres. Welfare food tokens were not issued to such families and therefore could not be used to obtain reduced price infant formula. **Table 3.16**

At aged nine weeks, the majority of all groups who received tokens for free milk, Bangladeshi (83%), Pakistani (81%), Indian (69%) and White mothers (72%) exchanged them at the clinic. Others exchanged them with the milkman or at a chemist, supermarket or other type of shop. By nine months, fewer mothers exchanged the tokens at the clinic – 66% of Bangladeshi, 56% of Indian, 50% of Pakistani and 49% of White mothers. Ten per cent of Bangladeshi and about 20% of all other mothers exchanged them with the milkman. Sixteen per cent of Bangladeshi, Pakistani and White mothers and 8% of Indian mothers exchanged the tokens at the local shop or post office. Less than ten per cent of all mothers exchanged them at a supermarket. **Table 3.17**

Notes

1   Those eligible for Income Support are people aged 18 or over whose income is below a certain level and who are not working for 16 hours or more a week. They must be available for work and taking reasonable steps to find a job (unless they are sick, disabled, a lone parent, 60 or over, getting invalid care allowance or pregnant). The amount paid depends on age, whether the person has a partner, the number and age of dependent children, whether anyone in the family has a disability, weekly income and savings. Income-based Job Seeker's Allowance was introduced on 7 October 1996 after the completion of fieldwork for this project.

Table 3.1

Feeding method at each stage by ethnic group

All Babies

Feeding Method	Ethnic group			
	Bangladeshi	Pakistani	Indian	White
	%	%	%	%
Aged 9 weeks				
Bottle fed	95	91	81	83
Bottle only	60	72	59	70
Breast and bottle	35	18	23	13
Breastfed only	5	9	19	17
Aged 5 months				
Bottle fed	94	91	87	88
Bottle only	78	84	74	79
Breast and bottle	16	7	13	9
Breastfed only	6	9	13	12
Aged 9 months				
Bottle fed	96	95	94	96
Bottle only	87	90	86	90
Breast and bottle	9	5	9	6
Breastfed only	4	5	5	4
Aged 15 months				
Bottle fed	92	93	91	75
Bottle only	88	92	88	74
Breast and bottle	4	1	2	1
Breastfed only	3	4	4	2
Neither	5	3	5	23
Base = 100%				
Aged 9 weeks	*610*	*731*	*934*	*619*
Aged 5 months	*552*	*668*	*841*	*594*
Aged 9 months	*513*	*636*	*810*	*564*
Aged 15 months	*477*	*590*	*758*	*548*

Table 3.2

Whether milk given from a cup at aged 15 months and frequency by ethnic group

All children

Milk from a cup	Ethnic group			
	Bangladeshi	Pakistani	Indian	White
	%	%	%	%
Yes	26	41	50	67
No	74	59	50	33
Base = 100%	*477*	*590*	*758*	*548*
Number of cups of milk drunk each day				
Less than one	49	39	42	26
One	20	39	32	31
Two	25	14	16	23
Three	6	4	8	10
Four or more	1	3	2	10
Base = 100%	*121*	*242*	*376*	*365*
Average (mean) number of cups of milk drunk each day	*0.9*	*0.9*	*1.0*	*1.6*

Table 3.3
Main type of non-human milk given at each stage by ethnic group

*All bottle fed babies**

Type of non-human milk	Bangladeshi				Pakistani			
	9 weeks	5 months	9 months	15 months	9 weeks	5 months	9 months	15 months
	%	%	%	%	%	%	%	%
Whey dominant	90	76	43	2	82	65	35	4
Casein dominant	8	20	22	2	16	28	26	3
Soya based	1	3	3	2	1	2	2	1
Follow on milk	–	–	3	1	–	1	5	2
Liquid cow's milk:								
whole	–	1	27	86	–	4	28	84
semi-skimmed	–	–	1	4	–	0	3	4
skimmed	–	–	0	1	–	–	0	1
Other	1	0	1	1	1	1	1	1
Base = 100%	*579*	*519*	*498*	*449*	*663*	*608*	*610*	*575*

	Indian				White			
	9 weeks	5 months	9 months	15 months	9 weeks	5 months	9 months	15 months
	%	%	%	%	%	%	%	%
Whey dominant	83	68	36	3	48	41	21	3
Casein dominant	14	25	20	1	47	51	28	3
Soya based	1	1	3	2	1	2	3	2
Follow on milk	–	2	16	6	–	4	25	4
Liquid cow's milk:								
whole	–	2	22	81	–	1	20	79
semi-skimmed	–	1	2	5	–	0	2	5
skimmed	–	–	0	0	–	–	–	0
Other	2 .	1	1	1	4	1	2	4
Base = 100%	*758*	*730*	*771*	*740*	*515*	*522*	*548*	*511*

*   At fourth interview (aged approx. 15 months) included those given milk in a cup, glass or beaker.

Table 3.4

Main type of non-human milk given at each stage to babies who were bottle fed exclusively and those who are also breastfed

All bottle fed babies

Type of non-human milk	Ethnic group							
	Bangladeshi		Pakistani		Indian		White	
							Babies bottle fed exclusively at:	
	9 weeks	5 months	9 weeks	5 months	9 weeks	5 months	9 weeks	5 months
	%	%	%	%	%	%	%	%
Whey dominant	91	75	81	64	81	66	42	38
Casein dominant	8	21	17	29	16	27	52	55
Soya based	1	3	1	1	1	1	1	2
Follow on milk	–	–	–	1	–	2	–	4
Liquid cow's milk:								
whole	–	1	–	4	–	2	–	1
semi-skimmed	–	–	–	1	–	1	–	0
skimmed	–	–	–	–	–	–	–	–
Other	0	0	1	1	2	1	5	0

							Babies who were also breastfed at:	
	9 weeks	5 months	9 weeks	5 months	9 weeks	5 months	9 weeks	5 months
	%	%	%	%	%	%	%	%
Whey dominant	90	78	88	81	89	82	79	74
Casein dominant	7	17	12	15	9	11	17	18
Soya based	1	2	–	3	1	2	–	2
Follow on milk	–	–	–	1	–	2	–	4
Liquid cow's milk:								
whole	–	1	–	–	–	3	–	–
semi-skimmed	–	–	–	–	–	1	–	–
skimmed	–	–	–	–	–	–	–	–
Other	2	1	–	–	1	–	4	2
Base = 100%								
Bottle fed exclusively	*365*	*433*	*528*	*560*	*547*	*618*	*433*	*468*
Also breastfed	*214*	*86*	*135*	*47*	*211*	*112*	*82*	*54*

Table 3.5

Reasons for choosing brand of formula milk by ethnic group

All bottle feeding mothers at third interview

Reasons for choosing brand of formula milk	Ethnic group			
	Bangladeshi	Pakistani	Indian	White
	%	%	%	%
Recommended by health professional	43	42	33	30
Recommended by family/friends	21	26	30	18
Previous experience	17	19	18	20
Baby likes it/suits baby	10	4	8	11
Advertising/coupon/free sample	2	2	4	7
Baby allergic to other formulas	3	2	3	4
First given in hospital	1	4	3	5
Religious/dietary reasons	6	3	3	0
Well known/quality brand	1	1	1	5
Continued with same brand	–	1	1	4
Closest to breast milk	1	0	2	2
Only one available	1	2	0	3
Low price	–	0	0	4
Heavier milk	–	1	2	2
Other	3	2	3	3
Base = 100%	356	419	583	431

Percentages do not add to 100 as some mothers gave more than one reason.

Table 3.6

Liquid cow's milk given at each stage by ethnic group

All babies

Ethnic group				
	Bangladeshi	Pakistani	Indian	White
	%	%	%	%
				Proportion of all babies given liquid cow's milk
Aged 5 months				
All given liquid cow's milk	1	4	3	1
Aged 9 months				
As main milk:	27	30	23	20
whole	25	26	21	18
semi-skimmed	1	3	2	1
skimmed	0	0	0	–
As second milk:	7	12	17	31
whole	5	12	15	26
semi-skimmed	1	1	2	5
skimmed	–	0	0	0
All given liquid cow's milk	34	42	40	50
Aged 15 months				
As main milk:	86	86	85	79
whole	81	82	79	74
semi-skimmed	4	4	5	5
skimmed	1	1	0	0
As second milk:	3	4	7	13
whole	2	4	5	6
semi-skimmed	1	1	1	6
skimmed	–	–	0	0
To mix food:	54	73	72	78
All given liquid cow's milk	94	95	94	94
Base = 100%				
Aged 5 months	*552*	*668*	*841*	*594*
Aged 9 months	*521*	*642*	*815*	*576*
Aged 15 months	*477*	*590*	*758*	*548*

Table 3.7

Average amount of milk given daily by bottle by ethnic group

All bottle fed babies

Ethnic group							
Bangladeshi		Pakistani		Indian		White	
Bottle only	Breast and bottle	Bottle only	Breast and bottle	Bottle only	Breast and bottle	Bottle only	Breast and bottle
Average (mean) amount (ounces) of milk							
Aged 5 months	19	12	25	14	25	12	28	12
Aged 9 months	17	*	23	*	22	11	20	*
Average (mean) number of bottles of milk given daily							
Aged 5 months	4.4	3.0	4.6	2.9	4.7	2.8	4.5	2.3
Aged 9 months	3.5	*	3.7	*	3.7	2.4	3.0	*
Base = 100%							
Aged 5 months	*432*	*85*	*559*	*46*	*617*	*111*	*468*	*53*
Aged 9 months	*443*	*45*	*571*	*33*	*695*	*68*	*500*	*33*

*   Means not shown because sample sizes small.

Table 3.8

Whether adds anything to milk in bottle by ethnic group

All bottle feeding mothers

Ethnic group			
Bangladeshi	Pakistani	Indian	White
%	%	%	%

Aged 9 weeks

	Bangladeshi	Pakistani	Indian	White
Yes	1	2	2	6
No	99	98	98	94

Aged 9 months

	Bangladeshi	Pakistani	Indian	White
Yes	22	12	9	8
No	78	88	91	92

Aged 15 months

	Bangladeshi	Pakistani	Indian	White
Yes	32	24	20	19
No	68	76	80	81

Base = 100%

	Bangladeshi	Pakistani	Indian	White
9 weeks	*580*	*662*	*757*	*514*
9 Months	*498*	*609*	*771*	*551*
15 Months	*449*	*575*	*740*	*511*

Table 3.9

What added to milk in bottle by ethnic group

All bottle feeding mothers

What added to milk*	Ethnic group			
	Bangladeshi	Pakistani	Indian	White
	%	%	%	%

Aged 9 months

	Bangladeshi	Pakistani	Indian	White
Rusks	11	5	4	2
Baby rice/cereal	8	1	1	0
Sugar	2	3	2	0
Milk shakes/other milk drinks	–	0	0	4
Egg custard	1	1	0	–
Fruit puddings	1	0	–	–
Honey	0	1	0	–
Tea/coffee	–	0	0	1
Other	1	1	2	1

Aged 15 months

	Bangladeshi	Pakistani	Indian	White
Rusks/biscuits/baby rice/cereal	23	7	4	1
Milk shakes/other milk drinks	1	3	5	13
Sugar	4	10	5	2
Egg custard/rice pudding/egg	2	0	1	–
Tea	–	0	1	2
Honey	0	1	1	0
Other	2	2	3	1

Base = 100%

	Bangladeshi	Pakistani	Indian	White
Stage 3	*498*	*609*	*771*	*551*
Stage 4	*449*	*575*	*740*	*511*

* Vitamins, colic drops, gripe water and other medicines are excluded.

Table 3.10

How bottles are sterilised by ethnic group

All mothers bottle feeding at either stage 1 or stage 2

How bottles are sterilised	Ethnic group			
	Bangladeshi	Pakistani	Indian	White
	%	%	%	%
Sterilising tablets	64	47	52	38
Sterilising fluid	30	43	21	15
Bottle steamer	1	5	19	38
Hot water	4	2	4	1
Microwave	0	0	2	5
Other	1	2	2	3
Base = 100%	*588*	*675*	*826*	*557*

Table 3.11

Who usually makes up the bottles by ethnic group

All mothers bottle feeding at either stage 1 or stage 2

Who usually makes up bottles	Ethnic group			
	Bangladeshi	Pakistani	Indian	White
	%	%	%	%
Baby's mother	98	98	96	92
Husband/partner	0	0	1	7
Other relative	1	2	2	0
Other person	0	–	0	0
Base = 100%	*587*	*676*	*826*	*557*

Table 3.12

Whether makes up more than one bottle at a time by ethnic group

All mothers bottle feeding at either stage 1 or stage 2

	Ethnic group			
	Bangladeshi	Pakistani	Indian	White
	%	%	%	%
Yes	9	13	21	84
No	91	87	79	16
Base = 100%	*588*	*676*	*825*	*556*

Table 3.13

Where usually stores the made up bottles by ethnic group

All mothers who made up more than one bottle at a time at either stage 1 or stage 2

Where made up bottles are stored	Ethnic group			
	Bangladeshi	Pakistani	Indian	White
	%	%	%	%
Fridge	66	72	84	95
Kitchen work surface	16	9	5	3
Cool place	6	7	4	2
Bedroom	6	2	1	0
Bag when go out	–	2	2	0
Other	7	8	4	0
Base = 100%	*55*	*88*	*176*	*468*

Table 3.14

Whether keeps unused feed to use later by ethnic group

All mothers bottle feeding at either stage 1 or stage 2

	Ethnic group			
	Bangladeshi	Pakistani	Indian	White
	%	%	%	%
Yes	9	8	9	6
Sometimes	7	6	9	5
No	84	86	82	88
Base = 100%	*587*	*676*	*825*	*556*

Table 3.15

Whether mother received tokens for free milk by ethnic group

All mothers

Whether received tokens for free milk	Ethnic group			
	Bangladesh	Pakistani	Indian	White
	%	%	%	%
Aged 9 weeks				
Yes	45	39	19	24
Aged 5 months				
Free milk	50	40	20	22
Aged 9 months				
Free milk	47	40	19	22
Base = 100%				
Aged 9 weeks	*599*	*712*	*898*	*607*
Aged 5 months	*552*	*668*	*841*	*593*
Aged 9 months	*520*	*639*	*815*	*576*

Table 3.16

Whether mother said she received milk tokens by whether received income support and ethnic group

All mothers

Whether received milk tokens[†]	Ethnic group							
	Bangladeshi		Pakistani		Indian		White	
							Whether received Income Support[*]	
	Yes	No	Yes	No	Yes	No	Yes	No
	%	%	%	%	%	%	%	%
Aged 9 weeks								
Yes, free milk	85	6	87	7	83	1	93	2
Yes, reduced price milk	2	6	3	11	5	3	1	2
No, neither	13	89	10	82	13	96	6	96
Aged 5 months								
Yes, free milk	93	8	91	4	84	2	95	2
Yes, reduced price milk	2	9	3	10	3	3	–	2
No, neither	6	83	6	86	12	94	5	96
Aged 9 months								
Yes, free milk	93	7	95	6	88	2	95	2
Yes, reduced price milk	1	7	0	8	2	3	–	2
No, neither	6	87	5	87	9	95	5	95
Base = 100%								
Aged 9 weeks	*287*	*304*	*282*	*425*	*190*	*703*	*142*	*465*
Aged 5 months	*270*	*279*	*273*	*385*	*178*	*662*	*129*	*464*
Aged 9 months	*245*	*273*	*241*	*390*	*165*	*647*	*124*	*452*

*   Based on answers to the question 'Have you (or your husband) drawn Income Support at any time in the last 14 days?'

†   Based on answers to the question 'Do you get milk tokens for free or reduced price milk?'

Table 3.17

Where milk tokens were exchanged by ethnic group

All mothers who received milk tokens for free milk

Where exchanged milk tokens	Ethnic group			
	Bangladeshi	Pakistani	Indian	White
	%	%	%	%
Aged 9 weeks				
Clinic	83	81	69	72
Milkman	5	8	12	10
Chemist	5	8	10	12
Local shop/post office	4	3	5	4
Supermarket	2	1	3	2
Aged 5 months				
Clinic	80	77	73	70
Milkman	5	8	8	11
Chemist	7	10	8	12
Local shop/post office	4	4	4	5
Supermarket	3	1	6	2
Aged 9 months				
Clinic	66	50	56	49
Milkman	10	22	20	22
Chemist	5	8	8	8
Local shop/post office	16	16	8	16
Supermarket	2	4	7	5
Base = 100%				
Aged 9 weeks	*266*	*277*	*169*	*143*
Aged 5 months	*276*	*270*	*166*	*131*
Aged 9 months	*245*	*254*	*158*	*129*

4 Antenatal care and advice

Summary

■ Almost all mothers in all groups had an *antenatal checkup*. A slightly higher proportion of mothers in Asian groups than White mothers had talked about feeding at the checkup.

■ Fewer Asian than White first time mothers had attended *antenatal classes*. Asian mothers were less likely to have been to a class which discussed feeding and the advantages of breastfeeding.

■ Most, but not all, health visitors and midwives visiting mothers who did not speak English, either spoke in the mother's own language or used an interpreter.

■ Asian mothers were more likely than White mothers to have received advice about their pregnancy from other family members.

■ Fewer Asian mothers (especially Bangladeshi) than White mothers had been given copies of the Health Education Authority publications for new mothers.

■ Of those whose main language was not English, Bangladeshi mothers were most likely to have been given published material in their own language.

4.1 Introduction

At the first interview, mothers were asked about the antenatal care and support they received. This chapter looks at whether mothers visited a health professional in connection with their pregnancy. It shows the proportion of mothers who were visited at home by a health visitor or midwife, and the language used at the visit when the mother did not speak English. It describes who attended antenatal classes and the reasons why others did not attend. It looks at other people who helped or advised the mothers during pregnancy, and whether their advice differed to that given by health professionals. Finally, it looks at the proportion of mothers who received written material about pregnancy and infant feeding.

4.2 Antenatal checkups and home visits

4.2.1 Antenatal checkups
Almost all mothers had received antenatal care. Nearly half the Asian mothers and 42% of White mothers had talked about how they would be feeding their baby at an antenatal visit.   Table 4.1

4.2.2 Antenatal home visits by health visitors and midwives
Around a third of Indian and Bangladeshi mothers were visited at home by a health visitor or midwife before they had the baby, compared with 45% of Pakistani and 42% of White mothers. A similar proportion of mothers having their second or a later baby were visited as those having their first baby.   Table 4.2

When visiting mothers who said that they did not understand spoken English very well or at all[1], health visitors and midwives spoke in English using an interpreter to translate, to two thirds of Bangladeshi mothers and a half of Pakistani and Indian mothers. A quarter of Pakistani mothers were spoken to in their own language, but this figure was lower for Bangladeshi (18%), and Indian mothers (15%). The 35% of Indian mothers who were spoken to in English without an interpreter were mothers who said they did not understand English very well, rather than not at all.   Table 4.3

4.3 Antenatal classes

4.3.1 Attendance at antenatal classes
A lower proportion of Asian than White first time mothers attended antenatal classes and the proportion who did, varied between the ethnic groups. Fifty three per cent of Indian, 24% of Pakistani, and 14% of Bangladeshi mothers attended classes, compared with 77% of White mothers. In 1990, the equivalent figure for Great Britain was 67% [2]. Three per cent of Bangladeshi and Pakistani mothers, and 10% of Indian and White mothers, having their second or a later baby, attended classes.

Not all those who had been to classes had attended one which discussed feeding. Sixty four per cent of White, 41% cent of Indian mothers, 16% of Pakistani and 9% of Bangladeshi mothers had attended a class which included a discussion about feeding. Almost all mothers who had done so had also discussed the advantages of breastfeeding.   Figure 4.1, Table 4.4

4.3.2 Reasons for not attending antenatal classes
Mothers from each group gave a wide range of reasons for not attending antenatal classes. The main reason given by first-time mothers for not attending was not wanting to go. About a third of first-time Asian mothers and 43% of White mothers who did not attend classes said they had not wanted to go. Asian mothers were more likely than White mothers to say that they had never heard of classes or that they did not know when or where they were held (Bangladeshi 22%, Pakistani 16%, Indian 14% and White 9%). Between 10 and 12 per cent of all Asian mothers mentioned language difficulties as a reason for not attending. Pakistani, Indian and White mothers were more likely than Bangladeshi mothers to say that the classes were held at an inconvenient time, or that they were too busy working, studying or looking after relatives to attend.   Table 4.5

Figure 4.1
Proportion of first time mothers attending antenatal classes by ethnic group

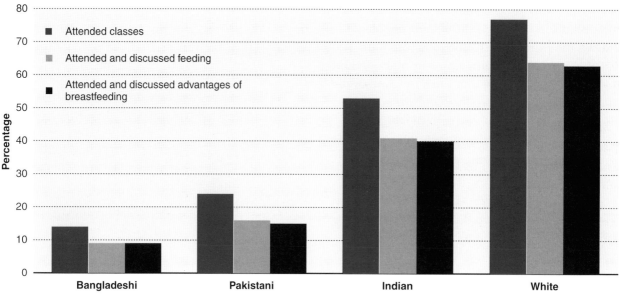

All first time mothers

Legend:
■ Attended classes
■ Attended and discussed feeding
■ Attended and discussed advantages of breastfeeding

(Y-axis: Percentage, 0–80; X-axis groups: Bangladeshi, Pakistani, Indian, White)

4.3.3 Characteristics of mothers attending classes

A logistic regression model was used in order to identify the social characteristics of mothers in each ethnic group which made them more likely to attend antenatal classes. The results of the analysis show that the most significant factor associated with attending classes, for all groups, was whether the mother was having her first baby. The other factor to affect whether Bangladeshi mothers attended classes was if they understood English. For Pakistani mothers, those with 14 years or more of education, living in London or the South of England, and who had come to England before 1990, were most likely to attend classes. Similar factors were important for Indian mothers and also age of mother and social class of husband or partner. White mothers aged 25 and over, with at least 12 years of education, were most likely to attend classes. Those with husbands or partners in a non-manual occupation, and who lived in Outer London or the South, were also more likely to attend. The model, the results, and the independence of variables included in it are given at the end of the chapter.[3] **Table 4.6**

4.4 Other sources of advice during pregnancy

4.4.1 Other people giving advice

Eighty two per cent of Indian, 71% of Pakistani, 66% of Bangladeshi and 64% of White first time mothers said that they had received advice from someone other than their health visitor or midwife when pregnant. About three quarters of Asian mothers and 60% of White mothers said most advice was given by their mother or sister (or mother- or sister-in-law). **Table 4.7-4.8**

4.4.2 Mothers receiving differing advice

White mothers were more likely than Asian mothers to say that the advice given by their health visitor or midwife differed from that given by others who advised them (White 37%, Indian 19%, Pakistani 17%, and Bangladeshi 14%).

Of those who said the advice given by the health visitor or midwife differed from that given by others, the most common theme amongst all groups was that family and friends gave practical advice, whereas health workers' advice was more theoretical, or that family and friends gave better or more personal advice. Other differences cited mainly by Indian mothers were that their families gave them traditional or cultural advice, and gave specific advice about the mother's diet or amount of exercise she should have e.g. "what to eat while pregnant, no fish and spicy things, plenty of milk", "mother said to eat certain foods, midwife would say not and vice versa", "traditional ideas to do with Indian diet – to eat or avoid foods".

Table 4.9

4.4.3 Advice received from voluntary groups

Asian mothers were unlikely to have received help or advice from a voluntary organisation (such as the National Childbirth Trust or La Leche League). Of first time mothers, 3% of Indian, 1% of Bangladeshi and less than 1% of Pakistani mothers had received advice from these organisations, compared with 10% of White mothers.

Table 4.10

4.4.4 Proportion of mothers given pregnancy books and leaflets about feeding

Mothers were asked if they had been given either *The Pregnancy Book* or *Birth to Five*, both published by the Health Education Authority (in English only), and available free to first time mothers. Of first time mothers who could read English at least fairly well, Bangladeshi mothers were least likely to have been given these books, 32% of

Bangladeshi mothers had not had either, compared with 16% of Pakistani, 12% of Indian, and 6% of White mothers. In the 1990 survey of infant feeding, 11% of mothers had not received either book[2]. The Health Education Authority target for 1994-6, is that 90% of first time mothers should receive a copy of 'The Pregnancy Book'[4].

Figure 4.2, Table 4.11

Of those whose main language was not English, Bangladeshi mothers were most likely to have received a leaflet, magazine, cassette or video in their own language (46%), compared with 38% of Pakistani, and 32% Indian mothers. When compared by language, 46% of Bengali-reading mothers received information in their own language, compared with mothers reading Punjabi (38%), Urdu (35%) and Gujarati (31%).

Tables 4.12-13

Figure 4.2

Percentage of first time mothers given HEA books by ethnic group

All first time mothers who said they could read English 'fairly well' or 'very well'

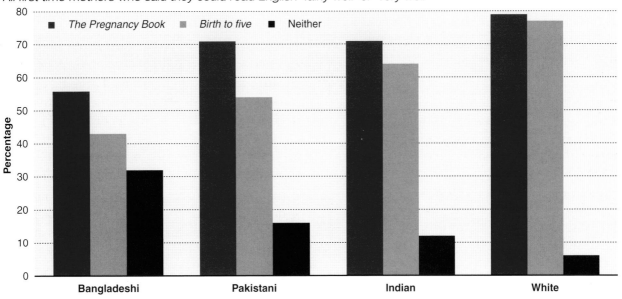

Notes

1 Fifty nine per cent of Bangladeshi, 32% of Pakistani and 17% of Indian mothers said that they did not understand spoken English very well or at all (Appendix B, Table B11).

2 White A, Freeth S, O'Brien M. *Infant Feeding 1990* HMSO (London 1992).

3 Logistic regression was used to identify which social characteristics have a significant independent effect on the dependent variable 'whether the mother attended antenatal classes or not'. The results of the analyses are shown in Table 4.6.

The characteristics in the first column are the independent variables included in the model. For each category of these variables, the logistic regression procedure produces a coefficient which represents the factor by which the odds of a mother attending classes differ from those in the reference group. These factors, or odds ratios are shown in the column headed 'Multiplying factors'. The reference categories have odds ratios of 1.00. In this model the reference group has been chosen as the group least likely to attend classes.

The multiplying factors can be used to calculate the odds of a mother attending classes. To do this, the baseline odds shown at the top of the table are multiplied by the appropriate factors. For example, from Table 4.6, the odds of an Indian mother expecting her first baby, aged 30 or over, with 14 years of education, whose husband was in a non-manual occupation, attending classes would be calculated as:

$0.001 \times 21.73 \times 6.96 \times 2.63 \times 3.05 = 1.21$

The odds of a mother with these characteristics attending classes would therefore be 1.21 to 1. To calculate this in percentage terms, the odds are divided by the odds plus one:

$[1.21 / (1+1.21)] \times 100 = 55\%$

Thus the model would predict that 55% of Indian mothers with these characteristics would attend antenatal classes.

Some of the variables in Table 4.6 are not truly independent. For example, region is related to variables such as social class and level of education. The model demonstrates the independent effect of each of the variables and shows that the effect of region is still significant even taking into account other characteristics of the mother.

4 Health Education Authority Quality Guidelines for the Distribution of *The Pregnancy Book* and *Birth to Five*, HEA (London 1994).

Table 4.1
Proportion of mothers who had an antenatal checkup and whether they talked about feeding by ethnic group

All mothers

| | Ethnic group | | | |
	Bangladeshi	Pakistani	Indian	White
	%	%	%	%
Had a checkup	97	98	99	100
Had a checkup and talked about feeding	47	50	46	42
Base = 100%	*609*	*728*	*934*	*619*

Table 4.2
Proportion of mothers who were visited at home by a midwife or health visitor by ethnic group

All mothers

| | Ethnic group | | | |
	Bangladeshi	Pakistani	Indian	White
	%	%	%	%
First births				
Visited at home	37	45	36	43
Not visited at home	63	55	64	57
Later births				
Visited at home	32	46	31	48
Not visited at home	68	54	69	52
All births				
Visited at home	34	46	33	46
Not visited at home	66	54	67	54
Base = 100%	*608*	*730*	*934*	*619*

Table 4.3
Language used by health visitor/midwife at the home visit by ethnic group

Asian mothers who said they did not understand English well or at all

| Language used by health visitor or midwife | Ethnic group | | |
	Bangladeshi	Pakistani	Indian
	%	%	%
English	82	75	85
Without an interpreter	16	26	35
With an interpreter	66	49	50
Other language	18	25	15
Base = 100%	*135*	*105*	*60*

Table 4.4

Proportion of mothers attending antenatal classes and whether they discussed feeding by ethnic group

All mothers

	Ethnic group			
	Bangladeshi	**Pakistani**	**Indian**	**White**
	%	%	%	%
Attended antenatal classes				
Mothers having their first baby	14	24	53	77
Mothers having a later baby	3	3	10	10
First–time mothers only				
Attended classes which included a discussion about feeding	9	16	41	64
Attended classes which included a discussion about the advantages of breastfeeding	9	15	40	63
Base = 100%				
First time mothers	*209*	*251*	*391*	*295*
All mothers	*609*	*730*	*934*	*619*

Table 4.5

Reasons for not attending antenatal classes by ethnic group

All first time mothers not attending antenatal classes

Reasons for not attending antenatal classes	Ethnic group			
	Bangladeshi	**Pakistani**	**Indian**	**White**
	%	%	%	%
Didn't want to	35	35	34	43
Never heard of them/didn't know where they were held	22	16	14	9
Classes held at an inconvenient time	7	14	17	18
Too busy to attend	8	10	19	10
Language difficulties	12	10	12	0
Too ill/tired	6	7	5	6
Away when pregnant	8	7	2	2
Wouldn't go alone/too shy or scared	3	5	4	6
Too far to go/no transport	4	5	4	3
None available	1	0	4	2
Not allowed to go	3	1	0	0
Other	6	7	7	18
Base = 100%	*180*	*190*	*183*	*67*

Percentages add to more than 100 because some mothers gave more than one reason.

Table 4.6

Odds of attending antenatal classes by ethnic group

Odds of attending antenatal classes	Ethnic group			
	Bangladeshi	Pakistani	Indian	White
Baseline odds	0.018	0.003	0.001	0.002
Characteristics				**Multiplying factors**
First baby	4.77	10.64	21.73	96.41
Later baby	1.00	1.00	1.00	1.00
Mother's age	ns	ns		
30 or over			6.96	9.71
25–29			6.36	11.55
20–24			3.83	1.79
Under 20			1.00	1.00
Mother's education	ns			
14 years or more		5.22	2.63	4.02
12–13 years		ns	ns	5.00
11 years		ns	ns	ns
10 years or less		1.00	1.00	1.00
Social class of husband/partner	ns	ns		
Non-manual			3.05	2.36
Manual			1.00	1.00
Region	ns			
South		2.59	5.00	3.96
Outer London		3.00	5.95	2.49
Inner London		2.57	ns	ns
Midlands		ns	2.15	ns
North		1.00	1.00	1.00
Understanding of English		ns	ns	ns
Understands well or fairly well	2.71			
Does not understand well or at all	1.00			
Length of residence in UK	ns			ns
16 years or more		3.42	3.37	
8–15 years		ns	2.16	
4–7 years		3.80	ns	
3 years or less		1.00	1.00	

ns Either the variable or the figure for a particular group was not significant at the 95% level in predicting the odds of a mother attending classes.

Table 4.7

Proportion of first time mothers receiving advice from people other than a health visitor or midwife during pregnancy and who advised them most by ethnic group

All first time mothers

	Ethnic group			
	Bangladeshi	Pakistani	Indian	White
	%	%	%	%
Whether mother received advice				
Mother received advice	66	71	82	64
Mother did not receive advice	34	29	18	36
Base = 100%	*209*	*250*	*391*	*295*
Person who advised mother most				
Mother (in-law)	44	48	40	40
Sister (in-law)	31	29	36	20
Friend or neighbour	13	12	12	24
Doctor	2	2	2	5
Husband	3	2	2	3
Other relative	4	5	6	4
Someone else	3	2	2	4
Base = 100%	*138*	*176*	*322*	*190*

Table 4.8

Person who advised first time mother most during pregnancy apart from the health visitor or midwife by ethnic group

All first time mothers who received advice

Person who advised mother most	Ethnic group			
	Bangladeshi	Pakistani	Indian	White
	%	%	%	%
Mother (in-law)	44	48	40	40
Sister (in-law)	31	29	36	20
Friend or neighour	13	12	12	24
Doctor	2	2	2	5
Husband	3	2	2	3
Other relative	4	5	6	4
Someone else	3	2	2	4
Base = 100%	*138*	*176*	*322*	*190*

Table 4.9

Proportion of first time mothers receiving advice during pregnancy which differed from that given by the health visitor or midwife, and type of differing advice received by ethnic group

All first time mothers

Whether received differing advice	Ethnic group			
	Bangladeshi	Pakistani	Indian	White
	%	%	%	%
Received differing advice	14	17	19	37
Did not receive differing advice	84	80	79	63
Did not answer question	2	3	2	0
Base = 100%	*238*	*317*	*511*	*295*
Type of differing advice received				
Family gave practical or better or more personal advice	[12]	42	28	44
Advice about exercise or mother's diet	[5]	20	23	6
Family gave traditional or cultural advice	[7]	7	20	0
Advice from family is old fashioned	[3]	6	8	10
Conflicting advice about whether to bottle feed or breastfeed	[0]	5	6	14
Other	[3]	13	12	15
No reason given	[5]	10	10	13
Base = 100%	*33*	*53*	*96*	*108*

Table 4.10

Proportion of first time mothers receiving help or advice from a voluntary group by ethnic group*

All first time mothers

Whether mother received help or advice from a voluntary group	Ethnic group			
	Bangladeshi	Pakistani	Indian	White
	%	%	%	%
Received help or advice	1	0	3	10
Did not receive help or advice	99	100	97	90
Base = 100%	*209*	*249*	*391*	*294*

* Such as the National Childbirth Trust or La Leche League.

Table 4.11

Proportion of mothers given HEA books by ethnic group

All mothers who said they could read English 'fairly well or very well'

Proportion of mothers given HEA books	Ethnic group			
	Bangladeshi	Pakistani	Indian	White
	%	%	%	%
First births				
'The Pregnancy book'	56	71	71	79
'Birth to five'	43	54	64	77
Neither	32	16	12	6
Later births				
'The Pregnancy book'	26	35	37	42
'Birth to five'	16	23	26	28
Neither	69	54	53	47
Total				
'The Pregnancy book'	41	50	52	60
'Birth to five'	29	36	43	51
Neither	50	38	35	28
Base = 100%	*238*	*432*	*747*	*618*

Percentages add to more than 100 because some mothers were given both books.

Table 4.12

Proportion of mothers given leaflets or other information in languages other than English by ethnic group

All mothers whose main language was not English and read another language

	Ethnic group		
	Bangladeshi	Pakistani	Indian
	%	%	%
During pregnancy	26	23	19
After the birth	15	13	10
Both during and after pregnancy	5	3	3
No leaflets or other information given	54	62	68
Base = 100%	*313*	*217*	*165*

Table 4.13

Proportion of mothers given leaflets or other information in languages other than English by main language

All mothers whose main language was not English and who read another language

	Language				
	Gujarati	Punjabi	Bengali	Urdu	Other
	%	%	%	%	%
During pregnancy	17	24	26	20	[3]
After the birth	12	12	15	11	[1]
Both during and after pregnancy	2	2	5	4	[0]
No leaflets or other information given	69	62	53	65	[9]
Base = 100%	*87*	*193*	*313*	*89*	*13*

5 Feeding problems and sources of advice during first 15 months

Summary

- A higher proportion of Asian than White mothers received help when feeding their baby for the first time.

- Fewer Asian than White mothers said they had experienced feeding problems in hospital.

- Fewer Asian than White mothers reported experiencing feeding problems when the child was around nine weeks old, but more reported problems when the child was between five and fifteen months old.

- Fewer Asian than White mothers took their child for a six week developmental checkup, but more visited a health professional, such as a family doctor, when the child was between nine and fifteen months.

- Fewer Asian than White mothers received information about looking after young children at all stages of the survey. Asian mothers who understood English were more likely to receive information than those who did not.

- Mothers in all groups said they received most advice over the first fifteen months from their own mother or mother-in-law. Between a quarter and a third of all mothers would have liked more advice about weaning and a healthy diet for the child.

5.1 Introduction

This chapter examines feeding problems experienced by mothers from their stay in hospital until their baby was about fifteen months old. Attendance at checkups and the sources of information and advice received by mothers are also described.

5.2 Feeding in hospital

5.2.1 Feeding the baby for the first time

More Asian than White mothers were helped when they first fed their baby. Of those who gave birth in hospital, eighty four per cent of Bangladeshi, 83% of Indian, 81% of Pakistani, and 65% of White first time mothers were helped. Twenty per cent of White, 12% of Indian, 11% of Pakistani and 7% of Bangladeshi mothers reported that they were not helped, but said that they would have liked some help.

Mothers in all ethnic groups having their second or a later baby were less likely to be helped than those having their first baby. Thirty nine per cent of Indian, 37% of Pakistani, 35% of Bangladeshi, and 22% of White mothers received help. Between 11% and 15% of mothers having their second or later baby were not given help but would have liked some.   Table 5.1

5.2.2 Feeding problems in hospital

Fewer Asian than White mothers having their first baby said that they experienced a feeding problem whilst in hospital. Thirty one per cent of Bangladeshi, 38% of Pakistani, 40% of Indian, and 50% of White first time mothers reported having problems. Fewer mothers who had given birth before experienced problems and there was less variation between groups in the proportion who did.   Table 5.2

The problems experienced by mothers in all groups were similar. Those most frequently mentioned were that the baby would not feed properly; that the baby was ill; breastfeeding was difficult or painful; or that the mother was generally ill or tired. More Bangladeshi and Pakistani mothers mentioned that the baby was ill or had problems with colic, than Indian or White mothers.   Table 5.3

5.2.3 Advice given to mothers about feeding problems

Bangladeshi mothers were least likely (65%) to report receiving help or advice with their feeding problems in hospital, compared with around three quarters of other mothers. Midwives were those most likely to help and advise mothers in all groups with their feeding problems in hospital, but a higher proportion of White than Asian mothers said they received such help. Asian mothers were more likely than White mothers to say they were helped by a nurse. Over four fifths of mothers in all ethnic groups said that help and advice was always or generally available in hospital.   Tables 5.4,5.5

5.3 Problems and advice after leaving hospital

5.3.1 Postnatal feeding problems

At the first interview (when the babies were on average nine weeks old), fewer Asian than White mothers said that they had experienced a problem feeding their baby since leaving hospital (or since birth for the one per cent who gave birth at home). Bangladeshi mothers were least likely to say they experienced a problem. Sixteen per cent of them had done so, compared with 19% of Indian, 22% of Pakistani and 28% of White mothers. At all other interviews this pattern reversed, with Bangladeshi mothers more likely to report problems than White and other Asian mothers. The proportion of mothers in all groups reporting problems increased between the second and later interviews. At the fourth interview, when the children were on average 15 months old, 42% of Bangladeshi mothers said they had experienced a problem with feeding or weaning since the previous interview, compared with 33% of Pakistani, 32% of Indian, and 23% of White mothers.   Figure 5.1, Table 5.6

Over the fifteen month period of fieldwork, Bangladeshi mothers were most likely to have experienced a feeding problem: 68% of Bangladeshi mothers mentioned a problem in at

Figure 5.1

Proportion of mothers experiencing feeding problems, since the previous interview, by age of baby and ethnic group

All mothers

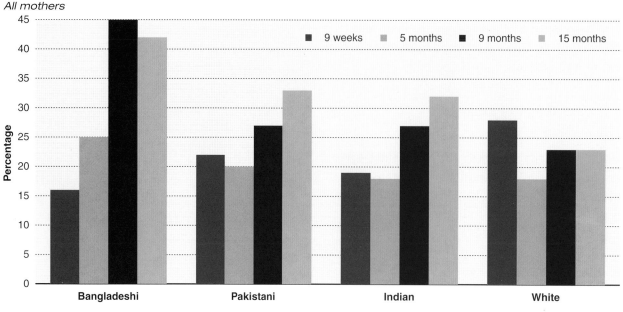

Figure 5.2

Proportion of mothers who ever experienced feeding problems during first 15 months by ethnic group

All mothers who gave four interviews

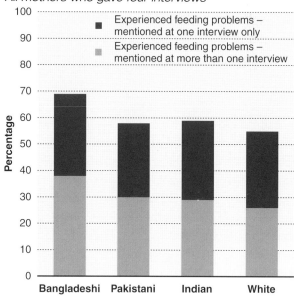

least one interview, compared with 58% of Pakistani, 59% of Indian, and 55% of White mothers. The proportion of mothers reporting a problem on only one occasion was similar for all groups (approximately 30%), but Bangladeshi mothers were more likely to have reported a problem at more than one interview (38%), compared with Pakistani (30%), Indian (29%), and White mothers (26%). Figure 5.2, Table 5.7

Mothers mentioned a variety of feeding problems. At the first interview, forty two per cent of Indian, 38% of Bangladeshi, 33% of White and 30% of Pakistani mothers said they had experienced a problem with breastfeeding. Forty per cent of Pakistani mothers said that the baby had been ill or suffered from an allergy. At the second interview (when the babies were on average five months old), illness or allergy was the most commonly mentioned problem in all groups. At the third interview (when the babies were approximately nine months old), weaning problems were common, with more mothers becoming concerned that the baby was not eating properly or not interested in food. This category also included mothers who said that the baby was only eating small amounts, losing weight or not gaining weight. At the fourth

interview (when the children were fifteen months old), Asian mothers were more likely than White mothers to say that their child was not eating enough and was not interested in food.

Table 5.8

5.3.2 Advice given to mothers about postnatal feeding problems

When the babies were aged approximately nine weeks, more Indian and White than other mothers said that they had been given help or advice with their feeding problems after leaving hospital (86% of both groups, compared with 74% of Bangladeshi and 73% of Pakistani mothers). Almost half of Pakistani, Bangladeshi and White mothers said that a midwife or nurse had given them help or advice with their problems, and a similar proportion of Indian mothers mentioned the health visitor. When the children were aged around 15 months, other family members were at least as important as a source of advice.   Tables 5.9-5.10

5.4 Checkups

Most mothers in all groups had taken their infant for a 'six-week' or 'developmental' checkup, although the proportion was slightly higher for White than Asian mothers. Of mothers whose infants were aged eight weeks or more at the time of interview, 94% of White, 89% of Indian, 86% of Bangladeshi and 85% of Pakistani mothers had taken their baby for a checkup.

Table 5.11

When the babies were aged about five months, approximately three quarters of Asian mothers, and four fifths of White mothers, said that they took their baby to a health professional such as a family doctor for checkups or advice. Over a half of Asian mothers in all groups and 70% of White mothers took their baby at least once a month. White mothers were more likely than Asian mothers to visit a health professional at least once a fortnight.

At the fourth interview, mothers were again asked if they had been for advice or a checkup since the previous interview, and their reason for going. Asian mothers were more likely to have done so than White mothers – Bangladeshi and Pakistani (82%), Indian (81%), and White mothers (76%). The most frequently mentioned reason for going was for a checkup – Bangladeshi (61%), Pakistani (53%), Indian (52%) and White mothers (47%). A minor or temporary illness was given as a reason for going by 30% of White, 28%

of Indian, 27% of Pakistani, and 24% of Bangladeshi mothers. Other reasons commonly mentioned were concern over their child's growth, immunisation, or because of a more serious medical problem. Similar proportions of mothers in all groups stated these reasons.

Table 5.12-5.13

5.5 Attendance at groups for mothers with young children

When the babies were aged about 5 months, mothers were asked if they attended any local groups for mothers with babies. Very few Asian mothers compared with White mothers, attended such a group: 1% of Bangladeshi, 3% of Pakistani, 7% of Indian, and 22% of White mothers did so. Most mothers who did attend a group said that they discussed feeding their child there. Groups were organised by a variety of people and organisations – health clinics or family doctors; religious organisations; voluntary organisations; and also mothers meeting informally themselves – "organised by women themselves after antenatal session", "group of friends meet".   Table 5.14

5.6 Other sources of information and advice

5.6.1 Information and advice about looking after young children

At the second, third and fourth interviews, all mothers were asked if they had read any books, leaflets or magazines, or watched any TV programmes or videos about looking after young children, since the last interview. At the second interview (when the babies were aged around five months), 71% of White, 59% of Indian, and 45% of Bangladeshi and Pakistani first time mothers had done so. Mothers with a second or later baby were less likely to do so – White (40%), Indian (32%), Pakistani (26%), and Bangladeshi (17%). As the babies got older, fewer mothers in all groups were receiving information, although the difference between the proportions of White and Asian mothers remained.   Figure 5.3, Table 5.15

Figure 5.3

Proportion of mothers who had read books, leaflets, magazines or watched TV programmes or videos about looking after young children by age of baby and ethnic group

All mothers

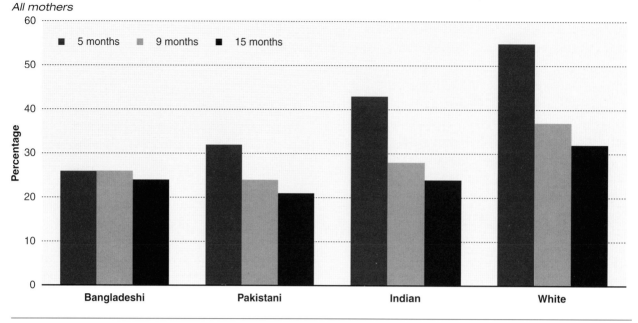

5.6.2 Language of information received by mothers

Some of the difference between the proportions of White and Asian mothers receiving information was due to language ability. Mothers in all Asian ethnic groups were more likely to receive or read information if they understood English. This did not change as the children got older.

Table 5.16

5.6.3 Sources of information on looking after children

For Pakistani, Indian and White mothers, the most commonly mentioned source of information on looking after children was commercially produced information obtained from shops or baby food companies. Bangladeshi mothers were more likely to obtain information from health clinics, possibly due to difficulties with understanding English. Health visitors, midwives, and hospitals were also commonly mentioned by all groups. Other sources mentioned more at the fourth interview than previously were doctors' surgeries (Bangladeshi mothers 12%); TV programmes (Bangladeshi 15%, and Pakistani mothers 18%); and family and friends (White mothers 12%).

Table 5.17

5.7 Views about advice received over first fifteen months

5.7.1 Person who advised mothers most

At the last interview, when the children were about 15 months old, mothers were asked who had given them most advice since the child was born. Of first time mothers, their mother or mother-in-law was mentioned most by all groups, but particularly by Bangladeshi and Pakistani mothers, (Bangladeshi 56%, Pakistani 50%, Indian 38% and White mothers 35%). Health visitors or midwives were mentioned by around a quarter of mothers in all groups. Other relatives were mentioned by 29% of Pakistani, 20% of Indian, 18% of Bangladeshi and 10% of White mothers. White mothers were more likely to mention friends (16%), than other relatives.

White first time mothers were also most likely to say that no-one gave them advice (15%) compared with Indian (3%), Pakistani and Bangladeshi mothers (1%). Indian first time mothers were most likely to say they had not needed any advice (12%) compared with Bangladeshi (6%), Pakistani and White mothers (3%). Between 40% and 60% of mothers having

their second or a later baby said they had not
needed any advice (not shown in table).

Table 5.18

5.7.2 Proportion of mothers who would have liked more advice

Mothers were asked if they would have liked
more advice about feeding their child during the
first fifteen months. Indian first time mothers
were most likely to say that they would have liked
more (33%), compared with Bangladeshi (27%),
Pakistani (26%), and White first time mothers
(25%). When asked what they would have liked
more help and advice with, most mothers
mentioned weaning (Bangladeshi 75%, Indian
and White 66%, and Pakistani mothers 62%).
Forty three per cent of Bangladeshi, 39% of
Pakistani, 36% of Indian, and 31% of White
mothers also wanted more information about a
healthy diet for the child.   **Figure 5.4, Table 5.19**

Figure 5.4

Proportion of mothers who would have liked
more advice about feeding their child by birth
order and ethnic group

All mothers

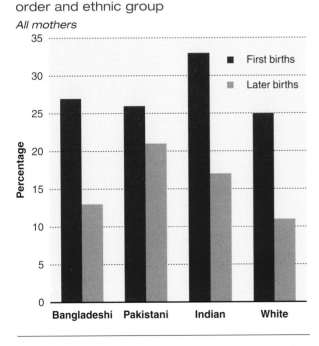

Table 5.1

Proportion of mothers reporting that they were given help or advice when feeding the baby for the first time by birth order and ethnic group

All mothers who gave birth in hospital

Whether given help or advice	Ethnic group			
	Bangladeshi	Pakistani	Indian	White
	%	%	%	%
First births				
Given help	84	81	83	65
Not given help, but would have liked help	7	11	12	20
Not given help, did not want any	9	8	5	15
Later births				
Given help	35	37	39	22
Not given help, but would have liked help	11	15	14	11
Not given help, did not want any	54	48	47	67
Base = 100%				
First births	*209*	*249*	*391*	*294*
Later births	*398*	*478*	*542*	*324*

Table 5.2

Proportion of mothers experiencing feeding problems in hospital by birth order and ethnic group

All mothers who gave birth in hospital

Proportion experiencing feeding problems	Ethnic group			
	Bangladeshi	Pakistani	Indian	White
	%	%	%	%
Birth order				
First births	31	38	40	50
Later births	18	24	21	22
Base = 100%				
First births	*208*	*241*	*390*	*294*
Later births	*396*	*474*	*539*	*317*

Table 5.3

Types of feeding problem experienced by mothers when in hospital by ethnic group

All mothers experiencing feeding problems in hospital

Type of feeding problem	Ethnic group			
	Bangladeshi	Pakistani	Indian	White
	%	%	%	%
Baby would not feed properly (breast or bottle)	37	42	46	46
Baby ill; vomiting; colic; wind	18	16	8	8
Breastfeeding difficult or painful for mother	16	14	16	15
Mother ill; tired; uncomfortable; or in pain	18	11	10	7
Lack of breast milk	4	7	7	4
Baby sleeping; slow to feed	3	6	6	8
Baby wanted feeding too often	1	4	4	6
Not enough help from staff; staff caused problems	2	–	1	4
Other	6	9	9	9
Base = 100%	*135*	*211*	*269*	*214*

Percentages add to more than 100 because some mothers had more than one problem.

Table 5.4
Proportion of mothers given help or advice with their feeding problems in hospital by ethnic group

All mothers experiencing feeding problems in hospital

Whether given help or advice	Ethnic group			
	Bangladeshi	Pakistani	Indian	White
	%	%	%	%
Given help or advice	65	72	79	75
No help or advice given	35	28	21	25
Base = 100%	*133*	*212*	*269*	*215*
Source of advice				
Midwife	58	67	68	73
Nurse	49	39	44	28
Doctor	9	6	6	6
Relative	2	3	2	3
Feeding specialist	1	1	0	2
Other	–	1	2	1
Base = 100%	*87*	*152*	*212*	*161*

Percentages add to more than 100 because some mothers were advised by more than one person.

Table 5.5
Availability of help and advice in hospital by ethnic group

All mothers who gave birth in hospital

Availability of help and advice	Ethnic group			
	Bangladeshi	Pakistani	Indian	White
	%	%	%	%
Always or generally available	81	84	85	87
Not available	19	16	16	13
Base = 100%	*599*	*721*	*924*	*611*

Table 5.6
Proportion of mothers experiencing feeding problems during first 15 months by ethnic group

All mothers

Whether experienced feeding problem	Ethnic group			
	Bangladeshi	Pakistani	Indian	White
	%	%	%	%
9 weeks	16	22	19	28
5 months	25	20	18	18
9 months	45	27	27	23
15 months	42	33	32	23
Base = 100%				
9 weeks	*603*	*721*	*929*	*609*
5 months	*552*	*668*	*841*	*594*
9 months	*513*	*636*	*810*	*564*
15 months	*477*	*590*	*758*	*548*

Question wording at 9 weeks: 'Since you left hospital have you had any problems with feeding your baby?';

at 5 months: 'Have you had any problems feeding or weaning your baby since I last spoke to you?';

at 9 months: 'Has your baby been difficult to wean onto solid food?'; and

'Have you had any (other) difficulties feeding your baby since I last spoke to you?';

at 15 months: 'Have you had any difficulty feeding (name) solid foods since I last spoke to you?'; and

'Have you had any other problems feeding him/her since I last spoke to you?'

Table 5.7

Proportion of mothers who ever experienced feeding problems during first 15 months by ethnic group

All mothers who gave four interviews

Whether ever experienced feeding problems	Ethnic group			
	Bangladeshi	Pakistani	Indian	White
	%	%	%	%
Experienced feeding problems	68	58	59	55
Problem mentioned at one interview only	31	28	30	29
Problem mentioned at more than one interview	38	30	29	26
Did not experience feeding problems	32	42	41	45
Base= 100%	*477*	*590*	*758*	*548*

Table 5.8

Types of feeding problem experienced by mothers during first 15 months by ethnic group

All mothers experiencing feeding problems

Type of feeding problem	Ethnic group			
	Bangladeshi	Pakistani	Indian	White
	%	%	%	%
9 weeks				
Breastfeeding problem	38	30	42	33
Child ill; had allergy	28	40	27	25
Not eating enough; not gaining enough weight	21	13	10	16
Child hungry; feeding too often	7	12	13	22
Not enough help	1	1	1	1
Other	4	3	5	4
5 months				
Breastfeeding problem	1	6	6	6
Bottle feeding problem	21	20	28	17
Child ill; had allergy	54	57	41	40
Not eating enough; not gaining enough weight	29	15	19	13
Child hungry; feeding too often	1	5	5	11
Would not eat solid food	20	18	10	26
Would not eat some solid foods	10	8	16	8
Other	–	–	1	1
9 months				
Child ill; had allergy	44	31	29	34
Not eating enough; not gaining enough weight	49	33	46	27
Would not eat solid food	28	36	18	21
Would not eat some solid foods	19	23	24	29
Teething	1	5	2	4
Messy eater; difficult to feed	1	5	4	6
Other	6	7	9	10
15 months				
Child ill; had allergy	38	35	34	43
Not eating enough; not interested in food	85	70	70	41
Would not eat some solid foods	36	34	30	27
Bottle feeding problem	10	6	3	6
Teething	2	12	22	6
Would not eat from spoon	0	5	3	1
Other	2	3	2	6
Base = 100%				
9 weeks	*95*	*162*	*179*	*168*
5 months	*138*	*136*	*156*	*109*
9 months	*220*	*160*	*198*	*103*
15 months	*198*	*195*	*246*	*128*

Percentages add to more than 100 because some mothers had more than one problem.

Table 5.9

Proportion of mothers given help or advice with feeding problems over first 15 months by ethnic group

All mothers experiencing feeding problems

Proportion given help or advice	Ethnic group			
	Bangladeshi	Pakistani	Indian	White
	%	%	%	%
9 weeks	74	73	86	86
5 months	69	76	78	72
9 months	71	70	71	72
15 months	71	66	64	62
Base = 100%				
9 weeks	*97*	*163*	*180*	*170*
5 months	*138*	*136*	*156*	*109*
9 months	*234*	*173*	*221*	*129*
15 months	*198*	*195*	*246*	*128*

Table 5.10

Source of help and advice at 9 weeks and 15 months by ethnic group

All mothers experiencing feeding problems

Source of help and advice	Ethnic group			
	Bangladeshi	Pakistani	Indian	White
	%	%	%	%
9 weeks				
Midwife or nurse	46	46	36	48
Health visitor	24	25	47	25
Doctor	32	39	30	26
Friend or relative	24	19	21	16
Other	4	5	3	11
Base = 100%	*72*	*119*	*154*	*147*
15 months				
Midwife or health visitor	46	42	36	35
Doctor or nurse	33	39	29	30
Mother or mother-in-law	46	41	49	42
Sister or sister-in-law	17	15	22	11
Husband	9	2	6	–
Other relative	20	8	9	4
Friend or neighbour	6	13	17	13
Other	6	9	6	19
Base = 100%	*140*	*129*	*158*	*79*

Percentages add to more than 100 because some mothers were helped or advised by more than one person.

Table 5.11

Proportion of mothers who took their baby for a six week checkup by ethnic group

All mothers whose baby was aged 8 weeks or more at the first interview

Whether took baby for a checkup	Ethnic group			
	Bangladeshi	Pakistani	Indian	White
	%	%	%	%
Took baby for checkup	86	85	89	94
Did not take baby for checkup	14	15	11	6
Base = 100%	*398*	*518*	*699*	*602*

Table 5.12

Proportion of mothers taking their child for advice or a checkup at age 5 months by ethnic group

All mothers

	Ethnic group			
	Bangladeshi	Pakistani	Indian	White
	%	%	%	%
Child taken for advice or checkup	73	72	75	81
Once a week	2	3	4	7
Once a fortnight	9	12	13	25
Once a month	43	38	41	38
Less than once a month	19	20	18	11
Child not taken for advice or checkup	27	28	25	19
Base = 100%	*552*	*663*	*841*	*594*

Table 5.13

Proportion of mothers taking their child for advice or a checkup at age 15 months, and reasons for doing so, by ethnic group

All mothers

	Ethnic group			
	Bangladeshi	Pakistani	Indian	White
	%	%	%	%
Child taken for advice or checkup	82	82	81	76
Reason*				
Checkup	61	53	52	47
Temporary illness	24	27	28	30
Concern over growth	9	9	8	6
Immunisation	9	8	6	9
Longer term illness/condition	5	5	5	7
Accident	1	2	1	1
Other	–	0	0	0
Child not taken for advice or checkup	18	18	19	24
Base = 100%	*476*	*589*	*758*	*548*

* Some mothers gave more than one reason.

Table 5.14

Proportion of mothers attending groups for mothers with babies at age 5 months; whether they discussed feeding; and who organised the group by ethnic group

All mothers

	Ethnic group			
	Bangladeshi	Pakistani	Indian	White
	%	%	%	%
Whether mother attended group				
Attended a group	1	3	7	22
Did not attend a group	99	97	93	78
Base = 100%	*552*	*667*	*841*	*594*
Whether discussed feeding				
Discussed feeding	[5]	[13]	71	70
Did not discuss feeding	[2]	[4]	29	30
Base = 100% (attended group)	*7*	*17*	*58*	*129*
Who organised group				
Health clinic or GP	–	[8]	27	16
Playgroup	[3]	[4]	41	19
Religious organisation	[2]	–	14	30
Health visitor or midwife	–	–	5	7
Informal group run by mothers themselves	[2]	[3]	9	20
Voluntary organisation for new mothers	–	–	4	22
Other	–	[1]	2	1
Base = 100% (attended group)	*7*	*17*	*56*	*128*

Table 5.15

Proportion of mothers who had read books, leaflets, magazines or watched TV programmes or videos about looking after young children by birth order and ethnic group

All mothers

Age of baby and birth order	Ethnic group			
	Bangladeshi	Pakistani	Indian	White
	%	%	%	%
5 months				
First births	45	45	59	71
Later births	17	26	32	40
All births	26	32	43	55
9 months				
First births	38	35	38	50
Later births	20	18	21	25
All births	26	24	28	37
15 months				
First births	34	33	32	45
Later births	19	15	19	21
All births	24	21	24	32
Base = 100% (15 months)				
First births	*165*	*197*	*306*	*256*
Later births	*312*	*392*	*450*	*292*
All births	*477*	*589*	*756*	*548*

Table 5.16

Proportion or mothers receiving information on looking after children by how well they understood English and ethnic group

All Asian mothers

Proportion receiving information	Ethnic group		
	Bangladeshi	Pakistani	Indian
	%	%	%
5 months			
Understands English well or fairly well	32	34	44
Does not understand English well or at all	20	22	27
9 months			
Understands English well or fairly well	31	26	29
Does not understand English well or at all	22	14	20
15 months			
Understands English well or fairly well	28	22	24
Does not understand English well or at all	20	14	9
Base = 100% (age 5 months)			
Understands English well or fairly well	*187*	*357*	*484*
Does not understand English well or at all	*275*	*183*	*117*

Table 5.17

Sources of information obtained by mothers on looking after young children, by ethnic group and age of child

All mothers who read leaflets, magazines, books about feeding or watched a TV programme or video

	Ethnic group and age of baby											
	Bangladeshi			Pakistani			Indian			White		
	9 weeks	5 months	15 months	9 weeks	5 months	15 months	9 weeks	5 months	15 months	9 weeks	5 months	15 months
	%	%	%	%	%	%	%	%	%	%	%	%
Shop or baby food company	22	30	24	33	34	31	38	46	50	52	55	55
Health clinic	34	34	34	29	29	21	20	21	13	15	14	8
Health visitor or midwife	20	20	12	24	20	15	31	25	18	32	8	14
Hospital	21	14	12	20	11	16	21	8	12	16	6	7
Doctor's surgery	7	1	12	4	3	6	5	4	7	3	3	5
Family and friends	1	4	4	3	4	5	2	1	9	4	5	12
TV programmes	5	9	15	2	3	18	2	2	7	1	4	9
Library or other public service	3	5	4	2	3	3	1	2	7	2	3	9
Voluntary group for new mothers	–	–	–	–	–	–	–	0	–	0	3	–
Other	1	–	–	2	2	–	1	3	–	1	–	–
Base = 100%	*146*	*137*	*113*	*213*	*151*	*125*	*363*	*228*	*182*	*326*	*214*	*176*

Table 5.18

Person who advised first time mothers most about feeding during child's first 15 months by ethnic group

All first time mothers

Who advised mothers most	Ethnic group			
	Bangladeshi	Pakistani	Indian	White
	%	%	%	%
Mother or mother-in-law	56	50	38	35
Health visitor or midwife	23	29	29	27
Other relative	18	29	20	10
Doctor or nurse	6	6	6	4
Friend	1	4	7	16
Books, leaflets, magazines	–	–	1	5
Other	–	–	1	1
No one gave advice	1	1	3	15
Did not need advice	6	3	12	3
Base = 100%	*165*	*197*	*307*	*256*

Table 5.19

Proportion of mothers who would have liked more advice on feeding their child during the first 15 months, and what they would have liked advice about by ethnic group

All mothers

Birth order	Ethnic group			
	Bangladeshi	Pakistani	Indian	White
	%	%	%	%
First births	27	26	33	25
Later births	13	21	17	11
All births	18	22	23	18
Base = 100%	*475*	*588*	*755*	*548*
Mothers wanted more advice about:				
Weaning	75	62	66	66
Healthy diet	43	39	36	31
Allergy or illness	–	6	6	3
Breastfeeding	4	9	8	18
Bottle feeding	6	6	9	17
Eating enough	2	9	6	5
Other	8	6	8	2
Base = 100%	*84*	*132*	*175*	*96*

6 Solid food, drinks and vitamins

Summary

- Over 90% of babies in all ethnic groups had started eating solid food by the age of four months. Asian mothers tended to introduce solid food at a later age than White mothers.

- Twenty four per cent of Indian households were vegetarian. At nine months, 38% of Indian children never ate meat. All or nearly all Bangladeshi, Pakistani and White households ate meat.

- Asian babies took longer than White babies to establish a mixed diet. Bangladeshi babies ate a narrower range of foods than other Asian groups, especially at about nine months old.

- Health and nutrition, baby or mother's preference, variety, and food given to the rest of the family were the most important factors in choosing food for their baby for all groups. Health and nutrition were mentioned most by White mothers. The baby or mother's preference were mentioned more by Asian mothers.

- The main foods which mothers said that they avoided giving their baby were spices and chillis, sugar, salt and meat or animal products.

- At about fifteen months, Pakistani children were most likely always to eat the same food as the rest of the family. White children were most likely to eat the same food as the rest of the family usually or always, and Bangladeshi children least likely.

- At aged fifteen months, White children were most likely to feed themselves; White, Indian and Pakistani were more likely than Bangladeshi children to drink from a cup, glass or beaker.

- Bangladeshi mothers were most likely to say their child had a poor appetite, that the child was difficult to feed or was a fussy eater. White mothers were least likely to say any of these things.

- Bangladeshi babies were most likely to drink water at all ages. White babies drank more fruit drinks and tea and coffee than other groups.

- Asian babies were more likely to be given vitamin supplements than White babies at all stages during the first fifteen months.

- Asian breastfeeding mothers were more likely to take vitamin supplements than White breastfeeding mothers when the babies were aged approximately nine weeks old.

6.1 Introduction

This chapter looks at the foods, drinks and vitamins consumed by the babies. It covers the introduction of solid food into the diet, the actual food eaten by the babies on the day before each interview, and additional information about their diets – how often they ate different types of foods, foods that they did not eat, and how mothers chose food to give to the baby. It looks at the babies diets in relation to their families – whether they lived in vegetarian households, whether they ate the same food as the rest of the family. It also covers the types of drinks given to the babies at all stages over the first fifteen months. It includes a section on vitamin supplements, looking at the proportion of mothers who gave their babies extra vitamins, the proportion of breastfeeding mothers who took vitamins themselves, and how the vitamins were obtained.

6.2 Introduction of solid food

6.2.1 Age at first introduction of solid food

White mothers tended to start giving their babies solid food earlier than mothers in the Asian groups. At eight weeks, 2% of Bangladeshi, 3% of Pakistani, and 5% of Indian mothers, compared with 18% of White mothers had given their baby some solid food. In all groups the majority of mothers introduced food between eight weeks and three months. By the age of three months, between 70% and 73% of Asian mothers, and 83% of White mothers had given some solid food. The Weaning and the Weaning Diet report of the Committee on Medical Aspects of Food and Nutrition Policy[1] recommends that 'the majority of infants should not be given solid foods before the age of four months, and a mixed diet should be offered by the age of six months.' By four months, more than nine out of ten children in all groups were being given solid food.

Figure 6.1, Table 6.1

6.2.2 Age when first started eating three meals a day

Having begun to eat solid food before those in other groups, White babies also started eating three meals of solid food a day earlier than others. Indian babies started eating three meals a day earlier than Pakistani and Bangladeshi babies. At six months, 88% of White, 75% of Indian, 61% of Pakistani and 51% of Bangladeshi babies were eating three meals a day. By nine months, 83% of Bangladeshi babies, 85% of Pakistani babies, 93% of Indian babies and 99% of White babies were doing so.

Figure 6.2, Table 6.2

Figure 6.1
Age of introduction of solid food by ethnic group
All mothers

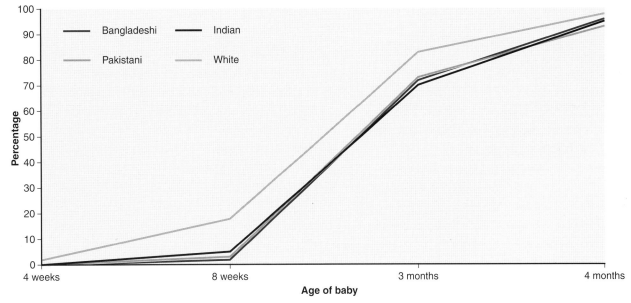

Figure 6.2

Proportion of children given three meals of solid food a day at different ages by ethnic group

All mothers who gave a fourth interview

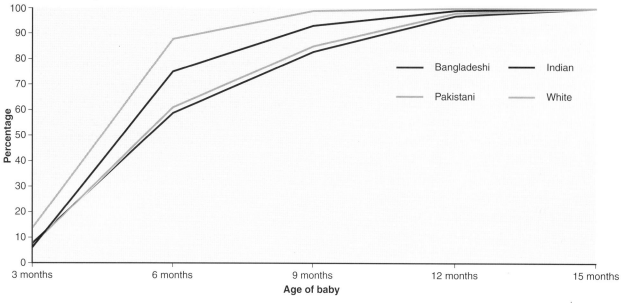

6.3 Whether household members eat meat

Mothers were asked if most members of the household ate meat. As a check, mothers in Muslim households who said they did not were also asked if they ever ate Halal meat. In Muslim households where most members did eat meat, mothers were asked if they ate Halal meat only. In all Bangladeshi households, and 99% of Pakistani households, most members ate meat. In 68% of Indian households most members ate meat, in 24% of Indian households most members were vegetarian, and in 9% there was an equal split between those who did and did not eat meat. Three per cent of White households did not eat meat, and 2% were split equally.

Table 6.3, Appendix Table B9

6.4 Food eaten by babies on the day before interview

At each interview, mothers were asked to recall all the food the baby had eaten on the day before the interview. At the first two interviews, the data were collected by recording each meal using open questions which were then coded. At the third and fourth interviews, the data were collected using computer-assisted coding from a large range of precodes. Interviewers were asked

to probe for snacks and small pieces of food given to the baby as a 'taster'. The codes given tend to summarise each meal or snack, rather than defining each ingredient in the food. There may therefore be some under-estimating of some foods, such as vegetables eaten as part of a meat dish and not coded separately. The tables show the proportion of babies who had eaten each type of food on the day before each interview, based on those who had ever eaten solid food. When the children were aged 9 and 15 months, mothers were also asked how often different types of food were given (see Tables 6.7, 6.8).

6.4.1 Aged approximately nine weeks

At the first interview, when the baby was approximately nine weeks old, rusks and rice cereal were the foods most frequently given, with rusks given more by Indian mothers (29%) than White mothers (18%). The number of Bangladeshi and Pakistani mothers in the sample giving solid food at this age was too small for analysis.

Table 6.4

6.4.2 Aged approximately five months

At the second interview, when the babies were aged approximately five months, mothers in all ethnic groups gave their babies cereals, vegetables, fresh fruit, desserts, sweets and chocolates. The largest differences between groups were in the proportion of mothers who gave cereals other than rice cereal (e.g. breakfast cereals), meat and desserts. White mothers (51%) were twice as likely to have given such cereals as Bangladeshi and Pakistani mothers (25%). Very few Bangladeshi or Pakistani mothers had given meat. Bangladeshi mothers (59%) were most likely to have given desserts on the day before interview, compared with Pakistani (44%), White (41%) and Indian mothers (31%). Indian (35%) and Pakistani (36%) mothers were most likely to have given rusks, and Bangladeshi mothers (8%) were least likely.   Table 6.5

6.4.3 Aged approximately nine months
Between the ages of five and nine months, consumption of cereals other than rice cereal increased significantly for babies in all groups. There was still a difference between the groups, with more White babies (82%) eating cereals, than Indian (63%), Pakistani (46%) and Bangladeshi babies (42%). Babies in all groups ate more bread aged 9 months, than previously – particularly White (46%) and Pakistani babies (44%). Consumption of meat also increased for babies in all groups.

Bangladeshi babies were most likely to eat desserts (50%), and Indian babies least likely (30%). White babies were most likely to eat yoghurt (58%) – over twice the proportion of Indian babies, and almost ten times the proportion of Bangladeshi babies. White babies were also twice as likely to eat biscuits and cakes as Asian babies. Eleven per cent of White babies ate sweets and chocolate on the day before interview, compared with 3% or less of Asian babies.

More babies in all groups ate fresh fruit than when aged 5 months, but fewer Bangladeshi babies did so than babies in other groups. Other differences were that Bangladeshi babies were most likely to eat rice or pasta; Indian babies were most likely to eat vegetables or potatoes, reflecting the 24% of Indian household who were vegetarian; and Pakistani and White babies were

most likely to eat egg or dairy products. Crisps were eaten by 10% or fewer babies.   Table 6.6

6.4.4 Aged approximately 15 months
The major change in diets between the ages of 9 and 15 months, was the increase in meat consumption by Bangladeshi and Pakistani children. The proportion eating meat increased to 45% and 43% respectively. This was still lower than the proportion of White children eating meat (78%).

More information on bread consumption was collected at the fourth interview, showing that Pakistani and Indian children were most likely to eat chapatis either on their own, or dipped in curry or a sauce. Forty seven per cent of Pakistani and 27% of Indian children ate chapati dipped in curry or sauce on the day before interview. White children were most likely to eat other types of bread, such as sandwiches and toast.

Bangladeshi children (40%) were still the most likely to have eaten desserts on the day before interview, and Indian children least likely. However fewer Asian children ate desserts than previously. Consumption of biscuits, cakes, sweets and chocolate increased for all groups, but were still consumed more by White children than Asian children. Thirty one per cent of White children ate sweets or chocolate on the day before interview, compared with 15% of Bangladeshi and Pakistani, and 12% of Indian children.

Other differences between the ages of nine and 15 months were an increase in the proportion eating fish in all groups, and also egg and dairy products. Bangladeshi children (8%) were less likely to eat egg and dairy products than other groups – Pakistani (28%), White (20%) and Indian children (18%). The proportion of children eating fruit increased in all groups with Pakistani children (67%) most likely to do so, and Bangladeshi children (45%) least likely. There was a large increase in the proportion in all groups eating crisps   Table 6.7

6.5 How often children ate different types of food

6.5.1 Bangladeshi children

At about nine months old, Bangladeshi children ate a smaller range of food than those in other groups. Foods most often eaten were cereal or rusks (66% ate these at least once a day); rice or pasta (38% at least once a day); and fruit (32% at least once a day). They were more likely to eat rice than children of other ethnic groups. Twenty one per cent had bread or chapati at least once a day; 40% never ate bread or chapati. Thirty four per cent had meat at least once a week, but 58% never ate meat. Twenty six per cent ate fish at least once a week. Bangladeshi children were less likely than those in other groups to eat potatoes, pulses and other vegetables. Most never ate eggs (71%) or yoghurt or cheese (66%). Bangladeshi children were the least likely to eat chocolate or sweets – 65% never ate them.

Figure 6.3, Table 6.8

By the age of 15 months, Bangladeshi children were eating a much broader range of food than previously. One of the largest increases was in the percentage eating meat. More Bangladeshi (53%) than Pakistani or Indian children ate meat every day. Eighty two per cent ate rice, pasta or potatoes at least once a day – higher than for any other group. Forty six per cent ate fresh fruit once a day and 89% at least once a week. Thirty five per cent never ate eggs, yoghurt or cheese. Thirty three per cent ate puddings or desserts at least once a day, which was the highest proportion of the Asian groups, but a further 38% never ate puddings or desserts. This was also a higher proportion than for other groups.

Figure 6.4, Table 6.9

6.5.2 Pakistani children

At about nine months old, Pakistani children ate a broader range of foods more frequently than Bangladeshi children, but ate some foods less frequently than White children. Ninety four per cent ate fruit at least once a week. Sixty seven per cent ate meat at least once a week, and 41% ate fish. These figures were higher than for Indian and Bangladeshi children but lower than for White children. Pakistani children were those most likely to eat bread or chapati at least once a day (59%). They were less likely than Indian and White children, to eat pulses and vegetables. Pakistani children were most likely to eat eggs (49% ate them at least once a week).

Figure 6.3, Table 6.8

Figure 6.3

Proportion of children aged 9 months who ate different foods at least once a day by ethnic group

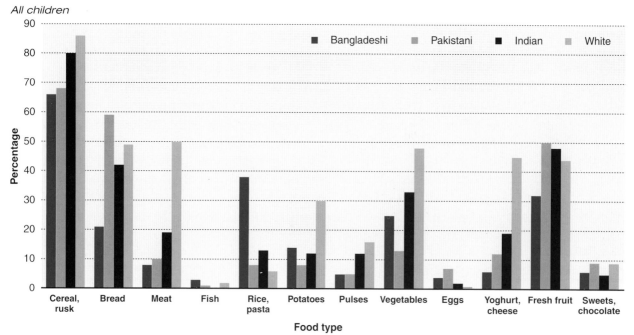

Figure 6.4
Proportion of children aged 15 months who ate different foods at least once a day by ethnic group

All children

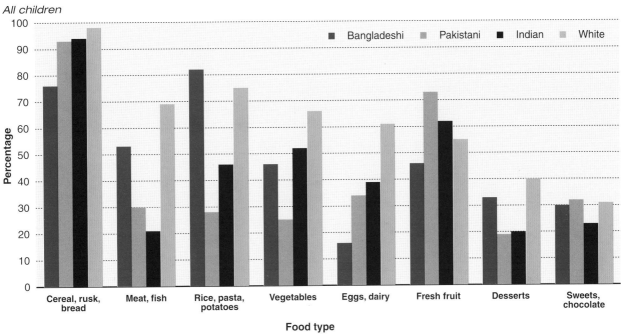

The proportion of Pakistani children eating meat or fish at least once a day increased to 30% at approximately 15 months, and to 95% for those eating it at least once a week. This was higher than for other Asian children. The proportion eating fresh or dried vegetables at least once a day (25%), was lower than for other groups. Pakistani children were more likely than others to eat fresh fruit both at least once a day (73%) and at least once a week (98%). Nineteen per cent had desserts at least once a day and a further 52% had desserts at least once a week.

Figure 6.4, Table 6.9

6.5.3 Indian children
In general, the diets of Indian children aged about nine months were similar to Pakistani children for some foods, and to White children for others. Eighty per cent had cereal or rusk at least once a day, and 42% had bread or chapati. Although 24% of Indian households were vegetarian and 38% of children never ate meat, 19% had meat at least once a day, and 40% at least once a week. Sixty five per cent of Indian children never ate fish. Indian children were less likely to eat pulses and vegetables regularly than White children. Fifty seven per cent never ate eggs, but 76% ate yoghurt or cheese at least once

a week. A similar proportion ate fruit to Pakistani and White children. Fifty six per cent never ate sweets or chocolate – twice as high as the proportion of White children.

Figure 6.3, Table 6.8

At around 15 months old, Indian children were least likely to eat meat – 27% never ate it. Twenty four per cent of Indian households were vegetarian (see Table 6.3). More Indian than Pakistani or Bangladeshi children regularly ate fresh or dried vegetables. Sixty two per cent ate fresh fruit at least once a day. This was more than White or Bangladeshi children. Twenty two per cent of Indian children never ate puddings or desserts and 25% never ate sweets or chocolate.

Figure 6.4, Table 6.9

6.5.4 White children
Compared with Asian children, White children had the most varied diets at around nine months old. They were most likely to eat cereal or rusk regularly, meat, fish, potatoes, pulses and other vegetables, yoghurt and cheese, and also chocolate or sweets.

Figure 6.3, Table 6.8

At about 15 months old, White children still had the most varied diets. The proportion eating meat each day had increased to 69% and vegetables to 66%. White children were less likely to eat fresh fruit daily than Pakistani or Indian children.

Figure 6.4, Table 6.9

6.6 Factors considered when choosing food for the child

Mothers who gave their child three meals of solid food a day were asked at the second, third and fourth interviews about how they chose food to give the child. Two factors mentioned by mothers in all groups on all three occasions were general nutrition or health, and the child or mother's preference. General nutrition or health was mentioned most when the children were aged five months, by 57% of White, 50% of Pakistani, 47% of Indian and 45% of Bangladeshi mothers. By 15 months, the child or mother's preference for type of food was more commonly mentioned by Asian than White mothers (Bangladeshi 48%, Pakistani 46%, Indian 40%, White mothers 31%).

By the age of 15 months, giving the children the same food as the rest of the family became the reason mentioned by the highest proportion of White (68%), Pakistani (63%) and Indian mothers (59%). It was also mentioned by 44% of Bangladeshi mothers.

Variety in the children's diet was mentioned by between a third and a half of mothers in all groups, when the children were aged five months. By the age of 15 months (when the children ate a broader range of foods), the proportion of mothers mentioning variety had fallen to a quarter or less.

At the second interview at about five months, a higher proportion of White than Asian mothers said they considered sugar and salt content when choosing food for the baby. Thirty eight per cent of White mothers mentioned sugar content, compared with 24% of Indian, 19% of Pakistani and 8% of Bangladeshi mothers. Both sugar and salt were mentioned by fewer mothers at later interviews.

Pakistani mothers were most likely to say that they considered vitamin, iron and mineral content. At the second interview it was

mentioned by 25% of Pakistani, 21% of Indian, 17% of White and 16% of Bangladeshi mothers.

The influence of home cooked food was greatest when the children were aged about nine months, mentioned by up to a fifth of mothers in all groups.

Table 6.10

6.7 Foods and ingredients which the mother avoided giving to the child

To find out more about the decisions made on how to feed the child, mothers were also asked whether there were foods they did not give the child and the reasons for this. Between a half and two thirds of mothers in all ethnic groups said they avoided giving some foods when the children were aged about nine months. The proportion of Bangladeshi, Indian and White mothers who said they avoided certain foods had increased by the time the children were aged 15 months, but decreased for Pakistani mothers.

Table 6.11

6.7.1 Foods and ingredients avoided

Spices and chillis were the most commonly avoided food by mothers in all Asian groups, when the children were aged both nine and 15 months. At about 15 months, 52% of Bangladeshi, 44% of both Indian and White, and 39% of Pakistani mothers said they avoided giving spices and chillis.

Mothers were more likely to say they avoided sugar and salt when the children were aged around nine months, than 15 months. At both ages, White mothers were more likely to say they avoided them (37% and 30% respectively), than mothers in other groups.

When the children were aged nine months, White mothers (27%) were most likely say they avoided additives, colouring and preservatives, compared with Indian (10%), Pakistani (7%), and Bangladeshi mothers (5%). However by the age of 15 months, less than 5% of mothers in all groups said they avoided giving them to their children. Indian mothers (13%) were most likely not to give egg and dairy products.

At the age of 15 months there was an increase in the proportion of Indian mothers who said they did not give fish (from 2% to 10%), and in the proportion of Indian and Pakistani mothers who said they did not give desserts.   Table 6.11

6.7.2 Reasons for avoiding certain foods

When the children were aged approximately nine months, mothers from all ethnic groups were most likely to say that they avoided a food or ingredient because it was harmful or not good for the child. At 15 months, mothers said that the spices and chillis were too strong or hot for the child.

Religion or tradition (for instance, avoiding non-Halal meat and animal products) was mentioned by mothers in the Asian groups, for example, at nine months by 30% of Indian, 20% of Pakistani and 18% of Bangladeshi mothers.

White mothers were more likely than Asian mothers to say that they avoided foods that were bad for the child's teeth or would encourage him/her to develop a sweet tooth. When the children were aged nine months, Bangladeshi mothers were more likely than others to avoid food that the child did not like, but this was more common in all groups when the children were 15 months.   Table 6.12

6.8 Eating food with the rest of the family

At the fourth interview, when the child was about 15 months old, mothers were asked if the child ate the same food as the rest of the family. Pakistani children were most likely always to eat the same food (42%), compared with White (36%), Bangladeshi (31%) and Indian children (29%). A majority of all children always or usually ate the same food as the rest of the family, White (86%), Pakistani (79%), Indian (74%) and Bangladeshi children (65%).   Table 6.13

6.9 Whether child feeds him/herself at aged 9 and 15 months

When aged approximately nine months, most children in all groups had fed themselves with either their fingers or a spoon, but the majority did not usually do so. White children were most likely to have done so (89%), compared with Indian (81%), Pakistani (80%) and Bangladeshi children (66%). By the age of fifteen months, most White (68%), Pakistani (59%) and Indian (52%) children usually fed themselves; 36% of Bangladeshi children usually did so.   Table 6.14

When they were aged about nine months old, most children in all ethnic groups had drunk from a cup, glass, or beaker or taken liquid from a spoon. Of those who had drunk from a cup or beaker, between 42% and 46% usually did so. By about 15 months, around 70% of Pakistani, Indian and White children, and just over a half of Bangladeshi children usually drank from a cup or beaker. Ninety four per cent of White children usually held the cup or bottle themselves when drinking, compared with Indian (86%), Pakistani (82%) and Bangladeshi children (73%). The Weaning and the Weaning Diet report[1] recommends that 'from six months of age, infants should be introduced to drinking from a cup and from age one year feeding from a bottle should be discouraged.' This survey showed that at fifteen months, at least nine out of ten children in each of the Asian groups and three quarters of White children were still bottle fed (Chapter 3, Table 3.1).   Table 6.15

6.10 Mother's assessment of child's eating habits

At the fourth interview (when the children were aged 15 months), mothers were asked three questions about how well they thought their child was eating. A clear pattern emerged with White mothers much more likely to say that the child was eating well, and Bangladeshi mothers least likely.

White mothers were most likely to say the child was very easy to feed (41%), compared with Pakistani (24%), Indian (21%) and Bangladeshi mothers (10%). Over a third of Bangladeshi mothers (38%) said that their child was difficult or very difficult to feed, compared with a quarter of Pakistani mothers, a fifth of Indian mothers and one tenth of White mothers.

When asked about the child's appetite, three quarters of White mothers said it was good, compared with approximately half of Pakistani and Indian and a quarter of Bangladeshi mothers. Bangladeshi mothers were most likely to say the child's appetite was poor (28%).

Eighty nine per cent of White mothers agreed that the child ate a variety of food, compared with 56% of Bangladeshi mothers. These findings are consistent with Chapter five, which found that Bangladeshi mothers reported more feeding and weaning problems than other groups as the children got older.   Figure 6.5, Table 6.16

6.11 Types of drinks other than milk

From an early age, Asian mothers were more likely than White mothers to give their child drinks other than milk. By the time the baby was aged around nine weeks, 67% of White mothers and over 80% of Asian mothers gave their baby drinks other than milk. When the babies were aged around 5 months, 76% of White mothers did so, compared with 90% of Indian, 91% of Pakistani and 94% of Bangladeshi mothers.

Table 6.17

6.12 Types of drinks given by mothers

When the babies were aged between nine weeks and nine months old, mothers were asked about the types of drinks apart from milk they usually gave their child. When the children were aged 15 months they were asked to recall all the drinks given the day before.

6.12.1 Drinks given when baby aged approximately 9 weeks

Plain or mineral water was by far the most popular drink given by mothers in all groups when the baby was about nine weeks old. Bangladeshi mothers were most likely to give water (71%), compared with Indian (53%), Pakistani (47%) and White mothers (41%). Sweetened water (e.g. with sugar or honey) was given most by Pakistani (16%) and Indian (15%) mothers. White mothers were most likely to give fruit drinks (17%). At this age, mothers in all ethnic groups who gave fruit drinks usually gave unsweetened drinks. Herbal drinks were most likely to be given by White (6%) and Pakistani (5%) mothers.   Table 6.18

Figure 6.5

Mother's assessment of how easy the child was to feed at 15 months by ethnic group

All mothers

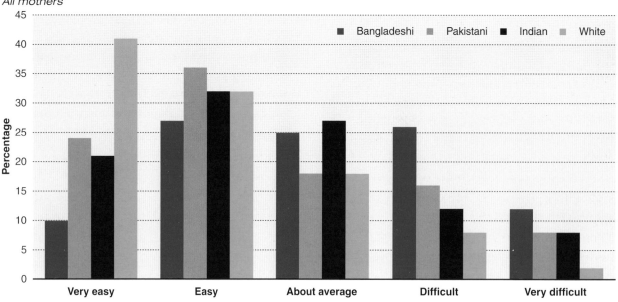

How easy the child is to feed

6.12.2 Drinks given when baby aged approximately five months

At about five months, Bangladeshi mothers were again most likely to give water. Seventy one per cent gave their baby boiled water, and 4% gave water from the tap. Pakistani, Indian and White mothers were less likely to give water at this age than previously. The other main difference from the previous interview was that a much greater proportion of mothers were giving fruit drinks. Seventy two per cent of Pakistani and White mothers, 63% of Indian and 61% of Bangladeshi mothers gave fruit drinks.

Mothers were asked whether any of the drinks they gave were commercially produced drinks for babies. Sixty two per cent of Pakistani mothers gave these baby drinks, compared with 57% of White, 48% of Indian, and 45% of Bangladeshi mothers.

Table 6.19

6.12.3 Drinks given when baby aged approximately nine months

When the babies were approximately nine months old, boiled water continued to be the most frequently given drink, but the proportion of babies drinking water from the tap had increased for all groups, and was higher among Pakistani (31%) and Bangladeshi (28%) babies, than among Indian (17%) and White babies (10%). Between a quarter and a third of mothers in all groups gave pure or fresh fruit juice. White babies were more likely than Asian babies to be given concentrated fruit drinks.

Twenty per cent of White babies drank tea or coffee at this age, compared with 6% of Indian, 3% of Pakistani and 1% of Bangladeshi babies. A low proportion of babies in all groups drank fizzy drinks at this age, the highest being Pakistani (6%).

Table 6.20

6.12.4 Drinks given when child aged approximately 15 months

When the children were aged about 15 months, mothers were asked to recall the drinks given to the child on the previous day. A major change at this age was that babies were drinking water straight from the tap rather than boiled water. Asian babies were still more likely to drink water than White babies – 68% of Pakistani, 62% of Bangladeshi, 47% of Indian, and 21% of White babies drank tap water.

At about 15 months, children in all groups were more likely to drink sweetened fruit drinks than before. A similar proportion of children in all groups drank sweetened fruit drinks. White children (48%) were more likely to drink unsweetened fruit drinks than Asian children (Pakistani 31%, Indian 29%, and Bangladeshi 25%).

White children (24%) were still more likely to drink tea and coffee than Asian children, but the proportions of Pakistani (12%) and Indian children (10%) drinking them had increased. Pakistani children (14%) were most likely to drink fizzy drinks.

Table 6.21

6.13 How often children drank different types of drink

When they were aged approximately 15 months, Asian children were much more likely than White children to drink water at least once a day. Thirty four per cent of White children never drank water. Pakistani and Indian children were most likely to drink pure or fresh fruit juice; about a half of those in both groups drank it at least once a day. White children were most likely to drink tea or coffee (27% drank either at least once a day) and Bangladeshi children were least likely (82%) ever to drink either. Pakistani children were most likely to drink fizzy drinks – 14% drank them at least once a day, and a further 34% at least once a week. White children were least likely to drink fizzy drinks. Very few children in any group drank herbal drinks.

Figure 6.6, Table 6.22

6.14 Reasons for giving drinks

Mothers were asked why they gave their baby drinks other than milk. The most commonly mentioned reason in all groups was that the baby was thirsty or dehydrated. This reason was always given more by White mothers than by Asian mothers. At all interviews, Asian mothers were more likely than White mothers to say it was because drinks were good for the baby; at the first interview for example, 26% of Bangladeshi,

Figure 6.6

Proportion of children aged 15 months who drank different types of non-milk drinks at least once a day by ethnic group

All children

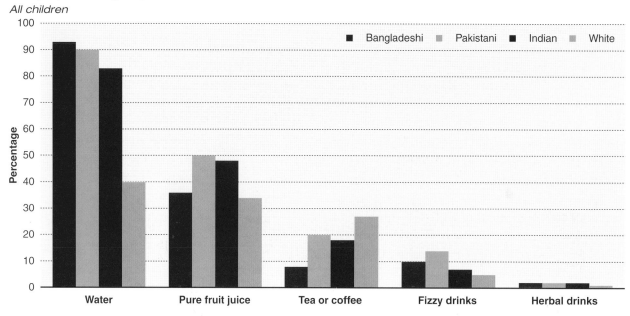

24% of Pakistani and 23% of Indian mothers, compared with 5% of White mothers, mentioned this.

Constipation and colic were mentioned less often at the ages of five and nine months than initially. Helping digestion and giving vitamins were mentioned more, especially at nine months.

Table 6.23

6.15 Vitamin supplements given to babies

At all stages of the survey, at least twice as many Asian mothers in all groups gave vitamin supplements to their babies as White mothers. At the second interview, when the babies were aged approximately five months, 41% of Pakistani, 39% of Indian and 32% of Bangladeshi mothers gave vitamin supplements to their babies, compared with 9% of White mothers. When the children were aged about 15 months, 58% of Indian, 54% of Pakistani, and 50% of Bangladeshi mothers gave vitamin supplements, compared with 26% of White mothers. The Weaning and the Weaning Diet report[1] recommends that 'from age six months, infants receiving breast milk as their main drink should be given supplements of A and D. Between the ages of one to five years, vitamin A and D

supplements should be given unless adequate vitamin status can be assured from a diverse diet containing vitamins A and D rich foods and from moderate exposure to sunlight.'

Figure 6.7, Table 6.24

Mothers in all groups were most likely to buy vitamins for their babies rather than getting them free (available to families on income support), or on prescription. When the children were aged about 15 months, 76% of White mothers giving vitamin supplements bought them, compared with 68% of Indian, 55% of Pakistani and 48% of Bangladeshi mothers. Bangladeshi mothers were most likely to get free vitamins (20% of mothers got them free at the fourth interview), compared with 16% of Pakistani, 8% of Indian and 4% of White mothers. Bangladeshi and Pakistani mothers were most likely to get vitamins on prescription.

Table 6.25

Most mothers in all groups who gave vitamins gave Children's vitamin drops from the child health clinic – when the children were aged about five months less than one in five gave other brands. By the age of 15 months, the proportion of mothers using other brands had increased slightly to 34% of White mothers, 25% of Indian and Bangladeshi mothers and 21% of Pakistani mothers.

Table 6.25

Figure 6.7

Proportion of mothers giving children vitamins at each stage by ethnic group

All mothers

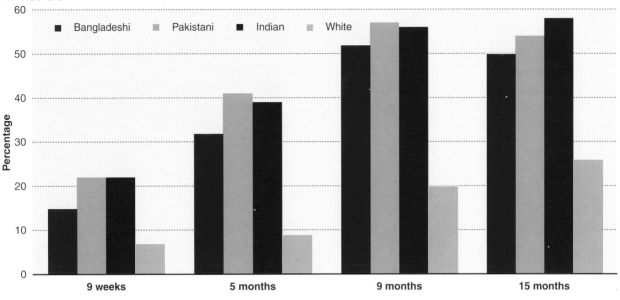

6.16 Vitamin supplements taken by breastfeeding mothers

One of the groups of babies most at risk from vitamin deficiency are those who are breastfed by a mother with poor vitamin status[1]. When the babies were aged between nine weeks and nine months old, breastfeeding mothers were asked whether they were taking extra vitamins. When the babies were aged nine weeks, mothers in all

Asian groups were more likely to take vitamin supplements than White mothers (Bangladeshi 43%, Pakistani 41%, Indian 40% and White mothers 31%). By nine months, the proportion was similar for all groups, with approximately one fifth of all mothers taking vitamin supplements.

Figure 6.8, Table 6.26

Figure 6.8

Proportion of breastfeeding mothers taking vitamins at each stage by ethnic group

All breastfeeding mothers

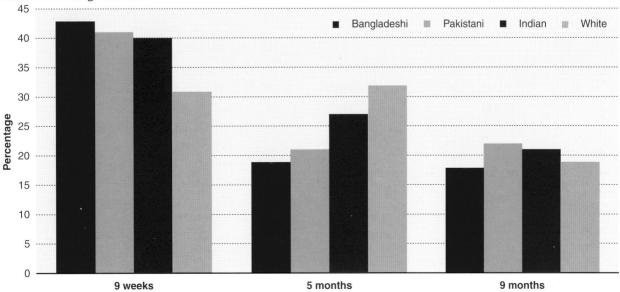

The majority of Asian breastfeeding mothers taking vitamin supplements obtained them on prescription (Bangladeshi 91%, Indian and Pakistani mothers 86%). Most White mothers bought their own supplements (74%).   **Table 6.26**

Notes

1   Department of Health. *Weaning and Weaning Diet.* Report on Health and Social Subjects 45. HMSO (London 1994).

Table 6.1

Cumulative proportion of children given solid food at different ages by ethnic group

All mothers who gave an interview at stage four

Proportion of children given solid food	Ethnic group			
	Bangladeshi	Pakistani	Indian	White
	%	%	%	%
4 weeks	0	0	0	2
6 weeks	1	1	1	6
8 weeks	2	3	5	18
3 months	72	73	70	83
4 months	96	93	95	98
6 months	99	98	99	99
9 months	100	100	100	100
Base = 100%	*476*	*590*	*758*	*548*

Table 6.2

Cumulative proportion of children given three meals of solid food a day at different ages by ethnic group

All mothers who gave a fourth interview

Proportion of children given 3 meals a day	Ethnic group			
	Bangladeshi	Pakistani	Indian	White
	%	%	%	%
3 months	8	7	6	14
6 months	59	61	75	88
9 months	83	85	93	99
12 months	97	98	99	100
15 months	100	100	100	100
Base = 100%	*430*	*551*	*738*	*544*

Table 6.3

Proportion of households where most members ate meat, and whether Muslim households ate only halal meat by ethnic group

All mothers

Proportion of households eating meat	Ethnic group			
	Bangladeshi	Pakistani	Indian	White
	%	%	%	%
Most members eat meat	100	99	68	95
Most members do not eat meat	–	0	24	3
Equal number do and do not eat meat	–	0	9	2
Base = 100%	*520*	*640*	*815*	*576*
Muslim households only				
Eats only halal meat	99	99	96	–
Does not eat only halal meat	1	1	4	–
Base = 100%	*511*	*620*	*123*	*–*

Table 6.4

Proportion of mothers giving different types of food to baby on day before 9 week interview by ethnic group

All mothers who had ever given solid food

	Ethnic group			
	Bangladeshi	Pakistani	Indian	White
	%	%	%	%
Rusk	[4]	[5]	29	18
Rice cereal	[5]	[4]	22	30
Other cereal	[1]	[2]	5	12
Bread, rice or pasta	[5]	[4]	–	3
Meat dish	–	–	1	10
Vegetables	[2]	[4]	4	12
Egg or dairy	[1]	[2]	3	3
Fresh fruit	[2]	[5]	6	9
Desserts, sweets and chocolate	[7]	[1]	3	8
Base = 100%	*35*	*38*	*93*	*299*

Table 6.5

Proportion of mothers giving different types of food to baby on day before 5 month interview by ethnic group

All mothers who had ever given solid food

	Ethnic group			
	Bangladeshi	Pakistani	Indian	White
	%	%	%	%
Rusk	8	36	35	27
Rice cereal	12	12	17	14
Other cereal	25	25	39	51
Bread, rice or pasta	5	4	7	7
Meat dish	3	6	23	52
Vegetables	33	34	46	43
Egg or dairy	1	6	3	7
Fresh fruit	23	28	25	30
Desserts, sweets and chocolate	59	44	31	41
Base = 100%	*480*	*581*	*783*	*579*

Table 6.6
Proportion of mothers giving different types of food to baby on day before 9 month interview by ethnic group

All mothers who had ever given solid food

| | Ethnic group | | | |
	Bangladeshi	Pakistani	Indian	White
	%	%	%	%
Rusk	12	34	35	21
Rice cere	17	12	10	3
Other cerea	42	46	63	82
Brea	12	44	35	46
Rice or pasta onl	26	12	16	2
Meat dish	12	28	33	71
Beef	1	2	3	35
Poultry	9	17	25	26
Other	3	10	8	23
Fish dish	5	6	4	9
Vegetables and potatoes	44	45	63	48
Egg or dairy	2	10	7	14
Fruit	30	48	44	45
Yoghur	6	12	24	58
Desser	50	41	30	35
Biscuits cakes	10	13	14	28
Sweets, chocolate	1	2	3	11
Crisps	4	9	8	10
Base = 100%	504	623	803	572

Table 6.7
Proportion of mothers giving different types of food to child on day before 15 month interview by ethnic group

All mothers

| | Ethnic group | | | |
	Bangladeshi	Pakistani	Indian	White
	%	%	%	%
Rusk	7	15	15	5
Cereals	54	58	70	85
Chapati only	1	26	28	0
Chapati dipped in curry sauce	1	47	27	–
Bread	33	35	38	75
Rice or pasta only	20	7	9	4
Meat dish	45	43	37	78
Beef	2	2	3	34
Poultry	6	11	17	27
Lamb	3	7	4	8
Pork, bacon, ham	0	0	3	14
Other meat, meat unspecified	36	27	13	10
Fish dish	18	12	9	16
Vegetables, vegetable dish	53	40	65	42
Egg or dairy	8	28	18	20
Fruit or nuts	45	67	53	53
Yoghurt	4	11	25	50
Other desserts	40	24	19	34
Biscuits, cakes	39	35	44	59
Sweets and chocolate	15	15	12	31
Crisps, savoury snacks	30	31	32	38
Base = 100%	468	573	750	547

Table 6.8
Frequency with which mothers gave baby aged 9 months different types of food by ethnic group

All mothers

Frequency with which food given	Ethnic group					Ethnic group			
	Bangladeshi	Pakistani	Indian	White		Bangladeshi	Pakistani	Indian	White
	%	%	%	%					
Cereal or rusk					**Pulses**				
At least once a day	66	68	80	86	At least once a day	5	5	12	16
At least once a week	20	22	14	11	At least once a week	34	56	63	63
Less than once a week	3	2	2	1	Less than once a week	5	7	8	8
Never	12	7	4	2	Never	56	32	18	13
Bread or chapati					**Other vegetables**				
At least once a day	21	59	42	49	At least once a day	25	13	33	48
At least once a week	34	28	42	40	At least once a week	33	53	54	49
Less than once a week	4	3	3	4	Less than once a week	4	5	3	1
Never	40	10	12	7	Never	39	29	10	2
Meat					**Eggs**				
At least once a day	8	10	19	50	At least once a day	4	7	2	1
At least once a week	26	57	40	44	At least once a week	16	42	30	30
Less than once a week	7	6	4	2	Less than once a week	8	12	11	20
Never	58	26	38	4	Never	71	40	57	49
Fish					**Yogurt or cheese**				
At least once a day	3	1	0	2	At least once a day	6	12	19	45
At least once a week	23	40	26	49	At least once a week	23	49	57	44
Less than once a week	7	12	9	26	Less than once a week	6	6	7	4
Never	68	46	65	23	Never	66	33	16	7
Rice or pasta					**Fruit**				
At least once a day	38	8	13	6	At least once a day	32	50	48	44
At least once a week	33	63	62	68	At least once a week	48	44	46	46
Less than once a week	5	13	8	12	Less than once a week	5	2	3	6
Never	24	17	16	13	Never	14	4	4	4
Potatoes					**Chocolate or sweets**				
At least once a day	14	8	12	30	At least once a day	6	9	5	9
At least once a week	52	72	69	64	At least once a week	19	23	25	39
Less than once a week	4	8	8	4	Less than once a week	10	12	14	25
Never	30	13	12	2	Never	65	56	56	28
Base = 100%	519	638	813	576	*Base = 100%*	519	638	813	576

Table 6.9

Frequency with which mothers gave child aged 15 months different types of food by ethnic group

All mothers

Frequency with which food given	Ethnic group				Frequency with which food given	Ethnic group			
	Bangladeshi	Pakistani	Indian	White		Bangladeshi	Pakistani	Indian	White
	%	%	%	%		%	%	%	%
Cereals, rusks, bread					**Eggs, yoghurt, cheese**				
At least once a day	76	93	94	98	At least once a day	16	34	39	61
At least once a week	19	6	6	2	At least once a week	40	55	52	36
Less than once a week	1	0	0	–	Less than once a week	9	4	4	2
Never	3	0	0	0	Never	35	8	5	2
Meat or fish					**Fresh fruit**				
At least once a day	53	30	21	69	At least once a day	46	73	62	55
At least once a week	34	65	48	29	At least once a week	43	25	32	35
Less than once a week	4	2	3	0	Less than once a week	5	1	4	6
Never	10	4	27	2	Never	6	1	2	5
Rice, pasta, potatoes					**Puddings, desserts**				
At least once a day	82	28	46	75	At least once a day	33	19	20	40
At least once a week	15	66	50	24	At least once a week	24	52	44	38
Less than once a week	0	3	1	0	Less than once a week	6	11	15	11
Never	2	2	2	0	Never	38	18	22	11
Fresh or dried vegetables					**Sweets, chocolates**				
At least once a day	46	25	52	66	At least once a day	30	32	23	31
At least once a week	34	62	40	32	At least once a week	35	35	36	47
Less than once a week	4	4	4	1	Less than once a week	8	8	16	12
Never	17	9	4	1	Never	27	25	25	10
Base = 100%	*477*	*590*	*758*	*548*	*Base = 100%*	*477*	*590*	*758*	*548*

Table 6.10

Factors considered when choosing food for the baby by ethnic group

All mothers who gave three meals a day

Factors considered when choosing food	Ethnic group											
	Bangladeshi			Pakistani			Indian			White		
	5 month	9 months	15 months	5 months	9 months	15 months	5 months	9 months	15 months	5 months	9 months	15 months
	%	%	%	%	%	%	%	%	%	%	%	%
Same food as rest of family	–	2	44	–	3	63	–	2	59	–	3	68
General nutrition or health food	45	33	14	50	37	17	47	42	26	57	52	35
Child or mother's preference	40	47	48	44	48	46	46	49	40	44	37	31
Variety	36	28	12	39	34	17	47	35	20	43	42	26
Sugar content	8	12	3	19	17	4	24	16	7	38	24	12
Vitamins, iron and mineral content	16	12	4	25	18	2	21	13	6	17	14	6
Salt content	6	8	1	7	5	1	9	9	5	22	18	9
Home cooked	2	14	8	9	16	10	8	18	16	15	19	9
Additives or preservatives	6	2	–	7	4	–	9	8	–	19	15	–
Ease of preparation	5	3	3	8	2	2	9	6	4	11	8	7
Price	1	1	1	2	1	–	4	1	1	6	4	1
Texture, consistency	2	2	4	3	3	1	1	3	1	3	4	2
Gluten free	–	–	–	1	–	–	2	–	–	6	–	–
Brand	1	–	–	2	–	–	2	–	–	4	–	–
Other	8	4	8	9	8	4	8	5	4	6	7	4
Base = 100%	*144*	*327*	*397*	*195*	*452*	*531*	*365*	*692*	*712*	*361*	*542*	*535*

Table 6.11

Foods and ingredients which the mother avoided giving the child by ethnic group

All mothers

Foods and ingredients avoided	Ethnic group							
	Bangladeshi		Pakistani		Indian		White	
	9 months	15 months	9 months	15 months	9 months	15 months	9 months	15 months
	%	%	%	%	%	%	%	%
Avoided giving some foods	53	69	61	54	61	70	66	73
Did not avoid giving some foods	47	31	39	46	39	30	34	27
Base = 100%	*518*	*475*	*636*	*590*	*810*	*758*	*576*	*548*
Spices, chillies	31	52	33	39	25	44	15	44
Sugar	17	8	21	6	23	9	37	15
Salt	11	5	12	6	16	7	30	22
Meat, animal products	11	11	12	8	18	25	3	9
Additives, colouring, preservatives	5	1	7	1	10	2	27	4
Egg or dairy	8	11	6	6	13	13	9	10
Fatty, oily foods	9	2	6	1	5	1	7	4
Fish, seafood	0	5	1	2	2	10	2	3
Desserts, sweets and chocolate	0	4	2	7	1	9	2	5
Nuts	0	1	0	0	0	1	2	6
Gluten, cereals	1	1	1	1	1	0	3	2
Fruit	–	2	–	1		2	0	2
Foods that are hard to chew	0	–	1	–	0	–	1	–
Other	5	4	6	2	4	1	8	4
Did not avoid giving some foods	47	31	39	46	39	30	34	27
Base = 100%	*518*	*475*	*636*	*590*	*810*	*758*	*576*	*548*

Table 6.12

Reasons for avoiding giving child some foods or ingredients by ethnic group

All mothers

Reason for avoiding some foods	Ethnic group							
	Bangladeshi		Pakistani		Indian		White	
	9 months	15 months	9 months	15 months	9 months	15 months	9 months	15 months
	%	%	%	%	%	%	%	%
Too strong or hot for child	–	58	–	45	–	42	–	32
Harmful for child	32	13	35	17	24	13	40	24
Not good for child	35	14	26	18	31	19	38	31
Religion, tradition	18	12	20	13	30	32	2	2
Bad for teeth	7	4	14	11	15	8	23	8
Child doesn't like them	15	15	12	18	9	10	8	18
Allergies, illness	12	15	10	10	10	11	16	14
Will develop a sweet tooth	7	2	8	5	8	5	14	6
Publicity, media, advice	2	0	2	0	3	3	9	10
Child is too young	6	–	6	–	4	–	5	–
Make child hyperactive	–	–	0	–	0	–	3	–
Other	2	2	3	1	2	1	2	2
Base = 100%	*273*	*329*	*389*	*319*	*494*	*531*	*380*	*396*

Table 6.13
Proportion of children aged 15 months eating the same food as the rest of their family by ethnic group

All children

Proportion eating the same food as the family	Ethnic group			
	Bangladeshi	Pakistani	Indian	White
Always eats same food	31	42	29	36
Usually eats same food	34	37	45	50
Occasionally eats same food	29	19	22	13
Never eats same food	6	2	4	2
Base = 100%	*477*	*590*	*758*	*548*

Table 6.14
Whether child ever feeds him/herself with fingers or spoon at ages 9 and 15 months by ethnic group

All children

	Ethnic group			
	Bangladeshi	Pakistani	Indian	White
	%	%	%	%
Aged 9 months				
Ever fed him/herself with:				
fingers	65	78	79	88
spoon	5	10	9	16
neither	33	20	19	11
Base = 100%	*519*	*638*	*813*	*576*
Usually feeds him/herself	7	11	7	10
Does not usually feed him/herself	93	89	93	90
Base = 100%	*349*	*510*	*659*	*513*
Aged 15 months				
Usually feeds him/herself with:				
fingers	26	43	32	23
spoon or fork	3	4	7	17
uses both fingers and spoon or fork	8	11	13	28
Does not usually feed him/herself	64	41	48	32
Base = 100%	*474*	*588*	*757*	*545*

Table 6.15

Whether child has ever or usually drunk from a cup or beaker or been given liquid from a spoon by ethnic group

All mothers who gave drinks

	Ethnic group			
	Bangladeshi	Pakistani	Indian	White
	%	%	%	%
Aged 9 months				
Ever drunk from:				
cup or beaker	61	75	78	86
spoon	31	15	22	18
neither	29	20	18	13
Base = 100%	*520*	*640*	*815*	*576*
Usually drinks from cup or beaker	43	44	42	46
Base = 100%	*319*	*482*	*633*	*493*
Aged 15 months				
Usually drinks from cup or beaker	54	71	71	69
Bottle	31	17	20	18
Uses both	15	11	10	12
Base = 100%	*469*	*588*	*751*	*534*
Child holds cup or bottle:				
usually	73	82	86	94
sometimes	17	14	11	5
never	10	4	4	1
Base = 100%	*469*	*588*	*753*	*534*

Table 6.16

Mother's assessment of child's eating habits at age 15 months by ethnic group

All mothers

Assessment of eating habits	Ethnic group			
	Bangladeshi	Pakistani	Indian	White
	%	%	%	%
How easy the child is to feed				
Very easy	10	24	21	41
Easy	27	36	32	32
About average	25	18	27	18
Difficult	26	16	12	8
Very difficult	12	8	8	2
Child's appetite				
Good	26	50	46	75
Average	48	35	40	21
Poor	28	15	14	4
Range of foods eaten				
Eats a variety of food	56	72	75	89
Is fussy about eating	44	28	25	11
Base = 100%	*476*	*589*	*758*	*547*

Table 6.17
Proportion of mothers who gave drinks other than milk by ethnic group

All mothers

Ethnic group	Bangladeshi	Pakistani	Indian	White
	%	%	%	%
9 weeks	86	84	80	67
5 months	94	91	90	76
9 months	98	99	99	97
15 months	99	100	99	97
Base = 100%				
9 weeks	*609*	*730*	*934*	*619*
5 months	*552*	*668*	*841*	*594*
9 months	*520*	*640*	*815*	*576*
15 months	*477*	*590*	*758*	*548*

Table 6.18
Proportion of mothers who gave drinks other than milk when baby aged 9 weeks by ethnic group

All mothers

Proportion of mothers who gave drinks	Ethnic group			
	Bangladeshi	Pakistani	Indian	White
	%	%	%	%
Plain or mineral water	71	47	53	41
Sweetened water	6	16	15	5
Gripe water	2	6	3	1
Herbal drinks	0	5	2	6
Fruit drinks – no added sweetener	7	8	7	14
Fruit drinks – added sweetener	2	3	1	1
Fruit drinks – sweetener unspecified	0	1	0	2
Other	0	1	0	0
No drinks given	14	16	20	33
Base = 100%	*610*	*731*	*934*	*619*

Table 6.19
Proportion of mothers who gave drinks other than milk when baby aged 5 months by ethnic group

All mothers

Proportion of mothers who gave drinks	Ethnic group			
	Bangladeshi	Pakistani	Indian	White
	%	%	%	%
Boiled water	71	40	31	34
Water from tap	4	1	4	1
Sweetened water	2	11	10	2
Other water	1	0	2	2
Gripe water	0	3	1	–
Herbal drinks	1	5	6	5
Fruit drinks – no added sweetener	43	44	45	50
Fruit drinks – added sweetener	15	22	15	14
Fruit drinks – sweetener unspecified	3	6	3	8
Other	–	1	1	1
No drinks given	6	9	10	24
Base = 100%	*552*	*668*	*841*	*594*
All mothers who gave drinks				
Gave drinks produced for babies	45	62	48	57
Base = 100%	*520*	*606*	*760*	*454*

Table 6.20
Proportion of mothers who gave drinks other than milk when baby aged 9 months by ethnic group

All mothers

Proportion of mothers who gave drinks	Ethnic group			
	Bangladeshi	Pakistani	Indian	White
	%	%	%	%
Boiled water	59	40	54	36
Water from tap	28	31	17	10
Sweetened water	1	3	5	1
Other water	2	3	3	3
Gripe water	1	5	–	–
Pure, fresh fruit juice	28	28	32	27
Concentrated fruit juice	18	24	20	32
Other fruit drink – no added sweetener	45	53	42	31
Other fruit drink – added sweetener	4	14	10	8
Tea, coffee	1	3	6	20
Fizzy drinks	1	6	3	1
Herbal	0	2	4	2
Other	0	2	3	3
No drinks given	2	1	1	3
Base = 100%	*520*	*640*	*815*	*576*

Table 6.21
Types of drinks other than milk given to child on day before 15 month interview by ethnic group

All mothers

Types of drinks given	Ethnic group			
	Bangladeshi	Pakistani	Indian	White
	%	%	%	%
Boiled water	23	9	25	8
Water from tap	62	68	47	21
Sweetened water	1	1	2	1
Other water	1	1	3	2
Pure, fresh fruit juice	19	28	28	20
Concentrated fruit juice	8	6	9	9
Other fruit drink – no added sweetener	25	31	29	48
Other fruit drink – added sweetener	22	26	24	18
Tea, coffee	4	12	10	24
Fizzy drinks	8	14	8	6
Herbal	0	1	1	1
Milk-based drinks	1	1	2	6
Other	1	2	2	1
Base = 100%	*471*	*588*	*753*	*534*

Table 6.22
How often mothers gave 15 month old children different types of drink by ethnic group

All mothers

How often drinks given	Ethnic group			
	Bangladeshi	Pakistani	Indian	White
	%	%	%	%
Water				
At least once a day	93	90	83	40
At least once a week	4	5	9	15
Less than once a week	1	1	2	10
Never	2	4	6	34
Pure fruit juice				
At least once a day	36	50	48	34
At least once a week	28	25	25	23
Less than once a week	5	6	6	12
Never	31	18	21	31
Herbal drinks				
At least once a day	2	2	2	1
At least once a week	2	2	4	1
Less than once a week	1	4	5	2
Never	96	92	89	96
Tea or coffee				
At least once a day	8	20	18	27
At least once a week	9	16	16	16
Less than once a week	1	4	5	7
Never	82	60	61	51
Fizzy drinks				
At least once a day	10	14	7	5
At least once a week	18	34	23	12
Less than once a week	7	11	11	14
Never	65	41	59	69
Base = 100%	*471*	*588*	*753*	*534*

Table 6.23
Reasons for giving drinks other than milk by ethnic group

All mothers who gave drinks other than milk

Reasons for giving drinks	Ethnic group											
	Bangladeshi			Pakistani			Indian			White		
	9 weeks	5 months	9 months	9 weeks	5 months	9 months	9 weeks	5 months	9 months	9 weeks	5 months	9 months
	%	%	%	%	%	%	%	%	%	%	%	%
Child thirsty or dehydrated	43	56	75	40	57	79	43	59	80	66	74	91
Good for the child	26	35	42	24	35	41	23	28	35	5	13	27
Helps digestion, with meal	–	14	31	–	18	25	–	25	34	–	13	19
Constipation	29	19	18	26	19	19	27	14	17	22	14	19
Colic, wind, hiccups	20	5	12	22	7	6	15	3	5	15	5	6
Hungry between feeds	4	4	8	12	4	9	14	7	8	15	7	6
To give child vitamins	–	4	11	–	2	10	–	2	8	–	2	8
Other health reason	3	2	–	4	2	–	3	2	–	3	1	–
Variety or change	0	2	–	1	3	–	1	3	–	2	6	–
Clean child's mouth	4	–	–	2	–	–	2	–	–	2	–	–
To comfort or settle child	0	–	0	1	–	1	1	–	0	2	–	2
Child likes it	–	2	–	–	2	–	–	2	–	–	1	–
Giving drinks to others	–	–	1	–	–	2	–	–	1	–	–	2
Other	7	3	4	6	3	3	6	2	3	6	4	4
Base = 100%	*517*	*518*	*511*	*609*	*604*	*633*	*747*	*760*	*808*	*414*	*453*	*560*

Table 6.24

Proportion of mothers giving children vitamins by ethnic group

All mothers

Proportion giving vitamins	Ethnic group			
	Bangladeshi	Pakistani	Indian	White
	%	%	%	%
9 weeks	15	22	21	7
5 months	32	41	39	9
9 months	52	57	56	20
15 months	50	54	58	26
Base = 100%				
9 weeks	*609*	*730*	*933*	*619*
5 months	*552*	*668*	*841*	*594*
9 months	*520*	*640*	*815*	*576*
15 months	*477*	*590*	*758*	*548*

Table 6.25

How mothers obtained vitamins for the child and type of vitamin drops given by ethnic group

All mothers giving children vitamins

	Ethnic group			
	Bangladeshi	Pakistani	Indian	White
	%	%	%	%
How vitamins obtained				
5 months				
Bought	37	47	52	60
Free	27	23	12	18
Prescription	36	29	35	22
Base = 100%	*176*	*277*	*331*	*55*
15 months				
Bought	48	55	68	76
Free	20	16	8	4
Prescription	32	30	24	20
Base = 100%	*180*	*231*	*332*	*140*
Type of vitamin drops given				
5 months				
Children's vitamin drops	89	89	86	82
Other brand	11	11	14	18
Base = 100%	*177*	*277*	*331*	*55*
15 months				
Children's vitamin drops	75	79	75	66
Other brand	25	21	25	34
Base = 100%	*241*	*317*	*437*	*143*

Table 6.26
Proportion of breastfeeding mothers taking vitamins and how they were obtained by ethnic group

	Ethnic group			
	Bangladeshi	Pakistani	Indian	White
	%	%	%	%
All breastfeeding mothers				
Proportion taking vitamins				
9 weeks	43	41	40	31
5 months	19	21	27	32
9 months	18	22	21	19
Base = 100%				
9 weeks	*243*	*203*	*387*	*186*
5 months	*119*	*107*	*223*	*126*
9 months	*67*	*64*	*114*	*58*
All mothers who took vitamins				
How vitamins obtained				
Bought	5	10	13	74
Free	4	4	1	–
Prescription	91	86	86	26
Base = 100% (baby aged 9 weeks)	*105*	*83*	*153*	*57*
Where vitamins obtained				
Child health clinic	9	8	10	19
Elsewhere	91	82	90	81
Base = 100% (baby aged 9 weeks)	*105*	*83*	*153*	*57*

Summary

- Birthweight as reported by the mothers was, on average, higher for White than Asian babies.

- At nine weeks old, White babies were heavier than Asian babies. At fifteen months, White boys were still heavier than Asian boys; White, Pakistani and Indian girls had on average a similar weight, and were heavier than Bangladeshi girls.

- Over the first fifteen months, Pakistani and Indian boys and girls gained more weight than Bangladeshi boys and girls.

- At nine weeks, White boys were longer than Asian boys but by fifteen months, Pakistani and Indian boys were longest. Indian and White girls were longest at nine weeks but by fifteen months, Indian girls were longest.

- The length of boys and girls in all Asian groups increased more over fifteen months than their White peers.

- Both White boys and girls had a larger head circumference at all ages than Asian babies.

- From the age of five months, White boys had a larger mid upper-arm circumference than Asian boys. White girls had the largest arm circumference up to nine months but by fifteen months, the arm circumference of Pakistani girls was similar to White girls.

- At all ages, White boys had a higher Body Mass Index (BMI) than Asian boys in all groups. White girls had a higher BMI until the age of fifteen months. At this age, their BMI was similar to Pakistani girls but still greater than Bangladeshi and Indian girls.

- The three main factors associated with weight at fifteen months in all groups were birthweight, sex and parental height. Feeding problems were related to the weight of Asian babies. Other factors related to weight were: whether the child was given extra vitamins (Bangladeshi and Pakistani children); mother's religion, whether the child ate rice, potatoes or pasta daily and whether the child was bottle fed at nine months and mainly given cow's milk (Indian children); birth order (Pakistani and White children).

- The two main factors associated with length at fifteen months in all groups were length at nine weeks and parents' height. Sex was associated with length in all groups except Indian children. Whether the child was bottle fed at nine months and mainly given cow's milk was associated with the length of Indian children. Factors relating to length in other groups were birth order (Pakistani and White children); feeding problems and whether the child drank water daily (Bangladeshi and Pakistani children); whether bottle fed at nine weeks and whether given vitamins at nine weeks (Bangladeshi children); whether the child ate rice, potatoes and pasta daily (Pakistani children); whether the family received income support and whether the child ate puddings (White children).

One of the aims of the survey was to measure the growth of young Asian children, to compare this with the growth of White children, and to relate it to feeding practices. Standard anthropometric measurements of body weight, supine length, head circumference, and mid upper-arm circumference were taken at each interview. This chapter reports how the measurements were taken and the proportion of measurements which were successfully achieved. For each measurement, it gives the actual results and the mean gain at each interview, for boys and girls in each ethnic group. It describes the results of modelling analysis explaining the variation in weight and length measurement at fifteen months. Tables comparing the survey data with national data are also presented.

Details of the protocols for carrying out the measurements are given in Appendix C and are summarised here. Many interviewers were already experienced in taking anthropometric measurements from previous health and dietary surveys, but all were trained to take the measurements at the pre-fieldwork briefings, where they were also given the opportunity to practise measuring babies.

7.2.1 Supine length
Supine length was measured using a Raven portable rollametre. This measurement required the help of the mother. The child was laid on a foam mat, with the mother holding the back of the head against a headpiece. The interviewer straightened the child's legs with one hand, and drew up the footrest attached to a measurement tape to touch both of the child's heels. The reading was recorded to the nearest millimetre. The results of a small study which was carried out to look at interviewer variability in measuring supine length are presented in Appendix C.

7.2.2 Weight
Children were weighed using Soehnle baby scales, with a detachable tray. Whilst the children were too young to sit on the scales unaided they

were placed in the tray. At later interviews the tray was removed and the child was weighed sitting or standing on the base of the scales. Children were normally weighed naked, and any clothing worn was noted. Weights were recorded to the nearest 10 grams.

7.2.3 Head circumference
Head circumference is a standard measure of development and growth. Lasso circumference tapes from the Child Growth Foundation were used to measure both head and mid upper-arm circumferences. The tape was placed around the child's head just above the brow ridges, at the point of maximum circumference. The measurement was taken over the child's hair under slight tension. The measurement was recorded to the nearest millimetre.

7.2.4 Mid upper-arm circumference
Mid upper-arm circumference gives information on body size. The measurement was taken at the mid point of a bare upper arm. The tape was positioned horizontally without compressing the tissues of the upper arm. Circumference measurements were taken to the nearest millimetre.

At the first interview, in all groups, at least 98% of children were measured. Two per cent of all measurements were excluded for each group because the date of measurement was either when the child was less than six weeks of age or greater than twelve weeks. This was to give an accurate picture of the measurements of children at around nine weeks old (see 7.4 below). Further individual measurements were not included in the analysis for two reasons: where the interviewer was unable to take a particular measurement, or because having attempted it she considered it unreliable. Measurements were considered unreliable for a variety of reasons, for instance, if the child was wearing heavy clothing, or if the child refused to keep still. Eight per cent of White, 12% of Pakistani, 15% of Indian, and 18% of Bangladeshi children had one or more measurements excluded from analysis at the first interview. Children were measured each time they were interviewed, even if a previous interview had been missed.

At the age of five months, the children were easier to measure, and four reliable measurements were obtained from at least 90% of eligible children. At nine and fifteen months the proportion of children with four reliable measurements was similar to that at nine weeks.

Table 7.1

7.4 Adjustment of data from first interview

In order to compare the measurements between groups, and allow for differences in age at interview, the measurement data for all interviews have been adjusted for exact age at measurement. Factors for age adjustment were calculated by running a linear regression model of each measurement at each age to obtain an equation showing the growth of each sex within each ethnic group. Ages were then standardised to the median age at interview. The effect of this was to increase the measurements of those interviewed when younger than average, and decrease the measurements of those interviewed when older than average.

Two examples of how the adjustment was calculated are given below:

The measurement of a Bangladeshi boy whose weight was 4.8kg when aged 8 weeks old, was adjusted to:

$$4.8 - (0.18 (8\text{-}9)) = 4.98 \text{ kg}$$

where

0.18 is the regression coefficient,

8 is the age (in weeks) at measurement, and
9 is the age (in weeks) to which the data are being standardised

The measurement of a White girl whose weight was 5.3kg aged 11 weeks old, was adjusted to:

$$5.3 - (0.17 (11\text{-}9)) = 4.96 \text{ kg}$$

where

0.17 is the regression coefficient,

11 is the age (in weeks) at measurement, and
9 is the age (in weeks) to which the data are being standardised

7.5 Results of the measurements

7.5.1 Mean body weight

At the first interview, mothers were asked the birthweight of their child. The mean reported birthweights of White boys (3.4kg) and White girls (3.3kg) were higher than the mean birthweights of Asian boys and girls. At all interviews, White boys were significantly heavier than Asian boys. At fifteen months, Pakistani, Indian and White girls had a similar mean weight and were heavier than Bangladeshi girls.

Figure 7.1, Table 7.2

Over the first fifteen months, Pakistani and Indian boys and girls had gained significantly more weight than Bangladeshi boys and girls.

Figure 7.2, Table 7.3

7.5.2 Supine length

At nine weeks, White boys were longer than Asian boys. At five and nine months, White, Pakistani and Indian boys had similar lengths and were all longer than Bangladeshi boys. By the age of fifteen months, Pakistani (81.0cm) and Indian boys (80.8cm) were longer than both White (80.1cm) and Bangladeshi boys (79.9cm). Indian, White and Pakistani girls were longer than Bangladeshi girls at nine weeks, but by the age of fifteen months, Indian girls (80.0cm) were longer than girls in all other groups (Pakistani 78.9cm, White 78.6cm and Bangladeshi 78.3cm).

Figure 7.1, Table 7.4

Pakistani and Indian boys and girls gained more in length up to nine months than White and Bangladeshi boys and girls. Over fifteen months, the length of boys and girls in all Asian groups had increased more than their White peers.

Figure 7.2, Table 7.5

7.5.3 Mean head circumference

At all interviews, White children had a larger mean head circumference than Asian children. At fifteen months the mean measurements for boys were – White 48.3cm; Indian 47.5 cm;

Bangladeshi 47.3cm and Pakistani 47.2cm. For girls the mean measurements were – White 46.9cm; Indian 46.3cm; Pakistani 46.2cm and Bangladeshi 46.0cm.
Figure 7.1, Table 7.6

Over fifteen months the head circumference of White girls increased more than Asian girls in all groups; the head circumference of Indian and White boys increased more than Pakistani and Bangladeshi boys.
Figure 7.2, Table 7.7

Figure 7.1

Mean measurements by age, sex and ethnic group

All babies

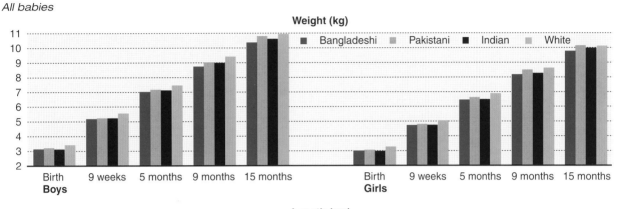

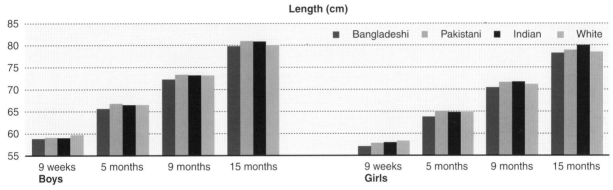

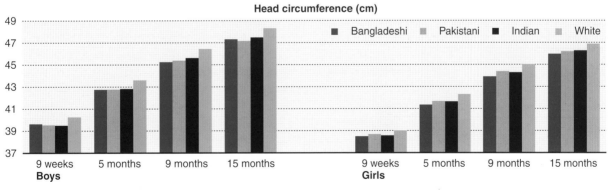

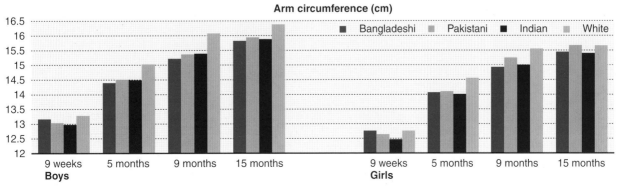

Figure 7.2

Mean gain in measurements by age, sex and ethnic group

All babies

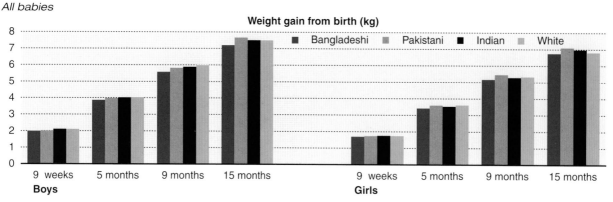

Weight gain from birth (kg)

Legend: Bangladeshi, Pakistani, Indian, White

Boys: 9 weeks, 5 months, 9 months, 15 months
Girls: 9 weeks, 5 months, 9 months, 15 months

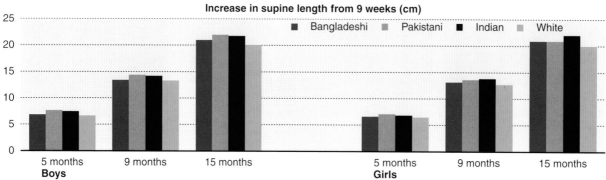

Increase in supine length from 9 weeks (cm)

Legend: Bangladeshi, Pakistani, Indian, White

Boys: 5 months, 9 months, 15 months
Girls: 5 months, 9 months, 15 months

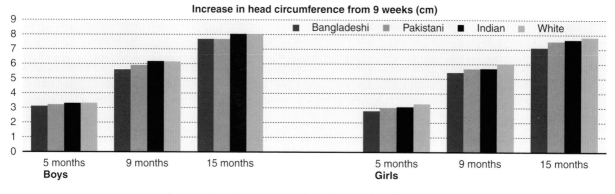

Increase in head circumference from 9 weeks (cm)

Legend: Bangladeshi, Pakistani, Indian, White

Boys: 5 months, 9 months, 15 months
Girls: 5 months, 9 months, 15 months

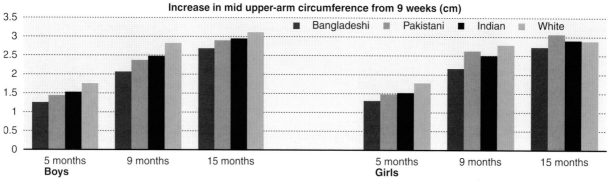

Increase in mid upper-arm circumference from 9 weeks (cm)

Legend: Bangladeshi, Pakistani, Indian, White

Boys: 5 months, 9 months, 15 months
Girls: 5 months, 9 months, 15 months

7.5.4 Mean mid upper-arm circumference

From the age of five months, White boys had a greater mean mid upper-arm circumference than Asian boys. At the age of fifteen months, the mean mid upper-arm circumference of White boys was 16.4cm, compared with Indian and Pakistani (15.9cm) and Bangladeshi boys (15.8cm). White girls had a greater mean measurement until the age of fifteen months. At this age, the only significant difference between the measurements for girls was that White and Pakistani girls (both 15.7cm) had a higher mean than Indian girls (15.4cm). **Figure 7.1, Table 7.8**

The arm circumference of White boys and girls increased more than boys and girls in all Asian groups over the first nine months. Over fifteen months, the arm circumference of White boys and girls increased significantly more than Bangladeshi boys and girls; the arm circumference of Pakistani girls increased as much as Indian and White girls and more than Bangladeshi girls. **Figure 7.2, Table 7.9**

7.5.5 Mean body mass index
Body Mass Index (or Quetelet), which controls for variations in body weight associated with height, is calculated as:

$$\text{weight (kg) / height (m)}2$$

For this survey, Body Mass Index (BMI) was calculated using the supine length measurement instead of standing height. At all ages, White boys had a higher BMI than Asian boys in all groups. At fifteen months, BMI was 17.1 for White boys, and ranged from 16.2 to 16.4 for Asian boys. White girls had a higher BMI than Asian girls

until the age of fifteen months. At this age, their BMI (16.5) was similar to Pakistani girls (16.3), but still greater than Bangladeshi (15.9) and Indian girls (15.5). Mean BMI increased for all groups between nine weeks and nine months but decreased at fifteen months. **Figure 7.3, Table 7.10**

7.6 Modelling the factors which affect weight and length

7.6.1 Using modelling analysis to explain body size
Many factors determine the size of young children, and some of these may be inter-related. By using a modelling analysis (multiple regression), it is possible to identify the factors that have the greatest impact on for example, the baby's weight or length, and those that have no significant impact once the main factors have been taken into account. The variables which were included in the analyses are those which might be expected from bi-variate analysis to have a significant effect on the growth of a child in this survey. **Table 7.11, Table 7.13**

There are separate models to analyse the characteristics associated with the weight and length of each group. Only variables found to be significant for any group have been included in

Figure 7.3
Mean body mass index by age, sex and ethnic group

All children

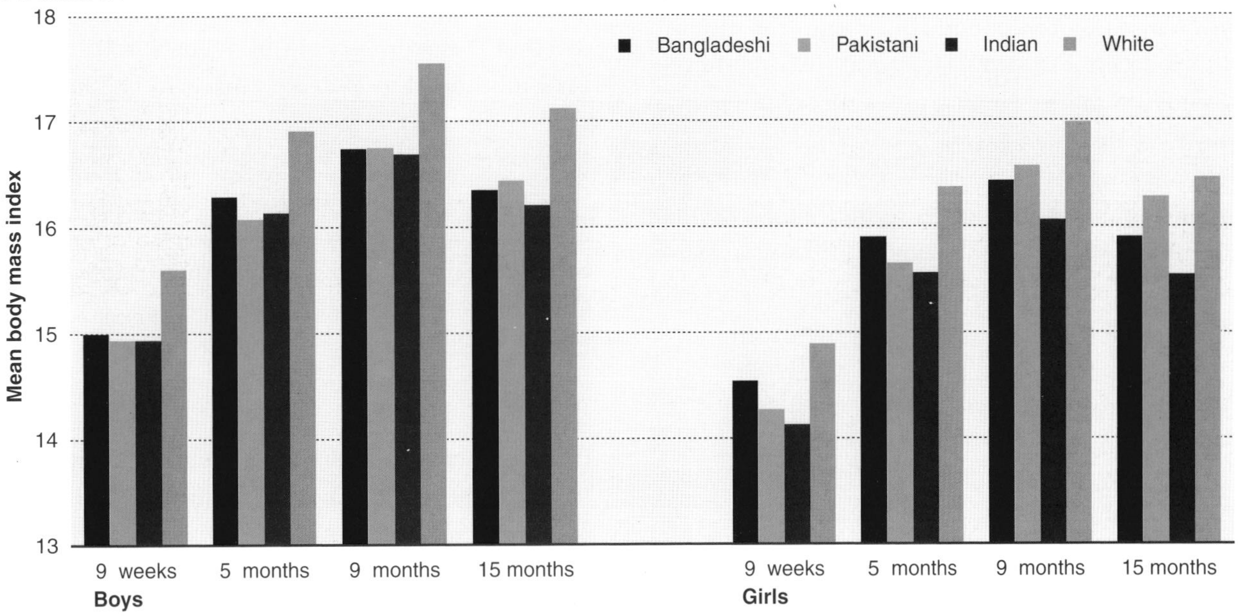

Legend: ■ Bangladeshi ■ Pakistani ■ Indian ■ White

Tables 7.12 and 7.14. Although the models indicate factors which affect the measurements, a large proportion of the variance is still unexplained. The proportion of variance explained by the models to predict weight ranged from 15% for Bangladeshi children to 25% for White, 26% for Pakistani and 28% for Indian children. A higher proportion of variance was explained by the models to predict length – Bangladeshi (28%), Indian (34%), Pakistani and White children (43%). Whilst these figures are not unusual for this type of modelling, the results should be used with care.   **Tables 7.12, 7.14**

7.6.2 Weight at 15 months
The three most significant factors affecting weight at fifteen months for all groups were:

- birthweight (children who were heavier at birth were also likely to be heavier at fifteen months)

- sex (girls were lighter than boys)

- parents' height (Children with taller parents were likely to be heavier than those with shorter parents)

Other factors associated with weight at fifteen months were not the same for all groups.

Feeding problems were related to the weight at fifteen months of all Asian children. Both Bangladeshi and Pakistani children were likely to be lighter if their mother reported feeding problems at more than one interview. Indian children were likely to be lighter if their mother considered that compared with other children, they were difficult to feed.

Whether the child was given vitamin supplements at nine weeks was a significant factor associated with the weight of both Bangladeshi and Pakistani children, but whereas Pakistani children were likely to be heavier at fifteen months if they were given vitamin supplements, Bangladeshi children were likely to be lighter. Further analysis showed that babies in all groups who were given vitamin supplements at nine weeks had on average a lower birthweight than those who were not given extra vitamins. By fifteen months, of those who were given extra

vitamins at nine weeks, Bangladeshi babies were still lighter than those who were not given extra vitamins but Pakistani babies were heavier (Table not shown).

At fifteen months, Indian children were likely to be lighter if their mother was a Hindu or Muslim or if they ate rice, potatoes or pasta daily. Indian children were likely to be heavier at fifteen months if they were bottle fed at nine months and mainly given cow's milk.

Both White and Pakistani children were likely to be lighter at fifteen months if they were a second or later child in the family.   **Table 7.12**

7.6.3 Supine length at 15 months
The two most important factors affecting length at fifteen months for all groups were:

- length at nine weeks (children who were longer at nine weeks were also likely to be longer at fifteen months)

- parents' height (children with taller parents were likely to be longer than those with shorter parents)

Sex was also an important factor affecting length (girls were likely to be shorter than boys) in all groups except Indian children.

Apart from their length at nine weeks and their parents' height, the only other significant factor which affected the length of Indian children was whether they were mainly given cow's milk at nine months. If so, they were likely to be longer.

Bangladeshi children were likely to be longer if they were bottle fed (including some who were also breastfed) at nine weeks. They were likely to be shorter if they were given vitamin supplements at nine weeks (see comment in section 7.6.2). Pakistani children were likely to be longer if they ate rice, pasta or potatoes daily.

Both Pakistani and Bangladeshi children tended to be shorter if their mother considered that, compared with other children of the same age, they were not easy to feed. Children in both of these groups were likely to be longer if they drank water daily. Although drinking water daily was significantly associated with length, not all significant factors necessarily imply causation and drinking water daily may be an indicator of other feeding behaviour or attitudes which affect length rather than having a direct impact on length itself.

Both Pakistani and White children were likely to be shorter if they were the second or later child in the family. White children were also likely to be shorter if the family was in receipt of income support but likely to be longer if they ate puddings or desserts daily. **Table 7.14**

7.6.4 Using the model to predict measurements
The models are additive. As shown in Tables 7.12 and 7.14, variables which are significant are given a value. For categorical variables, the value is added (or subtracted) when a characteristic or behaviour is observed. For example, in the model for weight, a Bangladeshi girl was likely to weigh 0.38kg less than a boy at fifteen months. For continuous variables, the value is multiplied by the actual value of the variable eg. the effect on weight at fifteen months for a Bangladeshi child weighing 3.0kg at birth would be: 3.0 x 0.7 = 2.1kg.

The factors found to be significant can be used to predict the weight or supine length of children with different characteristics. Each child can be thought of as having a base weight (or length), the 'constant' in Tables 7.12 and 7.14, to which various amounts are added or subtracted depending on the physical, social and feeding characteristics of the child.

For example, to predict weight at fifteen months for:

a Pakistani girl weighing 3.1kg at birth;
whose parents had a height of 164cm. (mother), 170cm. (father)
   - average height of both parents (167cm.)
who was a second or later child;
who drank water daily;
whose mother did not report feeding problems;
who was given vitamins at nine weeks
would be predicted using the values in Table 7.12

to weigh 9.48kg at 15 months.

	2.26	Base weight (constant)
+	3.32	Birthweight (3.1x1.07)
-	0.66	Girl
-	0.49	Second or later child
+	5.01	Parents'height (167x0.03)
-	0.38	Feeding problems
	<u>0.42</u>	Given vitamins at nine weeks
=	9.48	kg Weight at 15 months

Similar predictions for length can be made using the values shown in Table 7.14.

7.7 Comparison of survey and national measurement data
National measurement data are available for weight, height and head circumference. The national data used in this analysis are the 1990 nine centile United Kingdom charts, produced by the Child Growth Foundation[1, 2]. These data which relate only to White children were based on seven growth surveys between 1978 and 1990. The protocols for carrying out the measurements in the national growth surveys may not have been the same as in this survey so the data may not be strictly comparable.

Figures 7.4–7.9 and Tables 7.15–7.17 present the 2.3, 9, 25, 50, 75, 91 and 97.7 centiles for both this survey and the national data. Standard deviation scores (SDS) which allow the national growth charts to be adjusted for use with Bangladeshi, Pakistani and Indian babies are described in Appendix D.

7.7.1 Weight
At the age of nine weeks the median weights of boys and girls in all Asian groups in this survey were below the national median (boys – 5.4kg, girls 5.0kg). At fifteen months, both White boys and girls had a similar median weight to the national data but the median weights of Asian boys in all groups and Bangladeshi and Indian girls were below the national median.

Figures 7.4,7.5, Table 7.15

Figure 7.4

Comparison of weight at 9 weeks with national data by sex and ethnic group

All children

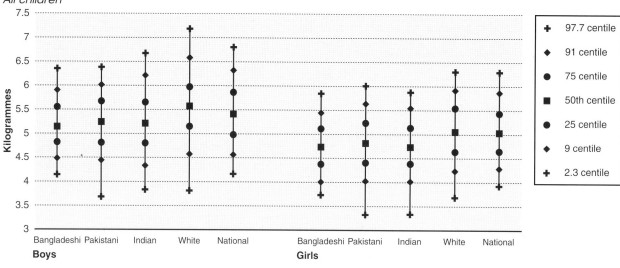

Figure 7.5

Comparison of weight at 15 months with national data by sex and ethnic group

All children

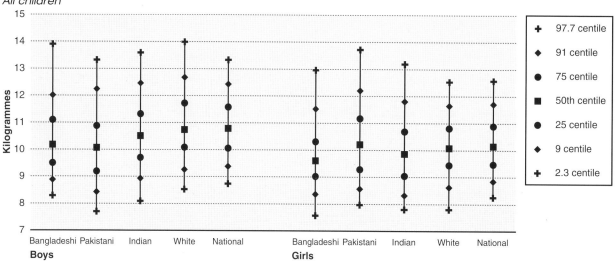

7.7.2 Head circumference

At nine weeks, the median head circumferences of boys and girls in all Asian groups were similar to the national median but by the age of fifteen months they were all below it. The median head circumferences of White boys and girls were also slightly below the national median at fifteen months.

At fifteen months, the head circumference of 75% of Asian boys (as shown by the 75th centile) was below the national median.

Figures 7.6, 7.7, Table 7.16

7.7.3 Supine length

In all ethnic groups, for both sexes, at the ages of nine weeks and fifteen months, the median supine length of the babies in the survey sample was greater than the national median. At the age of fifteen months, the median supine lengths of Pakistani and Indian boys and Indian girls were above the 75th centile of the national data.

Figures 7.8, 7.9, Table 7.17

Figure 7.6
Comparison of head circumference at 9 weeks with national data by sex and ethnic group

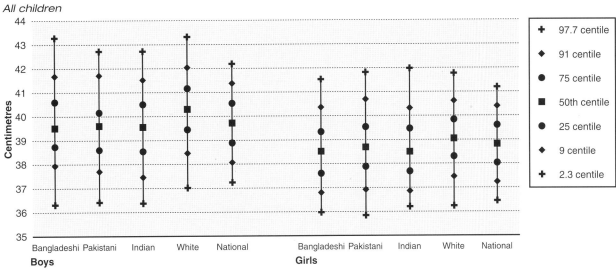

Figure 7.7
Comparison of head circumference at 15 months with national data by sex and ethnic group

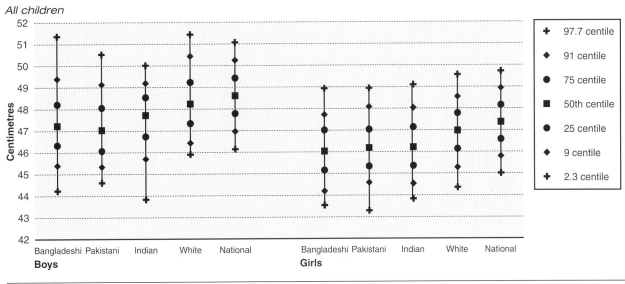

Figure 7.8

Comparison of supine length at 9 weeks with national data by sex and ethnic group

All children

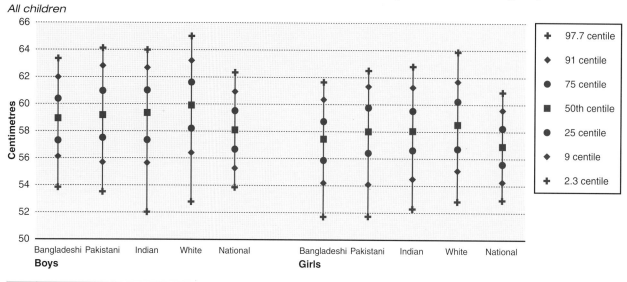

Figure 7.9

Comparison of supine length at 15 months with national data by sex and ethnic group

All children

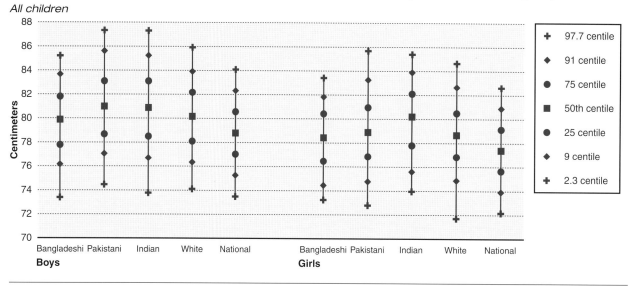

Notes

1 Hall D M B. *Monitoring children's growth. British Medical Journal,* vol 311, 1995, pp.583-584.

2 Cole T J. *Conditional reference charts to assess weight gain in British infants.* Archives of Disease in Childhood, vol.73, 1995, pp.8-16.

Table 7.1
Proportion of measurements* achieved at first interview by ethnic group

All babies

Proportion of measurements achieved	Ethnic group Bangladeshi		Pakistani		Indian		White	
	Number	%	Number	%	Number	%	Number	%
First interview								
Total babies eligible to be measured	610	100	731	100	934	100	619	100
of whom:								
no measurements obtained	7	1	8	1	9	1	5	1
some measurements obtained	3	0	6	1	1	0	3	0
all or some measurements obtained but all excluded from analysis	14	2	14	2	18	2	14	2
all measurements obtained and one or more excluded from analysis	107	18	89	12	140	15	52	8
All measurements used in analysis	479	78	614	84	766	82	545	88
Second interview								
Total babies eligible to be measured	552	100	668	100	841	100	594	100
All measurements used in analysis	509	92	618	92	755	90	548	92
Third interview								
Total babies eligible to be measured	521	100	642	100	815	100	576	100
All measurements used in analysis	423	81	555	87	708	87	514	89
Fourth interview								
Total babies eligible to be measured	477	100	590	100	758	100	548	100
All measurements used in analysis	371	78	463	78	619	82	480	88

*   The measurements taken were weight, supine length, head circumference, mid-arm circumference.

Table 7.2

Mean weight of baby by age, sex, and ethnic group

All babies

Mean weight (kg)	Ethnic group							
	Bangladeshi		Pakistani		Indian		White	
	Boys	Girls	Boys	Girls	Boys	Girls	Boys	Girls
Birth (reported by mother)								
Mean	3.2	3.0	3.2	3.1	3.1	3.0	3.4	3.3
Standard deviation	0.5	0.5	0.5	0.6	0.5	0.5	0.6	0.5
9 weeks								
Mean	5.2	4.8	5.2	4.8	5.2	4.8	5.6	5.1
Standard deviation	0.6	0.5	0.6	0.6	0.7	0.6	0.8	0.6
5 months								
Mean	7.0	6.5	7.2	6.6	7.1	6.5	7.5	6.9
Standard deviation	0.7	0.7	0.9	0.9	0.9	0.8	0.9	0.8
9 months								
Mean	8.8	8.2	9.0	8.5	9.0	8.3	9.4	8.7
Standard deviation	0.9	1.0	1.1	1.1	1.1	1.0	1.1	1.0
15 months								
Mean	10.4	9.8	10.8	10.2	10.6	10.0	11.0	10.1
Standard deviation	1.3	1.2	1.4	1.4	1.4	1.3	1.3	1.1
Base = 100%								
Reported weight at birth	*286*	*306*	*377*	*334*	*431*	*482*	*312*	*293*
9 weeks	*274*	*291*	*362*	*318*	*420*	*463*	*303*	*287*
5 months	*251*	*273*	*339*	*298*	*378*	*423*	*299*	*275*
9 months	*232*	*233*	*323*	*275*	*362*	*416*	*283*	*258*
15 months	*195*	*211*	*270*	*242*	*319*	*359*	*262*	*242*

Table 7.3

Mean weight gain from birth by age, sex and ethnic group

All babies

Mean weight gain (kg)	Ethnic group							
	Bangladeshi		Pakistani		Indian		White	
	Boys	Girls	Boys	Girls	Boys	Girls	Boys	Girls
9 weeks								
Mean	2.03	1.72	2.01	1.74	2.11	1.76	2.14	1.77
Standard deviation	0.42	0.40	0.44	0.45	0.47	0.42	0.59	0.49
5 months								
Mean	3.89	3.44	3.98	3.59	4.02	3.53	4.06	3.63
Standard deviation	0.59	0.63	0.62	0.75	0.69	0.68	0.78	0.66
9 months								
Mean	5.61	5.19	5.82	5.46	5.89	5.29	6.01	5.36
Standard deviation	0.85	0.89	0.93	1.01	0.94	0.94	0.99	0.89
15 months								
Mean	7.22	6.77	7.66	7.10	7.50	6.97	7.52	6.83
Standard deviation	1.18	1.20	1.29	1.33	1.21	1.22	1.22	1.06
Base = 100%								
9 weeks	*273*	*291*	*358*	*317*	*419*	*462*	*303*	*287*
5 months	*244*	*269*	*329*	*291*	*369*	*412*	*290*	*270*
9 months	*226*	*230*	*316*	*270*	*355*	*407*	*276*	*253*
15 months	*190*	*208*	*261*	*238*	*311*	*351*	*253*	*237*

Table 7.4
Mean supine length of baby by age, sex and ethnic group

All babies

Mean supine length (cms)	Ethnic group							
	Bangladeshi		Pakistani		Indian		White	
	Boys	Girls	Boys	Girls	Boys	Girls	Boys	Girls
9 weeks								
Mean	58.9	57.2	59.1	57.8	59.1	58.0	59.8	58.4
Standard deviation	2.5	2.4	2.8	2.7	3.1	2.6	2.7	2.7
5 months								
Mean	65.7	63.9	66.8	65.0	66.5	64.8	66.5	65.0
Standard deviation	2.3	2.2	2.7	2.7	2.8	3.0	3.3	2.6
9 months								
Mean	72.3	70.5	73.4	71.6	73.2	71.8	73.2	71.3
Standard deviation	2.6	2.4	2.8	2.8	2.9	2.7	2.6	2.6
15 months								
Mean	79.9	78.3	81.0	78.9	80.8	80.0	80.1	78.6
Standard deviation	3.0	2.8	3.2	3.1	3.3	2.9	3.0	3.0
Base = 100%								
9 weeks	245	264	348	309	385	427	285	281
5 months	259	275	343	302	372	422	297	270
9 months	229	236	314	277	351	392	279	254
15 months	211	221	287	245	320	371	277	244

Table 7.5
Mean increase in supine length from 9 weeks by age, sex and ethnic group

All babies

Mean increase in supine length (cms)	Ethnic group							
	Bangladeshi		Pakistani		Indian		White	
	Boys	Girls	Boys	Girls	Boys	Girls	Boys	Girls
5 months								
Mean	6.95	6.67	7.64	7.06	7.45	6.83	6.76	6.54
Standard deviation	2.04	2.01	2.06	1.96	2.44	2.61	2.72	1.88
9 months								
Mean	13.51	13.19	14.37	13.60	14.19	13.80	13.42	12.79
Standard deviation	2.55	2.15	2.31	2.44	2.79	2.33	2.26	2.29
15 months								
Mean	21.06	20.98	21.97	20.90	21.77	22.04	20.17	20.07
Standard deviation	2.79	2.68	2.83	2.74	3.30	2.64	2.58	2.64
Base = 100%								
5 months	220	238	312	276	331	372	266	257
9 months	198	207	288	258	312	350	253	239
15 months	180	189	266	227	285	327	247	229

Table 7.6

Mean head circumference of baby by age, sex and ethnic group

All babies

Mean head circumference (cms)	Ethnic group							
	Bangladeshi		Pakistani		Indian		White	
	Boys	Girls	Boys	Girls	Boys	Girls	Boys	Girls
9 weeks								
Mean	39.6	38.5	39.5	38.7	39.5	38.6	40.3	39.0
Standard deviation	1.6	1.4	1.5	1.4	1.6	1.4	1.6	1.3
5 months								
Mean	42.8	41.4	42.8	41.7	42.8	41.7	43.6	42.4
Standard deviation	1.3	1.4	1.3	1.3	1.4	1.3	1.3	1.1
9 months								
Mean	45.3	44.0	45.4	44.4	45.6	44.3	46.5	45.1
Standard deviation	1.3	1.3	1.4	1.3	1.3	1.4	1.4	1.2
15 months								
Mean	47.3	46.0	47.2	46.2	47.5	46.3	48.3	46.9
Standard deviation	1.7	1.3	1.4	1.4	1.4	1.3	1.4	1.2
Base = 100%								
9 weeks	*277*	*296*	*371*	*324*	*420*	*427*	*306*	*288*
5 months	*263*	*276*	*352*	*307*	*380*	*434*	*309*	*281*
9 months	*232*	*234*	*321*	*279*	*349*	*407*	*289*	*261*
15 months	*211*	*222*	*291*	*242*	*327*	*371*	*276*	*244*

Table 7.7

Mean increase in head circumference from 9 weeks by age, sex and ethnic group

All babies

Mean increase in head circumference (cms)	Ethnic group							
	Bangladeshi		Pakistani		Indian		White	
	Boys	Girls	Boys	Girls	Boys	Girls	Boys	Girls
5 months								
Mean	3.16	2.83	3.22	3.02	3.32	3.09	3.37	3.33
Standard deviation	1.30	1.46	1.14	1.05	1.15	1.15	1.14	0.92
9 months								
Mean	5.64	5.46	5.90	5.68	6.17	5.70	6.18	6.06
Standard deviation	1.47	1.33	1.40	1.21	1.26	1.26	1.32	0.99
15 months								
Mean	7.72	7.14	7.67	7.54	8.04	7.65	8.07	7.86
Standard deviation	1.67	1.35	1.48	1.31	1.44	1.31	1.41	1.14
Base = 100%								
5 months	*249*	*267*	*339*	*294*	*364*	*416*	*295*	*272*
9 months	*222*	*225*	*309*	*266*	*335*	*392*	*277*	*252*
15 months	*201*	*215*	*279*	*229*	*313*	*356*	*262*	*235*

Table 7.8
Mid upper-arm circumference of baby by age, sex and ethnic group

All babies

Mean mid upper-arm circumference (cms)	Ethnic group							
	Bangladeshi		Pakistani		Indian		White	
	Boys	Girls	Boys	Girls	Boys	Girls	Boys	Girls
9 weeks								
Mean	13.2	12.8	13.0	12.6	13.0	12.5	13.3	12.8
Standard deviation	1.1	1.1	1.2	1.1	1.2	1.1	1.2	1.1
5 months								
Mean	14.4	14.1	14.5	14.1	14.5	14.0	15.0	14.6
Standard deviation	1.0	1.1	1.2	1.2	1.2	1.1	1.2	1.1
9 months								
Mean	15.2	14.9	15.4	15.3	15.4	15.0	16.1	15.6
Standard deviation	1.1	1.2	1.3	1.3	1.2	1.3	1.3	1.2
15 months								
Mean	15.8	15.5	15.9	15.7	15.9	15.4	16.4	15.7
Standard deviation	1.4	1.3	1.4	1.3	1.3	1.3	1.4	1.2
Base = 100%								
9 weeks	*277*	*294*	*364*	*323*	*410*	*460*	*307*	*286*
5 months	*265*	*278*	*350*	*304*	*382*	*435*	*307*	*280*
9 months	*241*	*242*	*324*	*282*	*363*	*415*	*291*	*262*
15 months	*214*	*225*	*291*	*247*	*328*	*371*	*280*	*253*

Table 7.9
Mean increase in mid upper-arm circumference from 9 weeks by age, sex and ethnic group

All babies

Mean increase in mid upper-arm circumference (cms)	Ethnic group							
	Bangladeshi		Pakistani		Indian		White	
	Boys	Girls	Boys	Girls	Boys	Girls	Boys	Girls
5 months								
Mean	1.27	1.32	1.44	1.48	1.53	1.52	1.77	1.79
Standard deviation	1.16	1.18	1.18	1.00	1.02	1.05	0.95	0.90
9 months								
Mean	2.08	2.17	2.37	2.63	2.48	2.50	2.84	2.80
Standard deviation	1.33	1.26	1.26	1.27	1.13	1.25	1.21	1.03
15 months								
Mean	2.70	2.74	2.90	3.07	2.95	2.91	3.13	2.90
Standard deviation	1.58	1.43	1.39	1.39	1.24	1.31	1.32	1.21
Base = 100%								
5 months	*250*	*267*	*334*	*288*	*361*	*406*	*294*	*269*
9 months	*230*	*233*	*309*	*266*	*342*	*388*	*280*	*252*
15 months	*202*	*216*	*275*	*235*	*308*	*350*	*267*	*246*

Table 7.10
Mean body mass index by age, sex and ethnic group

All babies

Mean body mass index*	Ethnic group							
	Bangladeshi		Pakistani		Indian		White	
	Boys	Girls	Boys	Girls	Boys	Girls	Boys	Girls
9 weeks								
Mean	15.0	14.5	14.9	14.3	14.9	14.1	15.6	14.9
Standard deviation	1.2	1.5	1.3	1.4	1.9	1.3	1.5	1.5
5 months								
Mean	16.3	15.9	16.1	15.6	16.1	15.6	16.9	16.4
Standard deviation	1.4	1.5	1.4	1.5	1.6	2.1	2.1	1.4
9 months								
Mean	16.7	16.4	16.7	16.6	16.7	16.1	17.5	17.0
Standard deviation	1.4	1.6	1.5	1.6	1.5	1.6	1.6	1.5
15 months								
Mean	16.3	15.9	16.4	16.3	16.2	15.5	17.1	16.5
Standard deviation	1.4	1.5	1.5	1.6	1.4	1.6	1.6	1.4
Base = 100%								
9 weeks	*238*	*257*	*338*	*298*	*380*	*419*	*280*	*277*
5 months	*247*	*268*	*330*	*294*	*362*	*407*	*287*	*264*
9 months	*217*	*226*	*306*	*265*	*347*	*389*	*273*	*248*
15 months	*189*	*203*	*259*	*231*	*304*	*343*	*257*	*235*

*   For explanation of Body Mass Index see chapter 7, paragraph 7.5.5.

Table 7.11
Variables included in multiple regression to predict *weight* at 15 months

Variables significant for at least one group

Birthweight
Child's sex
Parent's height (average height of both parents)
Whether child was first or later child
Whether baby given extra vitamins at 9 weeks
Whether feeding problems reported at more than one interview
Whether ate rice, potatoes or pasta daily at 15 months
Whether main milk at 9 months - cow's milk
Whether child easy to feed
Mother's religion - Hindu
Mother's religion - Muslim

Variables not significant for any group

Age of mother
Mother's education (number of years)
Mother's country of birth
Whether family received income support
Whether baby breast of bottle fed at 9 weeks
Age at which baby first ate solid food
Age at which started eating three meals a day
Whether child ate meat or fish daily at 15 months
Whether child ate desserts daily at 15 months
Whether child ate cereal, rusk or bread daily at 15 months
Whether child ate eggs, yoghurt or cheese daily at 15 months
Whether child ate vegetables daily at 15 months
Whether child ate fresh fruit daily at 15 months
Whether child ate sweets or chocolate daily at 15 months
Whether child drank water daily at 15 months
Whether child drank fruit juice daily at 15 months
Whether avoids giving any foods or ingredients to child
Smoking (included only in model for White children)

Table 7.12
Characteristics associated with weight at 15 months

All children

Characteristics associated with weight at 15 months	Bangladeshi		Pakistani		Indian		White	
Constant: base weight (kg)	2.67		2.26		3.29		2.62	
Birthweight (kg)	0.70*	[1]	1.07*	[1]	0.82*	[1]	0.80*	[1]
Girl	−0.38*	[2]	−0.66*	[2]	−0.51*	[2]	−0.69*	[2]
Parent's average height (cm)	0.04*	[3]	0.03*	[3]	0.03*	[3]	0.03*	[3]
Feeding problems at more than one interivew	−0.30**	[4]	−0.38*	[5]	ns		ns	
Given vitamins	−0.38**	[5]	0.42*	[6]	ns		ns	
Second or later child	ns		−0.49*	[4]	ns		−0.32*	[4]
Eats rice, potatoes or pasta daily	ns		ns		-0.23**	[5]	ns	
Main milk at 9 mths - cow's milk	ns		ns		0.38*	[4]	ns	
Child not easy to feed	ns		ns		-0.33*	[6]	ns	
Hindu	ns		ns		-0.39*	[7]	ns	
Muslim	ns		ns		-0.5*	[8]	ns	
Percentage of variation explained by model	15		26		28		25	

ns   not significant
[ ]   indicates the order in which the characteristics entered the model
*   significance of value P 0.01
**   significance of value P 0.05

Table 7.13

Variables included in multiple regression to predict length at 15 months

Variables significant for at least one group

    Supine length at 9 weeks
    Parent's height (average height of both parents)
    Child's sex
    Whether breast or bottle fed at 9 weeks
    Whether baby given extra vitamins at 9 weeks
    Whether child easy to feed
    Whether child drank water daily at 15 months
    Whether child was first or later child
    Whether ate rice, potatoes or pasta daily at 15 months
    Whether main milk at 9 months - cow's milk
    Whether family receives income support
    Whether child ate puddings or desserts daily at 15 months

Variables not significant for any group

    Age of mother
    Mother's education (number of years)
    Mother's country of birth
    Age at which baby first ate solid food
    Age at which started eating three meals a day
    Whether feeding problems reported at more than one interview
    Whether child ate meat or fish daily at 15 months
    Whether child ate cereal, rusk or bread daily at 15 months
    Whether child ate eggs, yoghurt or cheese daily at 15 months
    Whether child ate vegetables daily at 15 months
    Whether child ate fresh fruit daily at 15 months
    Whether child ate sweets or chocolate daily at 15 months
    Whether child drank fruit juice daily at 15 months
    Whether avoids giving any foods or ingredients to child
    Smoking (included only in model for White children)

Table 7.14

Characteristics associated with length at 15 months

All children

Characteristics associated with length at 15 months	Bangladeshi		Pakistani		Indian		White	
Constant: base length (kg)	*36.8*		*35.52*		*30.01*		*26.64*	
Length at 9 weeks (cm)	0.41*	[1]	0.54*	[1]	0.43*	[1]	0.48*	[1]
Parent's height (cm)	0.10*	[2]	0.08*	[3]	0.15*	[2]	0.14*	[2]
Girl	−1.01*	[3]	−1.94*	[2]	ns		−0.81*	[4]
Bottle fed at 9 weeks	1.90*	[4]	ns		ns		ns	
Given vitamins	−1.08*	[5]	ns		ns		ns	
Child not easy to feed	−0.72**	[6]	−0.71*	[5]	ns		ns	
Drinks water daily	1.14**	[7]	1.09*	[4]	ns		ns	
Second or later child	ns		−0.73*	[6]	ns		−0.67*	[3]
Eats rice, potatoes or pasta daily	ns		0.69**	[7]	ns		ns	
Main milk at 9 months - cow's milk	ns		ns		0.96*	[3]	ns	
Receives income support	ns		ns		ns		−0.75*	[5]
Eats puddings & desserts	ns		ns		ns		0.60*	[6]
Percentage of variation explained by model	*28*		*43*		*34*		*43*	

ns   not significant

[ ]   indicates the order in which the characteristics entered the model

*   significance of value P 0.01

**   significance of value P 0.05

Table 7.15
Weight of children in the survey sample at 9 weeks and 15 months compared with national data*

Weight at 9 weeks

	2.3 centile	9 centile	25 centile	median	75 centile	91 centile	97.7 centile	Interquartile
Boys								
Bangladeshi	4.17	4.5	4.84	5.16	5.57	5.92	6.37	0.73
Pakistani	3.7	4.46	4.83	5.26	5.69	6.03	6.4	0.86
Indian	3.85	4.35	4.82	5.23	5.67	6.23	6.69	0.85
White	3.83	4.59	5.17	5.59	5.99	6.6	7.2	0.82
National	4.18	4.58	5	5.43	5.88	6.34	6.82	0.88
Girls								
Bangladeshi	3.75	4.02	4.39	4.75	5.13	5.46	5.86	0.74
Pakistani	3.34	4.04	4.42	4.83	5.25	5.65	6.02	0.83
Indian	3.35	4.03	4.4	4.75	5.15	5.56	5.89	0.75
White	3.7	4.25	4.65	5.07	5.56	5.93	6.32	0.91
National	3.94	4.3	4.66	5.05	5.45	5.88	6.31	0.79

Weight at 15 months

	2.3 centile	9 centile	25 centile	median	75 centile	91 centile	97.7 centile	Interquartile
Boys								
Bangladeshi	8.32	8.91	9.53	10.21	11.13	12.04	13.93	1.6
Pakistani	8.12	9.13	9.89	10.76	11.57	12.65	14.38	1.68
Indian	8.12	8.96	9.73	10.54	11.35	12.49	13.62	1.62
White	8.56	9.29	10.12	10.77	11.75	12.71	14.02	1.63
National	8.77	9.41	10.09	10.82	11.61	12.46	13.36	1.52
Girls								
Bangladeshi	7.6	8.39	9.05	9.63	10.34	11.55	12.99	1.29
Pakistani	7.73	8.46	9.22	10.1	10.91	12.27	13.35	1.69
Indian	7.83	8.35	9.07	9.89	10.72	11.83	13.22	1.65
White	7.83	8.65	9.47	10.11	10.84	11.67	12.56	1.37
National	8.28	8.87	9.5	10.18	10.92	11.73	12.6	1.42

* 1990 nine centile United Kingdom charts produced by the Child Growth Foundation.

Table 7.16
Head circumference of children in the survey sample at 9 weeks and 15 months compared with national data*

Head circumference (cms) at 9 weeks

	2.3 centile	9 centile	25 centile	median	75 centile	91 centile	97.7 centile	Interquartile
Boys								
Bangladeshi	36.28	37.9	38.70	39.48	40.56	41.64	43.24	1.86
Pakistani	36.38	37.66	38.56	39.57	40.41	41.67	42.68	1.85
Indian	36.34	37.42	38.50	39.52	40.46	41.48	42.67	1.96
White	36.98	38.42	39.41	40.26	41.12	42.00	43.28	1.71
National	37.20	38.03	38.85	39.68	40.50	41.33	42.15	1.65
Girls								
Bangladeshi	35.94	36.76	37.56	38.48	39.30	40.32	41.49	1.74
Pakistani	35.81	36.88	37.84	38.65	39.50	40.65	41.78	1.66
Indian	36.17	36.82	37.64	38.46	39.43	40.28	41.94	1.79
White	36.20	37.42	38.26	39.01	39.80	40.58	41.73	1.54
National	36.41	37.20	37.99	38.78	39.57	40.36	41.15	1.58

Head circumference (cms) at 15 months

	2.3 centile	9 centile	25 centile	median	75 centile	91 centile	97.7 centile	Interquartile
Boys								
Bangladeshi	44.20	45.36	46.30	47.20	48.18	49.36	51.32	1.88
Pakistani	44.57	45.30	46.04	47.00	48.02	49.10	50.49	1.98
Indian	43.80	45.66	46.70	47.68	48.50	49.16	49.98	1.80
White	45.87	46.40	47.30	48.20	49.20	50.40	51.40	1.90
National	46.11	46.93	47.75	48.57	49.39	50.21	51.03	1.64
Girls								
Bangladeshi	43.51	44.16	45.12	46.00	46.97	47.68	48.89	1.85
Pakistani	43.26	44.55	45.30	46.15	47.00	48.04	48.90	1.70
Indian	43.80	44.50	45.32	46.18	47.10	47.99	49.06	1.78
White	44.32	45.24	46.10	46.94	47.74	48.50	49.52	1.64
National	44.97	45.76	46.54	47.33	48.11	48.90	49.68	1.57

[1] 1990 nine centile United Kingdom charts produced by the Child Growth Foundation

Table 7.17

Supine length of children in the survey sample at 9 weeks and 15 months compared with national data*

Supine length (cms) at 9 weeks

	2.3 centile	9 centile	25 centile	median	75 centile	91 centile	97.7 centile	Interquartile
Boys								
Bangladeshi	53.84	56.11	57.30	58.93	60.37	61.97	63.34	3.07
Pakistani	53.51	55.68	57.50	59.17	60.95	62.81	64.11	3.45
Indian	52.02	55.64	57.34	59.34	61.00	62.67	63.98	3.66
White	52.78	56.40	58.20	59.90	61.60	63.20	65.00	3.40
National	53.85	55.26	58.09	58.09	59.50	60.91	62.33	2.83
Girls								
Bangladeshi	51.70	54.19	55.86	57.44	58.73	60.34	61.63	2.87
Pakistani	51.73	54.09	56.41	58.00	59.75	61.31	62.49	3.34
Indian	52.29	54.49	56.62	58.04	59.52	61.25	62.80	2.90
White	52.83	55.10	56.72	58.51	60.22	61.68	63.82	3.50
National	52.93	54.26	55.58	56.91	58.24	59.57	60.89	2.66

Supine length (cms) at 15 months

	2.3 centile	9 centile	25 centile	median	75 centile	91 centile	97.7 centile	Interquartile
Boys								
Bangladeshi	73.40	76.16	77.79	79.89	81.81	83.68	85.22	4.02
Pakistani	74.47	77.06	78.68	80.99	83.11	85.62	87.33	4.43
Indian	73.78	76.70	78.50	80.88	83.11	85.24	87.30	4.61
White	74.11	76.34	78.10	80.16	82.17	83.92	85.92	4.07
National	73.49	75.26	77.03	78.79	80.56	82.32	84.09	3.53
Girls								
Bangladeshi	73.24	74.45	76.47	78.43	80.42	81.82	83.42	3.95
Pakistani	72.79	74.77	76.86	78.89	80.95	83.26	85.68	4.09
Indian	73.96	75.60	77.80	80.20	82.10	83.90	85.40	4.30
White	71.71	74.87	76.84	78.67	80.49	82.66	84.65	3.65
National	72.17	73.91	75.66	77.40	79.14	80.88	82.62	3.48

Appendix A Methodology and response

1 Sample design

The sample was selected to represent births to mothers of Indian, Pakistani and Bangladeshi origin living in 41 local authority areas in England. For comparison, a sample of babies born to White mothers living in the same areas was also selected. The sampled areas cover 95% of the Asian population living in England at the time of the 1991 Census, and were divided into two strata: local authorities with the highest density of Asians and those with a lower density. The areas were selected so as to be able to make inferences about the Asian population as a whole. The sample of White babies is representative only of babies born to White mothers living in areas from which Asian families were recruited and is not representative of the White population as a whole. The location of the sampled areas is shown in Figure A.1.   **Figure A.1**

The aim was to schedule the first interview with mothers when their baby was aged 6–10 weeks. To achieve this, babies registered within four weeks of the birth were initially sampled from the birth register. This was later extended to babies registered within six weeks, then to eight weeks (the reason for this is described below in 1.1). Births are registered in the area where a baby is born. Because some mothers gave birth outside the registration district where they live, births were also selected from 39 registration districts with a maternity hospital used by mothers from the 41 selected areas. Babies living in the 41 selected areas were identified by postcode, with postcodes added by staff from the Office for National Statistics (ONS), where they were missing from the birth register. After the sample was selected, it was checked against the death register and any babies who had died were taken out of the sample.

1.1 Sample of Asian babies

All births to mothers with Asian names were included in the sample of Asian babies. In addition, a sample of babies born to mothers with non-Asian names was also selected. This was used for selecting the sample of White babies. It also ensured that any babies not already identified by their name as Asian, had a chance of being selected. Among the White sample, ten babies were identified with an Asian mother and transferred to the Asian sample.

A letter in English and five Asian languages (Hindi, Gujarati, Punjabi, Bengali, Urdu) was sent to each of the mothers of sampled Asian babies. The letter explained the purpose of the survey, gave some information about ONS and said that an interviewer would be calling. When the interviewer called, she explained that she was not sure whether she needed to speak to the mother, and using a card, asked to which ethnic group the mother considered she belonged. Those who turned out to be White or in a non-White group other than Indian, Pakistani or Bangladeshi were not eligible for interview.

The aim was to achieve interviews with approximately 800 Indian, 400 Pakistani and 400 Bangladeshi mothers at the time of the fourth contact, when the babies would be about fifteen months old. To achieve this, allowing for non-response at each new stage, it was estimated that interviews would be needed with approximately 1,140 Indian, 570 Pakistani and 570 Bangladeshi mothers at stage 1. Estimates from the Census and the Labour Force Survey indicated that to achieve this number of interviews at stage 1, two in three Indian, two in five Pakistani and all Bangladeshi mothers of babies sampled for stage 1, over a ten week period, should be interviewed. It was intended to sub-sample at the doorstep sift but the number of Asian babies sampled in the first two weeks was low, so it was decided not to sub-sample initially. Sub-sampling Pakistani babies was introduced after five weeks of interviewing, but the mothers of all Indian and Bangladeshi babies were interviewed for the entire field period.

Figure A.1
Location of sampled areas

After a few weeks of interviewing at stage 1, it became clear that it would be difficult to meet the target of 1,140 Indian interviews at this stage. A close examination of births registered in some of the areas with a high proportion of the population of Indian origin but with a low number of Asian babies sampled showed that many babies were registered late, some after the six week legal requirement. For example, in one week, 59% of Asian babies were registered late in Leicester and 64% of Asian babies were registered late in Brent. It is the custom in some Indian families to name the baby after (s)he is several weeks old and after consultation with the family, which may account for the late registration of some Indian babies. To include more of those registering late and to boost the Indian sample, the sample was first extended to those registering within six weeks and then to those registering within eight weeks.

To see if there was any bias in the survey data due to under-sampling babies registered later, the characteristics of those who registered 5–8 weeks after the birth were compared with those who registered up to 4 weeks after the birth. It was found that babies who were registered later were more likely to have mothers of Indian origin who were better educated, Hindu, and born outside the UK.

To correct for any bias, births registered later could have been weighted to allow for their lower chance of selection earlier in the sampling period. It was found however, that weighting had an insignificant effect on the estimates for key variables in comparison with large increases in the variance of the estimates. Because of the importance of providing precise estimates for each ethnic group, it was decided not to proceed with weighting for late registration.

Results have only been weighted to take account of sub-sampling Pakistani babies for part of the sampling period.

1.2 Sample of White babies

A White control sample was selected in the same areas as the Asian sample. One concern was that within the selected local authorities, the Asian population would be concentrated in a small area so that selecting the White sample from the local authority as a whole would dilute the matching effect. Although the clustering rates vary considerably by area, overall 90% of the Asian population are spread over 60% of the sectors. In seven areas where the Asian population was more clustered, the White sample was restricted to those sectors where the majority of the Asians lived.

One in three mothers with non-Asian names living in the 41 sampled local authority areas were selected. They were sent a letter/questionnaire which asked about ethnic origin and which explained that an interviewer would be calling on a sample of mothers. A reminder was sent to non-responders after two weeks. Mothers who were non-White, but not Asian, were eliminated from the sample. Then a sample was selected of both those who responded to the sift questionnaire and non-responders.

2. Fieldwork dates

Fieldwork for the first stage (when babies were on average nine weeks old) was October 1994–January 1995; the second stage (when babies were on average five months old) was January–March 1995; the third stage (when babies were on average nine months old) was May–July 1995 and the fourth stage (when babies were on average 15 months old) was November1995–January 1996. The age distribution of babies at each stage is shown in Figures A.2–A.5.

Figures A.2-A.5

3. Response

3.1 Stage 1

The overall response at stage 1 was 86% of eligible addresses with a similar response among the Asian (87%) and the White (85%) samples. This included 1% who gave an interview but no measurements were obtained (25); the interview was complete with only some measurements (14); it was a partial interview with no measurements (4).

Fourteen per cent of mothers selected for interviewing were lost to the sample altogether either because they did not wish to take part

Figure A.2

Age of babies at first interview by ethnic group

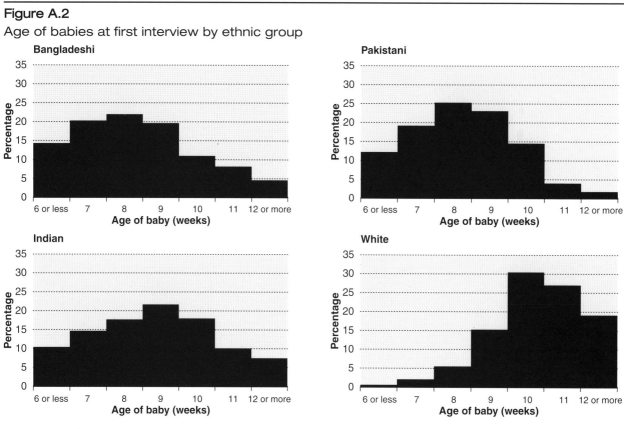

Figure A.3

Age of babies at second interview by ethnic group

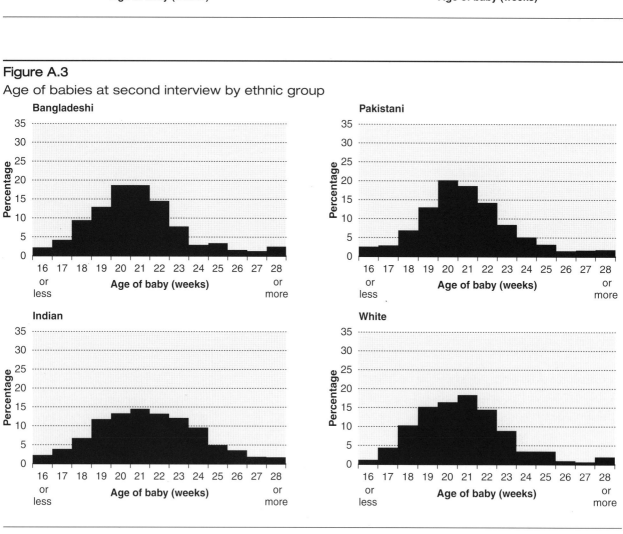

Figure A.4

Age of babies at third interview by ethnic group

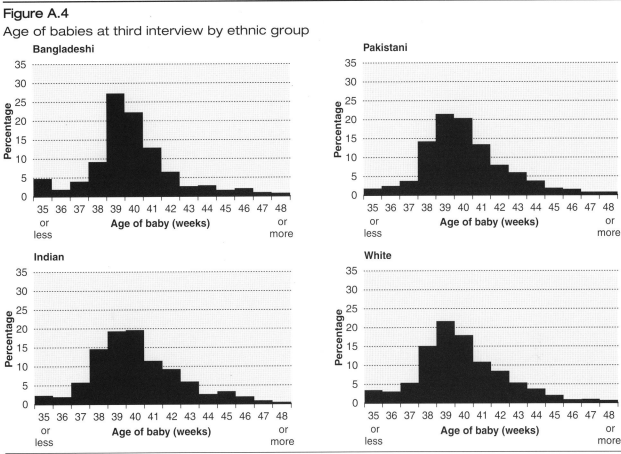

Figure A.5

Age of babies at fourth interview by ethnic group

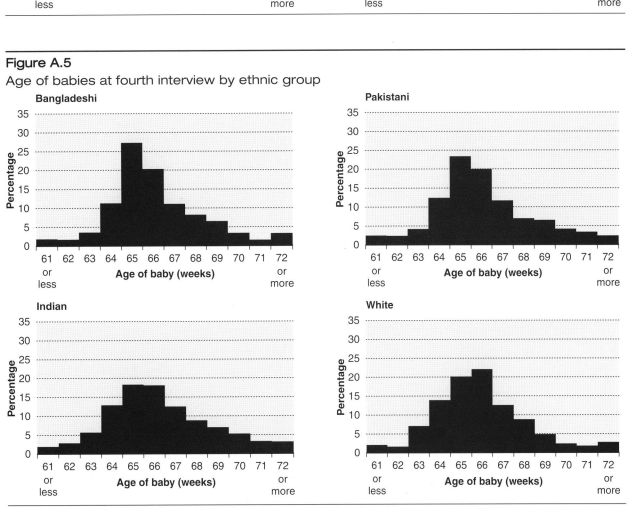

(4%) or because they could not be contacted (10%). The non-contact rate is higher than we would normally expect on a household survey because some respondents were away for the entire period of fieldwork, others were rarely at the address, and some babies were too old before the mother could be contacted.

Table A.1 also shows the total number of cases dealt with and the number ineligible. A large number (661) of the addresses at stage 1 were ineligible because they were sifted out on the doorstep either because the respondent did not fall into any of the ethnic groups in the study or because the respondent was Pakistani and was not selected for the 1 in 2 sample. Also ineligible were addresses which could not be traced (22); households where the baby was no longer with the mother (27); or there was an error on the birth certificate and the baby was actually older than stated (9).   **Table A.1**

Ninety nine per cent of mothers interviewed at stage 1 agreed to a follow-up interview.

3.2 Stage 2
The stage 2 sample of 2,874 addresses included all those who agreed at stage 1 to be interviewed again, including a few who gave complete interviews at stage 1 but without all or some of the measurements. Of these addresses, 32 were ineligible because the baby was no longer with the mother (4) or the respondent had moved and could not be traced (28). This resulted in a sample of 2,842 eligible addresses.

Table A.2 shows that of the eligible addresses, 94% were interviewed. The response was slightly higher among the White sample (97%) than among the Asian sample (93%), mainly because Asian mothers were more difficult to contact. Interviewers were unable to contact 5% of Asian compared with 2% of White mothers. Two per cent of the Asian sample and 1% of the White sample were unwilling to be interviewed at stage 2 although they had previously agreed to a follow-up interview. One in four refusals by Asians were made by a husband or mother-in-law on behalf of the respondent.   **Table A.2**

3.3 Stage 3
At stage 3, 2,756 addresses were issued. The sample consisted of all those who were interviewed at stage 2 and agreed to be interviewed again (2,649), plus some non-contacts (101) and refusals (6) from stage 2 where the interviewer indicated that the case was worth re-issuing. Of these addresses, 6 were ineligible because the baby was no longer with the mother, resulting in a sample of 2,750 eligible addresses.

Table A.3 shows that the overall response at stage 3 was 94% of eligible addresses. As in stage 2, response was slightly higher among the White (97%) than among the Asian (92%) sample. Again, this was because the non-contact rate was higher among Asians. The same proportion (2%) of the Asian and White samples refused to be interviewed at stage 3.   **Table A.3**

3.4 Stage 4
At stage 4, 2,626 addresses were issued. The sample consisted of all those who were interviewed at stage 3 and agreed to be interviewed again (2,551) plus 75 non-contacts at stage 3 who were interviewed at stage 2. The overall response at stage 4 was 92%. Again, response was lower among the Asian (91%) than among the White (96%) sample because of the higher non-contact rate among Asians.   **Table A.4**

3.5 Overall response
The target was to achieve interviews at stage 4 with mothers of 800 Indian, 400 Pakistani, 400 Bangladeshi and 400 White babies. The final sample included interviews with mothers of 764 Indian, 593 Pakistani, 477 Bangladeshi and 548 White babies. Table A.5 shows the response at each stage as a proportion of the initial sample. At stage 4, 70% of the original Asian sample and 75% of the original White sample were interviewed.   **Table A.5**

4 Language
Forty four per cent of all interviews with Asian mothers at stage 1, were done through an interpreter, ranging from 25% of interviews with Indian to 44% with Pakistani and 68% with

Bangladeshi mothers. The languages used in interpreted interviews were Bengali (45%), Punjabi (28%), Urdu (13%), Gujarati(11%), Hindi(1%), Other (2%).

At subsequent stages, the proportion of interviews done through an interpreter was slightly lower (41% at stages 2 and 3 and 39% at stage 4). There is no evidence that Asian respondents who had difficulty understanding English were more likely than others to drop out of the sample. Interviewers found that it was possible to do some interviews without an interpreter, particularly if the mother was Indian or Pakistani, even though one was used at the first interview (table not shown).

4.1 Interpreters

Several options for obtaining interpreters were recommended to interviewers if an interviewer speaking the appropriate language was not available to do the interview.

The first, was to ask who normally interprets for the informant and to arrange for that person to be present. Interviewers were asked to bear in mind that if at all possible, the interpreter should be female and of the same generation e.g. sister, female cousin or friend.

As a second option, interviewers were provided with a list of interpreters in their area. This included ONS employees in London who also work as interpreters, and interpreters recruited from other government departments in London, Birmingham, Bradford, Leicester, Manchester, Slough, Luton. Only female interpreters from these sources were used. They were all trained in basic interviewing techniques and were briefed about this survey.

Each interviewer also had a contact in their area who could help with providing an interpreter. In some cases, it was someone from the local authority who was able to suggest a council employee who could act as an interpreter. In other cases, it was an agency which provided interpreters.

The majority (68%) of interpreters at stage 1 were family or friends. This included 24% of interpreters who were the informant's husband, despite interviewers being advised to accept a husband as interpreter only if he insisted. Thirteen per cent of interpreters were from ONS or another government department and 10% were professional interpreters from the council or an agency. The 'other' category includes some (9%) interviewers who had local contacts and recruited their own interpreters. Similar arrangements were made with interpreters at subsequent stages. **Table A.6**

Table A.1

Response rates and non-response at stage 1

	Asian and White		Asian		White	
		%		%		%
Total response	2 904	86	2 285	87	619	85
Fully co-operating	2 861	85	2 250	85	611	84
Partly co-operating	43	1	35	1	8	1
Total non-response	462	14	352	13	110	15
Refusals	141	4	102	4	39	5
Non-contacts	321	10	250	9	71	10
Total eligible	3 366	100	2 637	100	729	100
Total ineligible	730		675		55	
Total cases dealt with	4 096		3 312		784	

Table A.2

Response rates and non-response at stage 2

	Asian and White		Asian		White	
		%		%		%
Total response	2 660	94	2 066	93	594	97
Fully co-operating	2 639	93	2 047	92	592	96
Partly co-operating	21	1	19	1	2	0
Total non-response	182	6	162	7	20	3
Refusals	55	2	48	2	7	1
Non-contacts	127	4	114	5	13	2
Total eligible	2 842	100	2 228	100	614	100
Total ineligible	32		28		4	
Total cases dealt with [*]	2 874		2 256		618	

[*] The 2,874 addresses issued at stage 2 included all those who gave a full or partial interview at stage 1 and agreed to be interviewed again.

Table A.3

Response rates and non-response at stage 3

	Asian and White		Asian		White	
		%		%		%
Total response	2 558	94	1 982	92	584	97
Fully co-operating	2 526	92	1 953	91	581	96
Partly co-operating	32	1	29	1	3	0
Total non-response	192	7	166	8	26	4
Refusals	52	2	42	2	10	2
Non-contacts	140	5	124	6	16	3
Total eligible	2 750	100	2 148	100	602	100
Total ineligible	6		4		2	
Total cases dealt with [*]	2 756		2 152		604	

[*] The 2,756 addresses issued at stage 3 included all those who gave a full or partial interview at stage 2 and agreed to be interviewed again (2,649); 101 non-contacts and 6 refusals at stage 2 where the interviewer indicated that the respondent might agree to an interview at stage 3.

Table A.4
Response rates and non-response at stage 4

	Asian and White		Asian		White	
		%		%		%
Total response	2 382	92	1 834	91	548	96
Fully co-operating	2 328	90	1 787	89	541	94
Partly co-operating	54	2	47	2	7	1
Total non-response	201	8	175	9	26	4
Refusals	30	1	23	1	7	1
Non-contacts	171	7	152	8	19	3
Total eligible	2 583	100	2 009	100	574	100
Total ineligible	43		32		11	
Total cases dealt with [*]	2 626		2 041		585	

[*] The 2,626 addresses issued at stage 4 included all those who gave a full or partial interview at stage 3 (2,551) and non–contacts at stage 3 (75) unless they were also a non-contact at stage 2.

Table A.5
Summary of response at the four stages

All mothers

	Asian and White		Asian		White	
		%		%		%
Stage 1						
Eligible	3 366	100	2 637	100	729	100
Response						
Stage 1	2 904	86	2 285	87	619	85
Stage 2	2 660	79	2 066	78	594	81
Stage 3	2 558	76	1 982	75	584	80
Stage 4	2 382	71	1 834	70	548	75

Table A.6
Who interpreted at stage 1 by language

Who interpreted	Gujarati	Punjabi	Bengali	Urdu	Total [*]
	%	%	%	%	%
Husband	41	20	25	19	24
Other family member	27	33	35	46	35
Friend	4	10	8	13	9
ONS/Govt. interpreter	15	18	12	3	13
Professional interpreter	0	14	12	5	10
Other	14	5	7	15	9
Base = 100%	*96*	*249*	*399*	*116*	*883*

[*] Includes 10 interviews interpreted in Hindi and 13 interviews interpreted in other languages.

Appendix B   Characteristics of the sample

Introduction

The results from this survey have been analysed by whether the mother was of Bangladeshi, Indian or Pakistani origin and a comparison made with a sample of White mothers who lived in the same areas as the Asian sample. The aim was to investigate infant feeding practices in each group separately. As described below, the characteristics of the groups are quite different.

Figures B1-B9, Tables B1-B23

Characteristics of the Bangladeshi sample

On average, Bangladeshi households were larger than other Asian households and Bangladeshi families had more children. A higher proportion of Bangladeshi households rented their home from a local authority or housing association than other Asian households and on average they had less space per person.

The majority of Bangladeshi mothers were born in Bangladesh, nearly all were Muslims and Bengali was the main language spoken at home by most of them. On average, Bangladeshi mothers were less able to understand or read English than other Asian mothers and were much less likely to have ever had paid employment. The average gross weekly income of a Bangladeshi mother and her husband/partner was less than other Asian couples and more Bangladeshi families were on income support or receiving family credit than other Asian families. Bangladeshi husbands/partners were more likely than other Asians to be unemployed.

Size of family and household

■ The average size of a Bangladeshi household in this sample was seven people[1]. Seventeen per cent of households had 10 or more people, including 3% with 14 people.

■ Nearly a half (46%) of the mothers of Bangladeshi babies had a female relative –

mother, mother-in-law, sister, sister-in-law – living in their household. Just over a third (38%) lived with their mother or mother-in-law

■ At stage 1, Bangladeshi families had on average, 2.8 children, including the new baby. Nineteen per cent had five or more children, including 5% with eight or more children.

■ This was the first baby in about a third of Bangladeshi families.

■ At stage 4 when the baby in this survey was about 15 months old, 10% of mothers had given birth again, 14% were pregnant and 5% planned to become pregnant in the next year.

■ Bangladeshi mothers were on average 25 years old, 10% were under 20 and nearly a half were aged 20-24.

Country of birth and religion

■ The majority (90%) of Bangladeshi mothers were born in Bangladesh. Only 8% were born in the UK.

■ Of those not born in the UK, 68% arrived in the UK since the beginning of 1985, including a third who arrived since the beginning of 1990.

■ All were Muslims.

Language

■ Bengali was the main language spoken at home by 96% of Bangladeshi mothers.

■ Sixteen per cent of Bangladeshi mothers had no understanding of English and a further 43% had very little understanding.

■ A third (32%) said that they could not read English at all and a further 29% said that they did not read English very well.

- About a half (49%) read Bengali but were unable to read English or did not read it very well.

- Nine per cent of all Bangladeshi mothers could not read any language.

Education and employment status

- On average, Bangladeshi mothers born in the UK had 11.6 years full-time education[2] (equivalent to leaving school at age 16–17), and those born elsewhere had 9 years full-time education (equivalent to leaving school at age 14). Seven per cent of Bangladeshi mothers born elsewhere had no full time education.

- About three quarters have never had paid employment.

- At stage 1 (when the baby was about nine weeks old), 1% of Bangladeshi mothers were working, 2% were on paid maternity leave and 3% were on unpaid maternity leave. At both Stage 2 (when the baby was about five months old) and Stage 3 (when the baby was about nine months old), 5% were working. At stage 4 (when the baby was about 15 months old), 6% were working.

- When they last worked, just over a half (53%) were in either a partly skilled or unskilled job; 33% had a skilled non-manual job; only 5% were in professional or managerial occupations.

- A third of husbands/partners were unemployed[3] in the week prior to the first interview.

Income

- About a half (49%) of all Bangladeshi families were receiving Income Support[4].

- Nearly a quarter (23%) of Bangladeshi families were in receipt of Family Credit[4].

- The average (mean) gross weekly income of the respondent and her husband/partner was £139[5].

Living conditions

- Fifty seven per cent of Bangladeshi households rented their home from the local authority or housing association, 30% were owner occupiers and 11% were private renters[6].

- On average Bangladeshi households occupied 0.7 rooms per person. Only 1% shared a kitchen and nearly all (99%) had the use of a cooker (99%) or refrigerator (98%). Forty three per cent had the use of a car[7].

Characteristics of the Indian sample

On average, Indian households were smaller than other Asian households and Indian families had fewer children. On average, Indian mothers were slightly older than either Pakistani or Bangladeshi mothers, had more full-time education, a better understanding of and ability to read English and were much more likely to have ever had paid employment. They were less likely than Pakistani mothers but considerably more likely than Bangladeshi mothers to have been born in the UK. Indian mothers were likely to be Hindu, Sikh or Muslim.

The gross weekly income of an Indian mother and her husband/partner was about 60% higher than an average Pakistani couple and about 75% higher than an average Bangladeshi couple. Indian households were more likely than other Asian households to be owner occupiers and to have more space per person in their accommodation.

Size of family and household

- The average size of an Indian household in this sample was 5.4 people[1].

- About four out of ten mothers of Indian babies had a female relative living in their household. Just over a third (37%) lived with their mother or mother-in-law.

- At stage 1, Indian families had on average, two children.

- This was the first baby in 42% of Indian families.

- At stage 4 when the baby in this survey was about 15 months old, 4% of Indian mothers had given birth again, 11% were pregnant and 11% planned to become pregnant in the next year.

- Indian mothers were on average 28 years old when this baby was born. A third (33%) were over 30 and only 2% were under 20.

Country of birth and religion

- Just over a half (54%) of Indian mothers were born in India, about a quarter (24%) were born in the UK, 15% were born in East Africa and 6% were born elsewhere.

- Of those born elsewhere, a third arrived in the UK before 1980 and a further third arrived since the beginning of 1990.

- 44% were Hindus, 37% were Sikhs, 16% were Muslims and 3% had other religions.

Language

- The main languages spoken at home were Gujarati (40%), Punjabi (34%), English (20%).

- Eighty three per cent spoke English at least fairly well. Only 2% had no understanding of English.

- Eighty per cent could read English at least fairly well. Only 6% could not read English at all.

- Fifteen per cent read either Gujarati or Punjabi and 2% read Hindi but were unable to read English or did not read it very well.

- Two per cent of all Indian mothers could not read any language.

Education and employment status

- On average, Indian mothers born in the UK and elsewhere had similar amounts of full-time education[2] (12.6 and 12.7 years respectively).

- Twenty seven per cent of those born in the UK and 39% of those born elsewhere had 14 years or more of full-time education which is

comparable to completing full-time education beyond the age of 18.

- About three quarters (74%) of Indian mothers have had paid employment.

- At stage 1 (when the baby was about nine weeks old), 5% of all Indian mothers were working, 26% were on paid maternity leave and 5% were on unpaid maternity leave. At stage 2 (when the baby was about five months old), 18% were working; at stage 3 (when the baby was about nine months old), 36% were working. At stage 4 (when the baby was about 15 months old), 43% were working.

- Of the Indian mothers who were working, 14% worked at home when their baby was about five months old, 12% worked at home when their baby was about nine months old and 16% worked at home when their baby was about fifteen months old.

- When they last worked, just over a half of Indian mothers were either in skilled non-manual (41%) or professional or managerial occupations (13%).

- 16% of husbands/partners were unemployed[3] in the week prior to the first interview.

Income

- Twenty one per cent of Indian families were receiving Income Support[4].

- Eight per cent of Indian families were receiving Family Credit[4].

- The average (mean) gross weekly income of the respondent and her husband/partner was £244[5].

Living conditions

- Eighty per cent of Indians were owner occupiers, 12% rented from a local authority or housing association, 6% were private renters[6].

- On average, Indian households occupied one room (ex. kitchens and bathrooms) per person. Only 2% shared a kitchen. Nearly all had the use of a refrigerator (99%) and cooker (100%). Eighty four per cent had the use of a car[7].

Characteristics of the Pakistani sample

On average, Pakistani households were larger than Indian households but not as large as Bangladeshi households; Pakistani families had more children than Indian families but fewer children than Bangladeshi families. Like Indian households, a high proportion of Pakistani households were owner occupiers but the amount of space they occupied was on average less than Indian households.

About two thirds of Pakistani mothers were born in Pakistan, nearly all were Muslims and the majority spoke Punjabi or Urdu at home. On average, their ability to understand and read English was better than Bangladeshi mothers but not as good as Indian mothers. Although nearly two thirds of Pakistani mothers had never had paid employment and just over a third of their husbands/partners were not working, these proportions were not as high as among Bangladeshis. The average gross weekly income of Pakistani couples was slightly higher than Bangladeshi couples but 60% less than Indian couples.

Size of family and household

- The average size of a Pakistani household in this sample was 6.4 people[1]. Eleven per cent of households had 10 or more people, including 2% with 14 people.

- Forty four per cent of mothers of Pakistani babies had a female relative living in their household. A third (33%) lived with their mother or mother-in-law.

- At stage 1, Pakistani families had on average, 2.4 children. Twelve per cent had 5 or more children.

- This was the first baby in about a third (35%) of all Pakistani families.

- At stage 4, when this baby was about 15 months old, 9% of mothers had given birth

again, a further 16% were pregnant and 10% planned to become pregnant in the next year.

- Pakistani mothers were on average 26 years old when this baby was born, 21% were over 30 and 7% were under 20.

Country of birth and religion

- About two thirds (67%) of Pakistani mothers were born in Pakistan. Thirty per cent were born in the UK.

- Of those not born in the UK, just over a half (56%) arrived here since the beginning of 1985, including a third who arrived since the beginning of 1990.

- Nearly all (98%) were Muslims.

Language

- The main languages spoken at home by Pakistani mothers were Punjabi (50%) and Urdu (36%).

- Nine per cent mainly spoke English at home and a further 60% said that they understood English at least fairly well, although it was not the main language they spoke at home.

- About a quarter (23%) could not read English at all and a further 17% said that they did not read English very well.

- Just over a quarter (27%) read Urdu but were unable to read English or did not read it very well.

- Eleven per cent of all Pakistani mothers could not read any language.

Education and employment status

- On average, Pakistani mothers born in the UK had 11 years full-time education[2] (equivalent to leaving school at the age of 16) and those born elsewhere had 9 years full-time education (equivalent to leaving school at the age of 14).

- Sixteen per cent of Pakistani mothers born elsewhere had no full-time education.

- About six out of ten (61%) Pakistani mothers have never had paid employment.

- At stage 1 (when the baby was about nine weeks old), 2% were working, 5% were on paid maternity leave and 3% were on unpaid maternity leave. At stage 2 (when the baby was about five months old), 6% were working. At stage 3 when the baby was about nine months old), 8% were working. At stage 4 (when the baby was about 15 months old), 9% were working.

- Of the Pakistani mothers who were working, 16% worked at home when their baby was about nine months old, and 13% worked at home when their baby was about 15 months old.

- When they last worked, nearly three quarters of Pakistani mothers were either in a skilled non-manual (31%) or partly skilled job (42%), 18% were in professional or managerial occupations.

- Thirty per cent of husbands/partners were unemployed[3] in the week prior to the interview.

Income

- Forty per cent of Pakistani families were receiving Income Support[4].

- Twenty per cent of Pakistani families were in receipt of Family Credit[4].

- The average (mean) gross weekly income of the respondent and her husband/partner was £152 per week[5].

Living conditions

- Nearly three quarters (73%) of Pakistanis were owner occupiers; 16% rented from a local authority or housing association; 8% were private renters[6].

- On average, Pakistani households occupied 0.8 rooms (ex. kitchens and bathrooms) per person. Only 1% shared a kitchen. Nearly all had the use of a refrigerator (98%) and cooker (99%). Seventy five per cent had the use of a car[7].

Characteristics of the White sample

On average, households in the White sample were smaller than Asian households and less crowded in their accommodation. An average mother in the White sample was more like an Indian than a Pakistani or Bangladeshi mother in terms of her age, level of education and number of children. She was more likely than an average Asian mother to have worked before the baby was born and to have returned to work after the birth. Her husband/partner was less likely to be out of work, than if he was Asian, particularly if he was Pakistani or Bangladeshi. The gross weekly income of a couple in the White sample was 20% higher than an Indian couple, 90% higher than a Pakistani couple and more than twice as high as a Bangladeshi couple.

The White sample was selected in the same areas as the Asian sample and is not representative of the Asian population as a whole.

Size of family and household

- The average size of a household in the White sample was 3.8 people[1].

- Five per cent of mothers of White babies lived in a household with a female relative, usually their mother or mother-in-law.

- Thirteen per cent of White babies lived in a family where the mother was a lone parent, either because she was single (10%) or divorced, separated or widowed (3%)[8].

- At stage 1, White families had on average 1.8 children.

- This was the first baby in 48% of the White families.

- At stage 4, 3% of White mothers had given birth again, 11% were pregnant and twelve per cent planned to become pregnant in the next year.

- White mothers were on average 28 years old when this baby was born. Twelve per cent were over 35 and 6% were under 20.

Education and employment status

- On average White mothers had 12.5 years of full-time education[2] which is equivalent to leaving school at age 17–18. Nearly a quarter (23%) had 14 years or more of full-time education which is comparable to completing full-time education beyond the age of 18.

- Nearly all (96%) White mothers have had paid employment.

- At stage 1 (when the baby was about 6 to 10 weeks old), 8% were working, 30% were on paid maternity leave and 10% were on unpaid maternity leave. At stage 2 (when the baby was about five months old), 25% were working; at stage 3 when the baby was about nine months old, 44% were working; at stage 4 when the baby was about 15 months old, 50% were working.

- Of the White mothers who were working, between 10% and 12% worked at home when their baby was between 5 and 15 months old.

- When they last worked, just over three quarters were in skilled or partly skilled occupations, 17% were in professional or managerial occupations.

- Eleven per cent of husbands/partners were unemployed[3] in the week prior to the first interview.

Income

- Twenty three per cent of White families were receiving Income Support[4].

- Five per cent of White families were receiving Family Credit[4].

- The average (mean) gross weekly income of the respondent and her husband/partner was £296[5].

Living conditions

- Two thirds of the White sample were owner occupiers, 26% rented from a local authority or housing association, 8% were private renters[6].

- On average, White households occupied one room (ex. kitchens and bathrooms) per person. Nearly all (99%) had the use of a refrigerator and cooker. Seventy eight per cent had the use of a car[7].

Notes

1 The average size of household in Great Britain in 1991 was: Bangladeshi (5.18 persons), Indian (3.83 persons), Pakistani (4.81 persons), White (2.44 persons).
Source: 1991 Census. Office for National Statistics.

2 So that a comparable measure of education could be derived for mothers educated in different countries, the number of years of full-time education was calculated as the difference between the age of starting and the age of completing full-time education. This assumed that full-time education was continuous.

3 The economic status of males aged 16 to 64 in Great Britain in Spring 1995 was:

	Working %	Unemployed %	Inactive %
Pakistani/ Bangladeshi	49	18	33
Indian	72	10	18
White	77	8	15

Source: Labour Force Survey. Office for National Statistics

4 Those eligible for Income Support are people aged 18 or over whose income is below a certain level and who are not working for 16 hours or more a week. They must be available for work and taking reasonable steps to find a job (unless they are sick, disabled, a lone parent, 60 or over, getting invalid care allowance or pregnant).

Those eligible for Family Credit are people who are working for at least 16 hours a week on a low or moderate wage and who have at least one child (aged under 16 or under 19 if in full-time education).

In 1994/5, 52% of Pakistani/Bangladeshi, 25% of Indian and 17% of White households were in receipt of Income Support.

Ten per cent of Pakistani/Bangladeshi, 6% of Indian, 2% of White households were in receipt of Family Credit.

Source: Family Resources Survey. Department of Social Security 1994.

5 In 1993/4, the average (mean) gross weekly income of head of household and partner was £307.
Source: General Household Survey. London HMSO 1993/1994.

6. In 1994/5 the tenure of households in England was:

	Owner Occupier %	Social Renter %	Private Renter %
Bangladeshi	36	59	5
Pakistani	68	18	14
Indian	83	8	9
White	68	22	10

Source: Housing in England 1994/5. London HMSO (1996)

7 In 1994/5, 56% of Bangladeshi/Pakistani, 72% of Indian, 66% of White households had a car continuously available for their use. *Source: Family Resources Survey.* Department of Social Security.

8 In 1994, 21% of families with dependent children in Great Britain were headed by a lone mother, 8% were single, 13% were widowed, divorced or separated. *Source: General Household Survey 1993/4.* London HMSO (1996)

Figure B.1
Average household size by ethnic group

All households

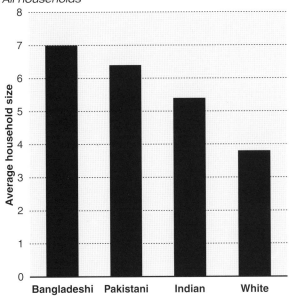

Figure B.2
Average number of children in family by ethnic group

All families

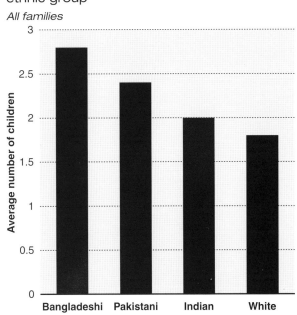

Figure B.3
Age of mother by ethnic group

All families

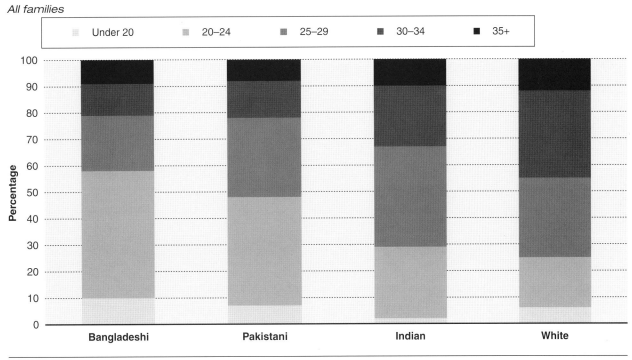

Figure B.4

Proportion of mothers born in UK by ethnic group

All families

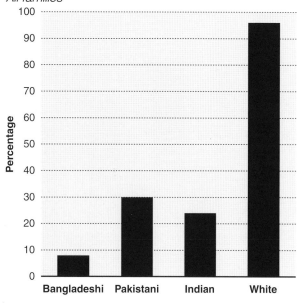

Figure B.5

Understanding of spoken English by ethnic group

All mothers

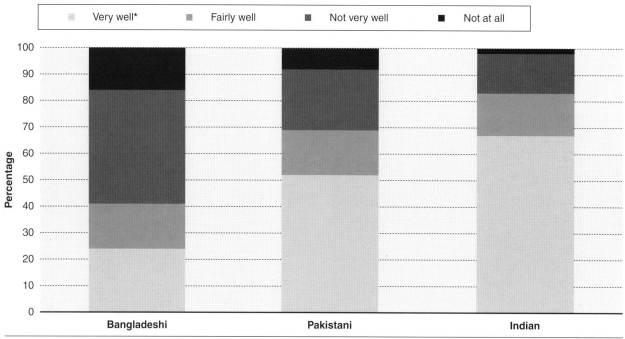

* Includes those who mainly spoke English at home.

Figure B.6
Ability to read English by ethnic group

All mothers

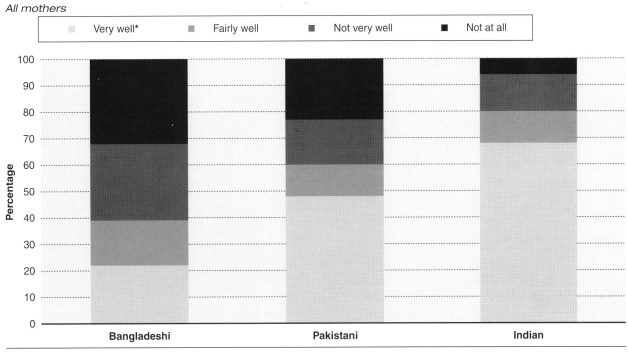

* *Includes those who mainly spoke English at home.*

Figure B.7
Average number of years of mother's full-time education by country of birth and ethnic group

All mothers

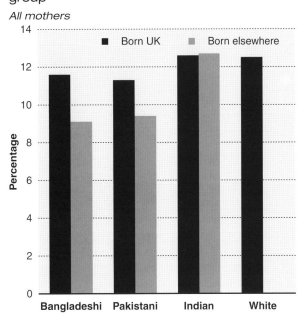

Figure B.8
Whether mother ever had paid employment by ethnic group

All mothers

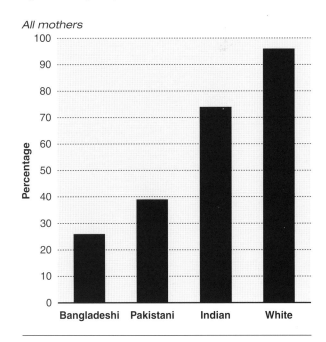

Figure B.9

Proportion of mothers working at each stage of interviewing by ethnic group

All mothers

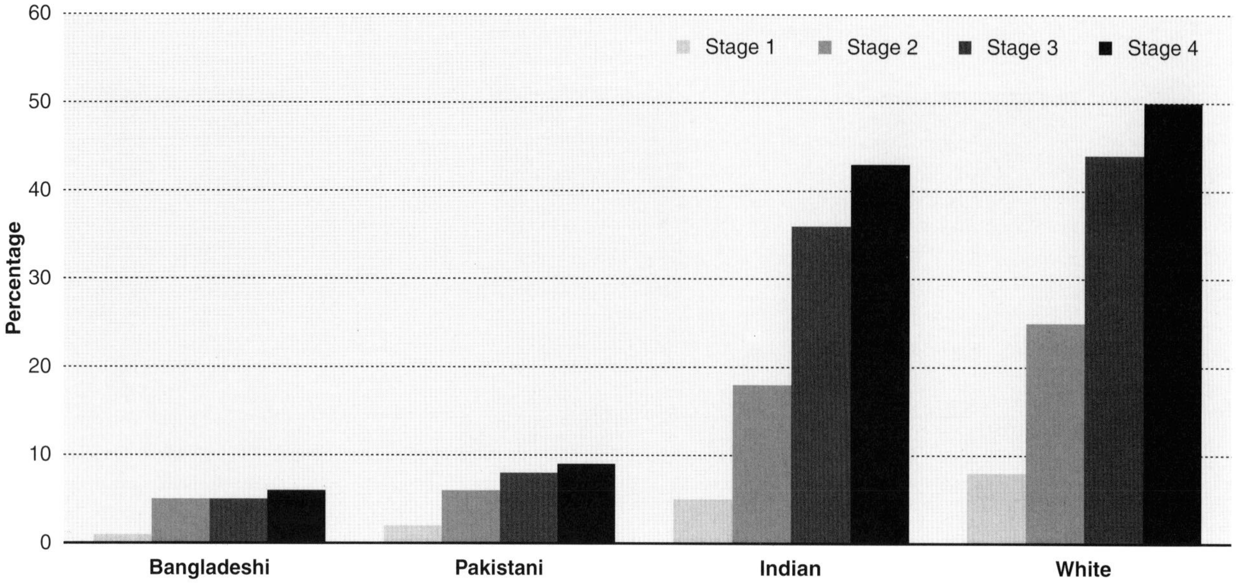

Table B.1
Household size by ethnic group

All households

Household size	Ethnic group			
	Bangladeshi	Pakistani	Indian	White
	%	%	%	%
Two	0	1	1	3
Three	6	11	17	43
Four	12	16	22	34
Five	14	14	21	14
Six	15	14	16	4
Seven	13	16	11	1
Eight	12	10	6	0
Nine	11	7	2	0
Ten or more	17	11	5	0
Base = 100%	*610*	*731*	*934*	*619*
Mean household size	*7.0*	*6.4*	*5.4*	*3.8*

Table B.2
Female relatives living in the household by ethnic group

All households

Proportion of households with:	Ethnic group			
	Bangladeshi	Pakistani	Indian	White
	%	%	%	%
Female relative	**46**	**44**	**41**	**5**
Mother/mother-in-law	38	33	37	4
Sister/sister-in-law	33	32	18	1
Base = 100%	*610*	*731*	*934*	*619*

Table B.3
Number of children in family by ethnic group

All families

Number of children in family	Ethnic group			
	Bangladeshi	Pakistani	Indian	White
	%	%	%	%
One	34	35	42	48
Two	23	28	32	31
Three	15	16	17	15
Four	9	10	6	4
Five	7	6	2	1
Six	5	3	1	0
Seven	2	2	0	0
Eight or more	5	1	0	0
Base = 100%	*607*	*727*	*930*	*617*
Mean number of children in family	*2.8*	*2.4*	*2.0*	*1.8*

Table B.4

Whether had another baby, was pregnant, or planned to become pregnant in next year when interviewed at stage 4 by ethnic group

All Mothers

	Ethnic group			
	Bangladeshi	Pakistani	Indian	White
	%	%	%	%
Had another baby	10	9	4	3
Pregnant	14	16	11	11
Planned to become pregnant in next year	5	10	11	12
No new baby, not pregnant, no plans to become pregnant	72	64	73	75
Base = 100%	*449*	*560*	*721*	*520*

Table B.5

Age of mother by ethnic group

All mothers

Age of mother	Ethnic group			
	Bangladeshi	Pakistani	Indian	White
	%	%	%	%
Under 20	10	7	2	6
20–24	48	41	27	19
25–29	21	30	38	30
30–34	12	14	23	33
35+	10	7	10	12
Base = 100%	*610*	*730*	*934*	*619*
Mean age of mother	*25*	*26*	*28*	*28*

Table B.6

Marital status of mother by ethnic group

All mothers

Marital status	Ethnic group			
	Bangladeshi	Pakistani	Indian	White
	%	%	%	%
Married	98	96	97	68
Living together	0	2	1	19
Single	1	2	1	10
Divorced, separated, widowed	1	2	1	3
Base = 100%	*610*	*731*	*934*	*619*

Table B.7
Mother's country of birth by ethnic group

All mothers

Mother's country of birth	Ethnic group			
	Bangladeshi	Pakistani	Indian	White
	%	%	%	%
UK	8	30	24	96
Bangladesh	90	0	0	0
Pakistan	0	67	0	0
India	0	0	54	0
East Africa	0	1	15	0
Elsewhere	2	1	6	4
Base = 100%	610	731	934	619

Table B.8
Year arrived in UK by ethnic group

All Asian mothers not born in UK

Year arrived in UK	Ethnic group		
	Bangladeshi	Pakistani	Indian
	%	%	%
1979 or earlier	14	26	37
1980–84	19	17	12
1985–89	33	22	17
1990–94	35	34	33
Base = 100%	563	509	706

Table B.9
Mother's religion by ethnic group

All mothers

Mother's religion	Ethnic group			
	Bangladeshi	Pakistani	Indian	White
	%	%	%	%
Hinduism	0	0	44	0
Islam	100	98	16	1
Sikhism	0	0	37	0
Christian	0	0	2	84
Other	0	1	1	2
No religion	0	0	1	13
Base = 100%	608	728	934	619

Table B.10

Main language spoken at home by ethnic group

All Asian mothers

Main language spoken at home	Ethnic group		
	Bangladeshi	Pakistani	Indian
	%	%	%
English	3	9	20
Punjabi	0	50	34
Bengali	96	0	0
Urdu	0	36	2
Gujarati	0	0	40
Other	0	4	4
Base = 100%	*610*	*729*	*930*

Table B.11

Mother's understanding of English by ethnic group

All Asian mothers

Understanding of spoken English	Ethnic group		
	Bangladeshi	Pakistani	Indian
	%	%	%
English main language*	3	9	20
English not main language but spoken			
Very well	21	43	47
Fairly well	17	17	16
Not very well	43	23	15
Not at all	16	9	2
Base = 100%	*610*	*731*	*934*

* Main language spoken at home.

Table B.12

Mother's ability to read English by ethnic group

All Asian mothers

Ability to read English	Ethnic group		
	Bangladeshi	Pakistani	Indian
	%	%	%
English main language*	3	9	20
English not main language but reads it:			
Very well	19	39	48
Fairly well	17	12	12
Not very well	29	17	14
Not at all	32	23	6
Base = 100%	*610*	*731*	*934*

* Main language spoken at home.

Table B.13
Languages read by mother by ethnic group

All Asian mothers

Languages read by mother	Ethnic group		
	Bangladeshi	Pakistani	Indian
	%	%	%
Reads English very or fairly well*	39	60	81
Little or no ability to read English but reads:			
Punjabi	0	2	7
Bengali	49	0	0
Urdu	0	27	1
Gujarati	0	0	8
Hindi	0	0	2
Other	2	1	1
Does not read any language	9	11	2
Base = 100%	*610*	*729*	*930*

* Includes those who mainly speak English at home.

Table B.14
Mother's full-time education by ethnic group and country of birth

All mothers

Number of years of full time education	Ethnic group						
	Bangladeshi		Pakistani		Indian		White
	Born UK	Born elsewhere	Born UK	Born elsewhere	Born UK	Born elsewhere	Born UK
	%	%	%	%	%	%	%
None	0	7	0	16	0	1	0
1–10 years	22	50	25	36	5	18	7
11 years	28	18	28	14	28	19	39
12–13 years	37	18	30	15	40	23	31
14 years or more	13	6	17	20	27	39	23
Base = 100%	*46*	*555*	*218*	*497*	*226*	*697*	*590*
Mean number of years of education	*11.6*	*9.1*	*11.3*	*9.4*	*12.6*	*12.7*	*12.5*

Table B.15
Whether mother ever had paid employment by ethnic group

All Mothers

Mother ever had paid employment	Ethnic group			
	Bangladeshi	Pakistani	Indian	White
	%	%	%	%
Yes	26	39	74	96
No	74	61	26	4
Base = 100%	*607*	*728*	*934*	*619*

Table B.16

Current employment status at each stage of interviewing by ethnic group

All mothers

Employment status	Ethnic group			
	Bangladeshi	Pakistani	Indian	White
	%	%	%	%
Stage 1 (baby 9 weeks old on average)				
Working	1	2	5	8
Paid maternity leave	2	5	26	30
Unpaid maternity leave	3	3	5	10
Not working / not on maternity leave	95	91	64	52
Base = 100%	*610*	*731*	*934*	*619*
Stage 2 (baby 5 months old on average)				
Working	5	6	18	25
Paid maternity leave	1	1	3	4
Unpaid maternity leave	1	2	13	17
Not working / not on maternity leave	94	91	66	54
Base = 100%	*552*	*668*	*841*	*594*
Stage 3 (baby 9 months old on average)				
Working	5	8	36	44
Paid maternity leave	0	0	0	0
Unpaid maternity leave	0	0	2	2
Not working / not on maternity leave	94	91	62	54
Base = 100%	*521*	*642*	*815*	*576*
Stage 4 (baby 15 months old on average)				
Working	6	9	43	50
Paid maternity leave	0	0	1	1
Unpaid maternity leave	0	0	1	0
Not working / not on maternity leave	94	90	56	48
Base = 100%	*477*	*590*	*758*	*548*

Table B.17

Whether mother works mainly at home or goes out to work by ethnic group

All mothers in employment

	Ethnic group			
	Bangladeshi	Pakistani	Indian	White
	%	%	%	%
Stage 2 (baby 5 months old on average)				
Works mainly at home	[1]	[6]	14	11
Goes out to work	[24]	[31]	86	89
Base = 100%	*25*	*37*	*148*	*148*
Stage 3 (baby 9 months old on average)				
Works mainly at home	[4]	16	12	10
Goes out to work	[20]	84	88	90
Base = 100%	*24*	*51*	*292*	*251*
Stage 4 (baby 15 months old on average)				
Works mainly at home	[2]	13	16	12
Goes out to work	[23]	87	84	88
Base = 100%	*25*	*54*	*321*	*275*

Table B.18
Mother's social class by ethnic group

All mothers who ever worked

Social class	Ethnic group			
	Bangladeshi	Pakistani	Indian	White
	%	%	%	%
Professional	0	2	2	1
Managerial and Technical	5	16	11	16
Skilled: non-manual	33	31	41	42
Skilled: manual	9	9	7	14
Partly skilled	51	42	35	21
Unskilled	2	2	3	5
Base = 100%	*123*	*219*	*355*	*299*

Table B.19
Economic status of husband/partner by ethnic group

All husbands/partners living in UK

Economic status of husband/partner	Ethnic group			
	Bangladeshi	Pakistani	Indian	White
	%	%	%	%
Working	56	64	81	86
Unemployed	33	30	16	11
Inactive	11	6	3	3
Base = 100%	*531*	*643*	*901*	*539*

Table B.20
Gross weekly income of respondent and husband/partner by ethnic group

All mothers

Gross weekly income	Ethnic group			
	Bangladeshi	Pakistani	Indian	White
	%	%	%	%
Less than £50	7	4	1	1
£50 less than £70	7	7	3	3
£70 less than £100	19	18	10	12
£100 less than £150	32	31	18	8
£150 less than £200	19	18	16	10
£200 less than £250	10	11	11	10
£250 less than £300	4	4	10	9
£300 less than £350	1	2	6	9
£350 less than £400	0	1	6	6
£400 less than £450	0	1	5	6
£450 less than £500	0	1	4	6
£500 or more	0	1	9	20
Base = 100%	*542*	*635*	*840*	*612*
Mean gross weekly income	*139*	*152*	*244*	*296*
Median gross weekly income	*125*	*125*	*225*	*275*

Table B.21

Receipt of income support and family credit by ethnic group

All families

Respondent/husband receiving:	Ethnic group			
	Bangladeshi	Pakistani	Indian	White
	%	%	%	%
Income support				
Yes	49	40	21	23
No	51	60	79	77
Family credit				
Yes	23	20	8	5
No	77	80	92	95
Base = 100%	*601*	*725*	*929*	*619*

Table B.22

Housing tenure by ethnic group

All households

Housing tenure	Ethnic group			
	Bangladeshi	Pakistani	Indian	White
	%	%	%	%
Owned outright	4	21	17	3
Buying with mortgage	26	52	63	63
Rented from:				
Council	48	12	10	22
Housing association	9	4	2	4
Rented privately:				
Unfurnished	4	2	2	4
Furnished	7	6	4	4
Rented with job or business	0	1	0	0
Rent free	1	1	2	0
Temporary accommodation	1	1	0	0
Base = 100%	*607*	*718*	*930*	*619*
Mean number of rooms per person	*0.7*	*0.8*	*1.0*	*1.0*

 Measurements – protocols and interviewer variability test

1 Measurement Protocols

1.1 Weight
We recommend that this is the first measurement you take as it is probably the easiest.

Equipment: Soehnle baby scales

1 Place the scales on a hard flat surface, preferably smooth and uncarpeted.

2 The battery should have already been inserted and the scales set to kg/g ready for use. It is possible to change them to lb/oz but this is quite difficult, so if the mother asks how much her baby weighs in lb/oz use the conversion chart (Show Card D).

3 To switch on, press the button once '8.8.8.8' will appear on the display. Then '0.00' will be displayed, indicating that the scales are ready for use. The scales are quite sensitive and can be affected even by a strong breeze. If anything other than '0.00' is displayed, check that the scales are on a smooth flat surface and that nobody is touching them, and press the button again until '0.00' is displayed.

4 The scales have a weight lock, so be sure to place the baby firmly and quickly either in the detachable tray or on the scales, so that they don't lock too soon.

5 The weight will be displayed in kg/g (to 10g) and will remain displayed after you have removed the baby. Record the weight then switch off, pressing the button once to display "0.00", then again to switch off. Alternatively, the scale will turn itself off automatically after two minutes.

1.2 Measurement of head circumference
Equipment: Lasso circumference tape

1 Thread the tapered end of the tape up at point marked 1, down through 2 and up through 3.

2 Pass the tape round the child's head, just above the brow ridges. Check that the tape is horizontal, in contact with the head throughout its length, and is under slight tension.

3 Record the measurement in centimetres, to 1 decimal place, at mark labelled 'read here'.

1.3 Measurement of mid upper arm circumference
Equipment: Lasso circumference tape, dermatological marker pen

The measurement is taken in two stages and the child must have a bare upper arm and shoulder to take the measurement accurately.

1 Find the length of the child's upper arm. To do this, their left arm should be across their body at a 90 degree angle at the elbow. The upper arm length measurement is from the tip of the acromium bone (we will demonstrate this at the briefing), to the tip of the elbow.

2 Divide this measurement in half and this will be the mid-point of the upper arm. Mark the mid-point with the dermatological marker pen.

3 Pass the tape horizontally around the arm (not sloping). The tape should be under tension, but not compressing the tissues of the arm.

4 Record the measurement in centimetres, to 1 decimal place.

1.4 Supine length
Equipment: Raven rollametre

1 Unroll the Rollametre fully and lie it as flat as possible on a smooth firm surface.

2 Pull the measuring rule up to the headpiece to check that it records '0', (you may need to

place something on the mat to stabilise it), then return it to the foot end of the Rollametre.

4 Place the baby on the foam pad with his/her head resting against the headpiece.

5 Ask the mother to hold the child's head in position. This is with the back of the head touching the headpiece, and the eyes and nose pointing upwards.

6 Straighten the baby's legs using one hand, and with the other, move the foot rest on which the measuring tape is mounted to touch the baby's heels.

7 Read the measurement (in centimetres) from the cursor in the tape window. It may be helpful to get the mother to distract the baby whilst you straighten the legs. Make sure you read the correct centimetre. The measure runs in the opposite direction to the tape measures.

1.5 General points

Each measurement need only be made once but if you are unhappy with any measurement, repeat it until you are satisfied you have done it correctly. Record the measurement which you consider to be the most reliable. Please remember to record the number of attempts at measuring and any circumstances which might have affected the measurement.

The baby should ideally be measured naked, so please ask the mother to remove the nappy. This is particularly important when measuring supine length and also weight which would be increased by a wet nappy. If the baby is wearing a nappy, please record this at both weight and supine length. It is acceptable for the baby to wear a vest.

2 Variability of supine length measurement

The measurement of supine length was considered to be the most difficult to achieve accurately. To gain some idea of interviewer variability in measuring this, a small exercise was set up before the start of fieldwork. Five interviewers with experience of measuring supine length from the feasibility study, visited a

local health centre and took measurements of babies and young children.

Unlike other measurement variability studies that have been completed in the past, this study was constrained by finding enough children of the right age, and by the maximum number of times that a young child could be measured at one time (this was considered to be three times). The aim was to measure ten children in two sets of five (each being measured three times). Each interviewer would measure three of the five children in each set. Interviewers did not see the results of previous measurements before measuring the child.

The analysis was severely limited because only six children of the right age visited the clinic on the chosen morning. The mean variation for children 1 to 6 was 1.3cm, excluding the fourth child. When measuring the fourth child, one interviewer recorded a very high measurement, which appeared as if she had misread the tape measure as 82cm instead of 62cm. To prevent this happening in the mainstage fieldwork, the measurement ranges that the questionnaire would accept were tightened, and the measurements of children who were genuinely outside the range were noted and entered separately before analysis.   Table C.1

Table C.1

Interviewer measurements of supine length taken at variability test

	Baby 1	Baby 2	Baby 3	Baby 4	Baby 5	Baby 6	Baby 7	Baby 8	Baby 9	Baby 10
Sex	Boy	Girl	Girl	Girl	Girl	Boy	–	–	–	–
Age	8 months	1 year	1 month	6 months	2 months	8 months	–	–	–	–
Interviewer	1	2	3	4	5	3	5	4	2	1
Measurement 1(cm)	73	71	52	63.5	59	68	–	–	–	–
Interviewer	2	1	5	3	4	2	1	3	5	4
Measurement 2(cm)	73	71	53	62	60	70	–	–	–	–
Interviewer	3	5	4	2	1	5	3	1	4	2
Measurement 3(cm)	72	72	53	82	58.5	69	–	–	–	–

Appendix D — Standard deviation scores

Standard deviation scores for this survey relative to the 1990 National data have been calculated for weight, supine length and head circumference for each of the ethnic groups in the survey. This allows the national charts to be used for Bangladeshi, Pakistani and Indian babies by incorporating an adjustment to the centiles.

Tables D1-D3

The following is an example of adjusting the National growth charts so that they can be used for Pakistani girls of nine weeks. Similar adjustments can be made for babies in other groups.

At nine weeks, the weight of Pakistani girls was on average 0.44 standard deviation scores (SDS) less than White girls of the same age in the National sample (Table D1). The published charts have centile lines 0.67 SDS apart. A mean SDS of -0.44 is approximately two thirds of this and corresponds to a shift downwards to two thirds of a centile band. So an average Pakistani girl of nine weeks will be approximately on the 33rd. centile.

Table D.1

Mean standard deviation scores relative to the national data for weight by age, sex and ethnic group

All babies

| | Ethnic group | | | | | | | |
| | Bangladeshi | | Pakistani | | Indian | | White | |
	Boys	Girls	Boys	Girls	Boys	Girls	Boys	Girls
Birth								
Mean SDS	−0.85	−0.86	−0.72	−0.81	−0.91	−0.95	−0.28	−0.25
Standard deviation	1.01	1.11	1.08	1.29	1.14	1.18	1.28	1.19
9 weeks								
Mean SDS	−0.34	−0.52	−0.30	−0.44	−0.45	−0.67	−0.41	−0.66
Standard deviation	1.04	1.12	1.13	1.27	1.24	1.25	1.31	1.17
5 months								
Mean SDS	−0.55	−0.66	−0.43	−0.44	−0.53	−0.71	−0.02	−0.05
Standard deviation	0.97	1.10	1.16	1.29	1.19	1.21	1.13	1.13
9 months								
Mean SDS	−0.63	−0.64	−0.33	−0.27	−0.42	−0.56	0.11	−0.06
Standard deviation	1.01	1.16	1.15	1.22	1.16	1.23	1.09	1.13
15 months								
Mean SDS	−0.47	−0.56	−0.18	−0.06	−0.32	−0.39	0.05	−0.13
Standard deviation	1.13	1.21	1.25	1.23	1.19	1.24	1.12	1.06
Base = 100%								
Birth	286	306	377	334	431	482	312	293
9 weeks	274	291	362	318	420	463	303	287
5 months	251	273	339	298	378	423	299	275
9 months	232	233	323	275	362	416	283	258
15 months	195	211	270	242	319	359	262	242

Table D.2

Mean standard deviation scores relative to the national data for supine length by age, sex and ethnic group

All babies

	Ethnic group							
	Bangladeshi		Pakistani		Indian		White	
	Boys	Girls	Boys	Girls	Boys	Girls	Boys	Girls
9 weeks								
Mean SDS	0.37	0.13	0.46	0.44	0.30	0.38	0.19	0.10
Standard deviation	1.35	1.34	1.41	1.44	1.55	1.41	1.33	1.36
5 months								
Mean SDS	0.13	0.02	0.59	0.60	0.37	0.36	0.51	0.58
Standard deviation	1.17	1.16	1.31	1.28	1.34	1.52	1.59	1.32
9 months								
Mean SDS	0.07	0.03	0.51	0.51	0.43	0.54	0.47	0.37
Standard deviation	1.13	1.11	1.20	1.25	1.21	1.20	1.15	1.18
15 months								
Mean SDS	0.30	0.23	0.70	0.47	0.63	0.88	0.40	0.35
Standard deviation	1.15	1.07	1.21	1.24	1.26	1.11	1.13	1.16
Base = 100%								
9 weeks	*245*	*264*	*348*	*309*	*385*	*427*	*285*	*281*
5 months	*259*	*275*	*343*	*302*	*372*	*422*	*297*	*270*
9 months	*229*	*236*	*314*	*277*	*351*	*392*	*279*	*254*
15 months	*211*	*221*	*287*	*245*	*320*	*371*	*277*	*244*

Table D.3

Mean standard deviation scores relative to the national data for head circumference by age, sex and ethnic group

All babies

	Ethnic group							
	Bangladeshi		Pakistani		Indian		White	
	Boys	Girls	Boys	Girls	Boys	Girls	Boys	Girls
9 weeks								
Mean SDS	−0.02	−0.22	−0.12	−0.11	−0.28	−0.31	−0.09	−0.40
Standard deviation	1.45	1.34	1.31	1.30	1.41	1.27	1.39	1.16
5 months								
Mean SDS	−0.60	−0.86	−0.63	−0.60	−0.64	−0.73	0.12	−0.20
Standard deviation	1.19	1.21	1.16	1.21	1.29	1.24	1.17	1.07
9 months								
Mean SDS	−1.11	−1.24	−1.02	−0.87	−0.82	−0.97	−0.09	−0.26
Standard deviation	1.13	1.18	1.23	1.14	1.13	1.24	1.20	1.06
15 months								
Mean SDS	−1.05	−1.19	−1.20	−1.01	−0.94	−0.96	−0.24	−0.40
Standard deviation	1.37	1.12	1.18	1.16	1.16	1.12	1.16	1.06
Base = 100%								
9 weeks	*277*	*296*	*371*	*324*	*420*	*472*	*306*	*288*
5 months	*263*	*276*	*352*	*307*	*380*	*434*	*309*	*281*
9 months	*232*	*234*	*321*	*279*	*349*	*407*	*289*	*261*
15 months	*211*	*222*	*291*	*242*	*327*	*371*	*276*	*244*

Appendix E Sampling errors

1 Sources of error in surveys

Like all estimates based on samples, the results of this survey are subject to various possible sources of error. The total error in a survey estimate is the difference between the estimate derived from the data collected and the true value for the population. The total error can be divided into two main types: systematic error and random error.

Systematic error, or bias, covers those sources of error which will not average to zero over repeats of the survey. Bias may occur, for example, if certain sections of the population are omitted from the sampling frame, because non-respondents to the survey have different characteristics to respondents, or if interviewers systematically influence responses in one way or another. When carrying out a survey, substantial effort is put into the avoidance of systematic errors but it is possible that some may still occur.

The most important component of random error is sampling error, which is the error that arises because the estimate is based on a sample survey rather than a full census of the population. The results obtained for any single sample may, by chance, vary from the true values for the population but the variation would be expected to average to zero over a number of repeats of the survey. The amount of variation depends on the size of the sample and the sample design and weighting method.

Random error may also arise from other sources, such as variation in the informant's interpretation of the questions, or interviewer variation. Efforts were made to minimise these effects through interviewer training and through pilot work.

2 Confidence intervals

Although the estimate produced from a sample survey will rarely be identical to the population value, statistical theory allows us to measure the accuracy of any survey result. The standard error can be estimated from the values obtained for the sample and this allows calculation of confidence intervals which give an indication of the range in which the true population value is likely to fall.

This report gives the 95% confidence intervals around selected survey estimates. The interval is calculated as 1.96 times the standard error on either side of the estimated percentage or mean since, under a normal distribution, 95% of values lie within 1.96 standard errors of the mean value. If it were possible to repeat the survey under the same conditions many times, 95% of these confidence intervals would contain the population value. This does not guarantee that the intervals calculated for any particular sample will contain the population values but, when assessing the results of a single survey, it is usual to assume that there is only a 5% chance that the true population value falls outside the 95% confidence interval calculated for the survey estimate.

The 95% confidence interval for a sample percentage estimate, p, is given by the formula:

$$p +/- 1.96 \times se(p)$$

where se(p) represents the standard error of the percentage estimate.

For results based on a simple random sample, which has no clustering or stratification or weighting, estimating standard errors is straightforward. In the case of a percentage, the standard error is based on the percentage itself (p) and the subsample size (n):

$$se(p) = \sqrt{p(100-p)/n}$$

When, as in the case of this survey, the sample design is not simple random, the standard error needs to be multiplied by a design factor (deft). The design factor is the ratio of the standard error with a complex sample design to the standard error that would have been achieved with a simple random sample of the same size. The 95% confidence interval for a percentage from this survey is therefore calculated as:

$$p +/- 1.96 \times deft \times \sqrt{p(100-p)/n}$$

The 95% confidence for a mean (x) is given by:

$$x +/- 1.96 \times deft \times \sqrt{variance(x)/n}$$

The standard errors, design factors and 95% confidence intervals for selected percentages and means are given in Tables E1-E3 for each ethnic group. The errors shown are for weighted data.

3 How to estimate sampling errors for other characteristics

For percentages based on the full sample of an ethnic group, standard errors can be estimated using the formula:

$$p +/- 1.96 \times deft \times \sqrt{p(100-p)/n}$$

For characteristics not shown in tables E1-E3, a design factor could be used which is likely to be clustered in the same way as a variable in the tables. However, since most of the design factors are relatively small, the effect of adjusting sampling errors to take account of the survey's complex design will be small and it is probably sufficient to use the basic estimates of standard errors assuming a simple random sample.

Tables E1-E3

Table E.1

Sampling errors: percentages

Characteristic	Percentage (p)	Base	Standard error of p	95% confidence interval	Design factor
	%	number	%	%	number
All mothers					
Whether ever breastfed					
Bangladeshi	89.8	610	1.18	87.5–92.2	0.97
Pakistani	76.4	731	1.86	72.8–80.1	1.19
Indian	82.0	934	1.34	79.4–84.7	1.07
White	62.5	619	2.02	58.5–66.5	1.04
Given vitamins at 9 weeks					
Bangladeshi	15.1	609	1.44	12.3–17.9	0.99
Pakistani	21.5	730	1.75	18.0–24.9	1.15
Indian	21.4	934	1.59	18.5–24.8	1.18
White	6.8	619	1.02	4.8–8.8	1.01
Experienced a feeding problem during first 15 months					
Bangladeshi	68.3	477	2.06	64.3–72.4	0.97
Pakistani	58.4	590	2.14	54.2–62.6	1.05
Indian	58.6	758	1.74	55.3–62.2	0.97
White	55.1	548	2.09	51.0–59.2	0.98
Given meat or fish daily at 15 months					
Bangladeshi	52.8	477	2.30	48.4–57.4	1.00
Pakistani	29.8	590	2.08	25.7–33.9	1.10
Indian	21.1	758	1.48	18.1–23.9	1.00
White	68.6	548	2.15	64.4–72.9	1.10
Eats rice, pasta or potatoes daily at 15 months					
Bangladeshi	82.2	477	1.75	78.8–85.6	1.00
Pakistani	28.4	590	1.94	24.6–32.2	1.04
Indian	46.4	758	2.26	41.6–50.6	1.25
White	74.8	548	1.89	71.1–78.5	1.02
Drinks water daily at 15 months					
Bangladeshi	92.8	471	1.19	90.5–95.1	0.99
Pakistani	89.9	588	1.31	87.3–92.5	1.05
Indian	83.4	753	1.25	80.9–85.8	0.92
White	39.9	534	2.05	35.9–44.0	0.97
First time mothers					
Attended antenatal classes	13.9	209	2.37	9.2–18.5	0.99
Pakistani	23.8	250	2.68	18.5–29.1	1.00
Indian	53.2	391	2.54	47.9–58.0	1.00
White	77.3	295	2.38	72.7–82.0	0.97

Table E.2
Sampling errors: mean measurements of male babies at 15 months

All male babies

Measurement	Mean	Base	Standard error of p	95% confidence interval	Design factor
Mean weight at 15 months					
Bangladeshi	10.4	195	0.10	10.20–10.58	1.04
Pakistani	10.8	270	0.09	10.63–11.00	1.05
Indian	10.6	319	0.07	10.47–10.76	0.96
White	11.0	262	0.08	10.82–11.13	0.97
Mean length at 15 months					
Bangladeshi	79.9	211	0.22	79.42–80.30	1.08
Pakistani	81.0	287	0.19	80.58–81.34	1.02
Indian	81.0	320	0.21	80.39–81.24	1.14
White	80.1	277	0.17	79.77–80.44	0.95
Mean head circumference at 15 months					
Bangladeshi	47.3	211	0.11	47.11–47.56	0.98
Pakistani	47.2	291	0.10	46.96–47.34	1.17
Indian	47.5	327	0.08	47.33–47.63	0.95
White	48.3	276	0.11	48.12–48.54	1.26
Mean arm circumference at 15 months					
Bangladeshi	15.8	214	0.09	15.64–16.01	1.01
Pakistani	15.9	291	0.09	15.75–16.11	1.14
Indian	15.9	328	0.07	15.74–16.01	0.98
White	16.4	280	0.09	16.21–16.57	1.12

Table E.3
Sampling errors: mean measurements of female babies at 15 months

All female babies

Measurement	Mean	Base	Standard error of p	95% confidence interval	Design factor
Mean weight at 15 months					
Bangladeshi	9.8	211	0.09	9.63–9.97	1.00
Pakistani	10.2	242	0.09	9.97–10.34	1.06
Indian	10.0	359	0.06	9.86–10.12	0.94
White	10.1	242	0.68	10.02–10.28	0.96
Mean length at 15 months					
Bangladeshi	78.3	221	0.19	77.98–78.72	1.00
Pakistani	78.9	245	0.21	78.50–79.34	1.05
Indian	80.0	371	0.16	79.68–80.32	1.05
White	78.6	244	0.19	78.20–78.96	1.00
Mean head circumference at 15 months					
Bangladeshi	46.0	222	0.09	45.82–46.18	1.04
Pakistani	46.2	242	0.10	46.00–46.38	1.11
Indian	46.3	371	0.07	46.12–46.39	0.99
White					
Mean arm circumference at 15 months					
Bangladeshi	15.5	225	0.08	15.29–15.62	0.96
Pakistani	15.7	247	0.09	15.49–15.84	1.08
Indian	15.4	371	0.06	15.28–15.52	0.92
White	15.7	253	0.08	15.53–15.84	1.05

Appendix F The Questionnaires

INFANT FEEDING SURVEY
WAVE 1 QUESTIONNAIRE

The survey was carried out using computer assisted interviewing. This is a list of the questions.

I would like to start by asking about you and your household

1. NPERSONS How many people normally live in this household ?

2. NADULTS How many people aged 16 or over are normally living in this household ?

3. NCHILD How many children aged under 16 are there normally living in this household ?

4. TWINTRIP Is your baby one of twins or triplets ?

1 No
2 Twin
3 Triplet

IF TWINS OR TRIPLETS PLEASE ASK QUESTIONS WITH RESPECT TO THE FIRSTBORN

5. SEX1 Is your baby a boy or a girl ?

1. Boy
2. Girl

6. NAME1 What is your baby's first name ?

7. BIRTHDAT What is ..... date of birth ?

8. FIRSTBBY Is this your first baby ?

1 Yes
2 No

IF NO AT FIRSTBBY

9. OTHCHILD How many other children have you given birth to, including any who are not living here and any who may have died since birth ?
EXCLUDE ANY STILLBORN

HOUSEHOLD BOX

INFORMATION COLLECTED FOR EACH PERSON IN HOUSEHOLD

10a. NAME OR IDENTIFIER

10b. SEX Code (....)'s sex

1 Male
2 Female

10c. AGE Can I just check, what is your (....) age now ?

10d. MARSTAT Are you ..... ?

1 Married
2 Living together
3 Single
4 Widowed, divorced or separated

10e. RELTOMUM What is the relationship of (....) to mother ?

1 Husband
2 Partner
3 Son/daughter
4 Father
5 Mother
6 Father-in-law
7 Mother-in-law
8 Sister
9 Brother
10 Sister-in-law
11 Brother-in-law
12 Other relative
13 Other non-relative

IF MARRIED AT MARSTAT

11. HUSB Is your husband living in this country or abroad ?

ALL

12. ETHNIC (Can I just check) To which ethnic group do you consider you belong ?
ASK OR RECORD

1 White
2 Black-Caribbean
3 Black-African
4 Black-Other
(Describe at next question)
5 Indian
6 Pakistani
7 Bangladeshi
8 Chinese
9 Other
(Describe at next question)

12a. XETHNIC WRITE IN NAME OF OTHER ETHNIC GROUP

13. RESPCOB In which country were you born ?
ASK OR RECORD

1 England
2 Other GB
3 East Africa
4 India
5 Bangladesh
6 Pakistan
7 Other

1

IF NOT BORN IN ENGLAND OR ELSEWHERE IN GB AT RESPCOB

14. ARRIVEUK In what year did you first arrive in the United Kingdom ?

IF INDIAN, PAKISTANI, BANGLADESHI AT ETHNIC

15. LANGUAG What is the main language you speak at home ?

1 English
2 Gujarati (include Kitchi)
3 Punjabi (include Mirpuri)
4 Bengali (include Sylheti)
5 Hindi
6 Urdu
7 Other

16. LANGUAG WRITE IN NAME OF OTHER LANGUAGE

IF MAIN LANGUAGE NOT ENGLISH

17. ENGUND (May I just check) How well do you understand English when it is spoken to you ?

1 very well
2 fairly well
3 not very well
4 or not at all

18. ENGREAD (May I just check) How well do you read English ?

1 very well
2 fairly well
3 not very well
4 or not at all

IF NOT VERY WELL OR NOT AT ALL AT ENGREAD

19. READOTH Do you read any other languages ?

1 Yes
2 No

IF YES AT READOTH

20. OTHLANG Which other language, apart from English, do you mainly read ?

1 Gujarati
2 Punjabi
3 Bengali
4 Hindi
5 Urdu
6 Other

Now I would like to ask you some questions about how you feed your baby

21. FEEDMODE At the moment is your baby ...

1 Breastfed
2 Bottle fed
3 Breast and bottle fed

IF BREASTFED AT FEEDMODE

22. BOTTLE1 Do you give your baby milk in a bottle at present ? (apart from expressed breast milk) even if only occasionally

1 Yes (if even occasionally)
2 No

IF BOTTLE FED AT FEEDMODE

23. BRSTEVER Did you ever put your baby to the breast ?

1 Yes (even if it was once only)
2 No

IF YES AT BRSTEVER

24. LBRW1 How old was your baby when you last breast fed him/her ?

PLEASE ENTER NUMBER OF WEEKS. ENTER 1 IF LESS THAN ONE WEEK

25. LBRST What were your reasons for stopping breast feeding ?
(Code at most 5 reasons)
PROMPT AS NECESSARY

1 Insufficient milk
2 Painful breasts or nipples
3 Baby would not suck/rejected
4 Breast feeding took too long/ tiring
5 Mother was ill
6 Baby was ill
7 Didn't like breastfeeding
8 Inverted nipples
9 Returned to work
10 Baby could not be fed by others
11 Other
(Please specify at next question)

25a. XLBRST WRITE IN OTHER REASON FOR STOPPING BREAST FEEDING

26. LONGBRI Would you like to have continued breast feeding for longer ?

1 Yes
2 No

2

27. MILKTYP — IF EVER BOTTLE FEEDS (CODE 2 OR 3 AT FEEDMODE) OR (CODE 1 AT FEEDMODE AND CODE 1 AT BOTTLE1)
(When you bottle feed) which kind of milk do you give your baby most of the time at the moment? ENTER 20 IF NOT IN LIST AND SPECIFY AT NEXT QUESTION
1 Cow & Gate Premium (powder)
2 Cow & Gate Nutrilon Premium (powder)
3 Cow & Gate Premium (ready-to-feed)
4 Cow & Gate Plus (powder)
5 Cow & Gate Nutrilon Plus
6 Cow & Gate Plus (ready-to-feed)
7 Cow & Gate Formula S (powder)
8 Cow & Gate Infasoy
9 SMA Gold Cap (powder)
10 SMA Gold Cap (ready-to-feed)
11 SMA White Cap (powder)
12 SMA White Cap (ready-to-feed)
13 SMA Wysoy (powder)
14 Milupa Milumil (powder)
15 Milupa Aptamil (ready-to-feed)
16 Milupa Prematil (powder)
17 Farley's Junior milk
18 Farley's First milk
19 Farley's Ostersoy
20 Other kind of milk (Please specify at next question)

27a. XMILKTYP — WRITE IN NAME OF MILK IF CODED OTHER AT Q27
If liquid cow's milk please specify whether:
1 ordinary (whole) milk
2 semi-skimmed
3 skimmed milk

ALL
28. MTOKEN1 — Do you get milk tokens for free or reduced price milk?
1 Yes, free milk
2 Yes, reduced price milk
3 No, neither

IF FREE OR REDUCED PRICE MILK AT MTOKEN1
29. MTOKEXCH — Where do you exchange the tokens for milk?
1 Clinic
2 Milkman
3 Elsewhere (Please specify at next question)

29a. XTOKECH — WRITE IN WHERE MILK TOKENS ARE EXCHANGED IF ELSEWHERE

IF MILKMAN OR ELSEWHERE AT MTOKEXCH
30. CHCMILK1 — Do you ever buy your baby's milk from the child health clinic?
1 Yes, always
2 Sometimes
3 No

31. HOWSTER — IF EVER BOTTLE FEEDS (CODE 2 OR 3 AT FEEDMODE) OR (CODE 1 AT FEEDMODE AND CODE 1 AT BOTTLE1)
How do you usually sterilise the bottles?
1 Sterilising tablets
2 Sterilising fluid
3 Bottle steamer
4 Hot water
5 Microwave
6 Other method (Please specify at next question)

31a. XHOWSTER — What other method do you use to sterilise the bottles?

32. WHOMAKES — Who usually makes up the bottles?
1 Self
2 Husband or partner
3 Other children in family
4 Other (Please specify at next question)

32a. XWHOMAKES — Write in who else usually makes up the bottles.

33. ADDMILK — Do you ever add anything to the milk in the bottle?
1 Yes
2 No

IF YES AT ADDMILK
34. WHATADD — What do you add to the milk?
1 Sugar
2 Other (Please specify at next question)

34a. XWHATADD — WRITE IN WHAT ELSE IS ADDED TO THE MILK

3

35. BOTMORE — IF EVER BOTTLE FEEDS (CODE 2 OR 3 AT FEEDMODE) OR (CODE 1 AT FEEDMODE AND CODE 1 AT BOTTLE1)
Do you ever make up more than one bottle at a time?
1 Yes
2 No

IF YES AT BOTMORE
36. STORMADE — Where do you usually store the made up bottles?
1 Fridge
2 Cool place
3 Kitchen work surface
4 Other (Please specify at next question)

36a. XSTORE — WRITE IN WHERE MADE UP BOTTLES ARE STORED

37. BOTLATER — IF EVER BOTTLE FEEDS (CODE 2 OR 3 AT FEEDMODE) OR (CODE 1 AT FEEDMODE AND CODE 1 AT BOTTLE1)
If your baby doesn't take all of its feed, do you ever keep it to use later?
1 Yes
2 No
3 Sometimes

ALL
38. SOLIDS1 — Has your baby ever had any foods such as cereal, rusk, or any other kind of solid food (soft weaning food)?
1 Yes
2 No

IF YES AT SOLIDS1
39. SOLAGE1 — How old was your baby when he/she first had any food apart from milk? PLEASE ENTER NUMBER OF WEEKS

40. SOLFRST — What was the first food your baby had, apart from milk? DESCRIBE NAME OF FOOD AND BRAND

41. SOLMEAL1 — At which feed did you first offer your baby solid food (soft weaning food)? PROMPT AS NECESSARY
1 Morning (before noon)
2 Afternoon (before 6pm)
3 Evening (6pm to midnight)
4 Some other feed (please specify at next question)

41a. XSOLMEAL — WRITE IN WHEN BABY FIRST OFFERED SOLID FOOD (soft weaning food)

42. SOLREG — At present, are you giving your baby cereal, rusks or any other solid food (soft weaning food) to eat everyday?
1 Yes
2 No

IF YES AT SOLREG
43. SOLYEST — Did you give your baby any cereal, rusks or solid food (soft weaning food) to eat yesterday?
1 Yes
2 No

IF YES AT SOLYEST
44. TWEAN — SOLIDS DIARY
Information collected about each type of food eaten on previous day

44a. TYPEFOOD — What type of food did he/she eat?

44b. BRAND — What was the brand? PLEASE WRITE IN IF HOME-MADE

44c. AMOUNT — How many teaspoons of ....did he/she eat?

44d. ANYMORE — INTERVIEWER - IS THERE ANYTHING ELSE?
1 Yes
2 No

IF YES AT SOLREG
45. SOLR1M — At which feed do you regularly offer your baby solid (soft weaning food) at the moment? PROMPT AS NECESSARY
1 Morning (before noon)
2 Afternoon (before 6pm)
3 Evening (6pm to midnight)
4 Some other feed (please specify at next question)

45a. XSOLR1M — WRITE IN NAMES OF OTHER FEEDS AT WHICH BABY IS OFFERED SOLID (WEANING) FOOD

ALL
46. DRINK1 — Apart from milk, do you give your baby water or anything else to drink at the moment?
1 Yes
2 No

4

66a. XWHODAY — WRITE IN WHO LOOKS AFTER HIM/HER DURING THE DAY

67. NTLOOK — ALL
Does anyone else regularly look after ... during the night?
1 Yes
2 No

68. WHONT — IF YES AT NTLOOK
Who else looks after him/her during the night?
1 Husband or partner
2 Mother
3 Mother-in-law
4 Other female relative
5 Child minder
6 Nursery or creche
7 Someone else
(Please specify at next question)

68a. XWHONT — WRITE IN WHO ELSE LOOKS AFTER HIM/HER DURING THE NIGHT

69. FEEDPLAN — ALL
Now a few questions about when you were pregnant. Thinking back to before you had your baby, how did you plan to feed him/her?
1 Bottle
2 Breast
3 Both Breast and Bottle
4 Not decided

70. FEEDPLMA — IF BOTTLE OR BOTH BREAST AND BOTTLE AT FEEDPLAN
Why did you think you would bottle feed your baby?
(CODE AT MOST 5 ITEMS)
1 Other people can feed baby
2 More convenient
3 Previous experience
4 Disliked idea of breastfeeding
5 Embarrassed to breastfeed
6 Can see how much baby has had
7 Medical reasons
8 Expect to return to work soon
9 No particular reason
10 Other
(Please specify at next question)

70a. XFDPLMA — WRITE IN OTHER REASON

---

61. WHOFEED — IF BOTTLE FED OR BREAST AND BOTTLE FED AT FEEDMODE
Who usually feeds your baby?
1 Self
2 Someone else
(Please specify at next question)

61a. XWHOFEED — WRITE IN OTHER PERSON WHO USUALLY FEEDS BABY

62. ELSEFEED — IF SELF AT WHOFEED
Does anyone else ever feed your baby?
1 Yes
2 No

63. WHOELSE — IF YES AT ELSEFEED
Who else sometimes feeds him/her?
(CODE AT MOST 4 PERSONS)
1 Husband or partner
2 Mother
3 Mother-in-law
4 Other female relative
5 Older children in the family
6 Other person
(Please specify at next question)

63a. XWHOELSE — WRITE IN WHO ELSE SOMETIMES FEEDS BABY

64. SELFEED — IF BOTTLE OR BREAST AND BOTTLE AT FEEDMODE
Do you ever give your baby a bottle to feed him/herself?
1 Yes
2 No

65. DAYLOOK — ALL
Does anyone else regularly look after (...) during the day?
1 Yes
2 No

66. WHODAY — IF YES AT DAYLOOK
Who else looks after him/her during the day?
1 Husband or partner
2 Mother
3 Mother-in-law
4 Other female relative
5 Child minder
6 Nursery or creche
7 Someone else
(Please specify at next question)

6

---

47. WATER1 — IF YES AT DRINK1
Does your baby usually have plain water or some other type of drink?
1 Plain Water
2 Water with sugar or honey added
3 Other

48. TDRINK — IF OTHER AT WATER1
DRINKS DIARY
Information collected about each type of drink other than water

48a. TYPDRINK — What is the drink?

48b. BRAND — What is the name of the brand?

48c. FLAVOUR — What is the flavour of the drink?

49. RDRINKIM — IF YES AT DRINK1
Why do you give your baby drinks?
PROMPT AS NECESSARY
1 Because he/she is thirsty
2 Hungry between feeds
3 To give him/her extra vitamins
4 To help his/her colic/wind
5 To help his/her constipation
6 Good for baby
7 or for some other reason

49a. XRDRNKIM — WRITE IN OTHER REASONS FOR GIVING BABY DRINKS

50. VIT1 — ALL
Do you give your baby any extra vitamins (apart from the vitamin drinks you have already mentioned)?
1 Yes
2 No

51. VITDROP1 — IF YES AT VIT1
Do you use Children's Vitamin Drops from the child health clinic or another brand?
1 Children's vitamin drops
2 Other
(Please specify at next question)

51a. XVITDRP1 — WRITE IN NAME OF OTHER BRAND

52. VITBUY — IF CHILDREN'S VITAMIN DROPS AT VITDROP1
Do you buy the vitamins or do you get them free from the clinic or on prescription?
1 Buy
2 Free
3 Prescription

53. VITOTHER — IF OTHER AT VITDROP1
Do you buy the vitamins or do you get them on prescription?
1 Buy
2 Prescription

54. VITM1 — ALL
Are you taking any extra vitamins or iron tablets yourself either in tablet or powder form?
1 Yes
2 No

55. VITM1GET — IF YES AT VITM1
How do you usually get the vitamins?
1 Child health clinic
2 Elsewhere

56. VITM1BUY — IF CHILD HEALTH CLINIC AT VITM1GET
Do you buy the vitamins/iron tablets or do you get them free or on prescription?
1 Buy
2 Free
3 Prescription

57. VITM1OTH — IF ELSEWHERE AT VITM1GET
Do you buy the vitamins or do you get them on prescription?
1 Buy
2 Prescription

58. FDTIMES1 — ALL
Do you feed your baby on demand or do you generally keep to set feeding times?
1 On demand
2 Set times
3 Depends

59. FEEDSET — IF SET TIMES AT FDTIMES1
How many times do you usually feed your baby in 24 hours?
PLEASE ENTER NUMBER OF TIMES
(Enter a number between 3 and 20)

60. FEEDLONG — ALL
How long does it usually take to feed him/her on average?
1 Less than 15 minutes
2 15 mins to less than 30 mins
3 30 mins to less than 45 mins
4 45 mins to less than 1hr
5 1 hr or more

5

Page 8

83. MWLANG

IF MAIN LANGUAGE NOT ENGLISH AND NOT VERY WELL OR NOT AT ALL AT ENGUND

Did the midwife speak to you mainly in English?

1 Yes
2 No

IF YES AT MWLANG

84. MWUND

Did you understand her.....

1 All of the time
2 Most of the time
3 Some of the time
4 Not at all
5 Or did someone interpret?

ALL

85. ADVELSE

Did anyone else including family and friends give you advice about your pregnancy?

1 Yes
2 No

IF YES AT ADVELSE

86. ADVWHO

Who (else) gave you advice? (CODE AT MOST 8 PERSONS)

1 Mother
2 Mother-in-law
3 Sister
4 Sister-in-law
5 Husband
6 Other relatives
7 Friend/neighbour
8 Doctor/GP
9 Someone else (Please specify at next question)

WRITE IN WHO GAVE ADVICE

86a. XADWHO

IF MORE THAN ONE PERSON GAVE ADVICE AT ADVWHO

87. MOSTADV

Who gave you most advice apart from the health visitor or midwife? PROMPT WHERE NECESSARY

1 Mother
2 Mother-in-law
3 Sister
4 Sister-in-law
5 Husband
6 Other relatives
7 Friend
8 Doctor/GP
9 Someone else (Please specify at next question)

88. DIFFADV

Do you think the advice given by (...) was any different from the advice that would have been given by a midwife or health visitor?

1 Yes
2 No

IF YES AT DIFFADV

89. WAYDIFF*

In what way? PROBE FULLY

ALL

90. KNOWMUMS

Do you know any other mothers with babies?

1 Yes
2 No

IF YES AT KNOWMUMS

91. OTBRORBO

Would you say that most of the mothers you know with babies bottle fed or breast fed?

1 Bottle fed
2 Breastfed
3 Half bottle/half breast

ALL

92. KBRORBO

Do you know whether you were breast fed when you were a baby?

1 Breastfed entirely
2 Bottle fed entirely
3 Both breast and bottle fed

93. BIRTH

Was your baby born at home or in hospital?

1 at home
2 in hospital

IF HOSPITAL AT BIRTH

94. LONGHOSP

How long after the baby was born did you stay in hospital?

1 Answer given in hours (Please specify at question 95)
2 Answer given in days (Please specify at question 96)

IF HOURS AT LONGHOSP

95. HRSHOSP

RECORD NUMBER OF HOURS

IF DAYS AT LONGHOSP

96. DAYSHOSP

RECORD NUMBER OF DAYS

8

Page 7

71. FEEDPLMB

IF BREAST OR BREAST AND BOTTLE AT FEEDPLAN

Why did you think you would breast feed your baby? (CODE AT MOST 5 ITEMS)

1 Best for baby
2 More convenient
3 Bond between mother and baby
4 Cheaper
5 Previous experience
6 Breastfeeding is natural
7 Best for mother
8 No particular reason
9 Other (Please specify at next question)

71a. XFDPLMB

WRITE IN OTHER REASON

ALL

72. CHECKUPS

While you were pregnant did you have any (antenatal) checkups?

1 Yes
2 No

IF YES AT CHECKUPS

73. TALKFEED

At the checkups did anyone talk to you about feeding your baby?

1 Yes
2 No

ALL

74. CLASSES

While you were pregnant with this baby did you go to any classes to prepare you for having the baby?

1 Yes
2 No

IF YES AT CLASSES

75. CLASSM

Who were the classes organised by? (CODE AT MOST 2 ITEMS)

1 Hospital
2 Clinic
3 G.P
4 Other (Please specify at next question)

75a. XCLASSM

WRITE IN NAME OF OTHER ORGANISATION

76. CLASSFED

IF YES AT CLASSES

Did you attend any classes that included talks or discussions about feeding babies?

1 Yes
2 No

77. CLSSADBR

IF YES AT CLASSFED

Did the classes talk about the advantages of breast feeding?

1 Yes
2 No

78. CLSSBOTL

Were you taught how to make up bottles of milk at the classes you attended?

1 Yes
2 No

IF NO AT CLASSES

79. CLASSNOT

Why didn't you go to any classes? (CODE AT MOST 3 ITEMS)

1 None available
2 Never heard of them
3 Other children to look after
4 Went for previous child
5 Working
6 Inconvenient time
7 Language difficulties
8 Didn't want to go
9 Other (Please specify at next question)

79a. XCLNOT

WRITE IN OTHER REASONS FOR NOT ATTENDING CLASSES

ALL

80. HVISITM

Did a midwife or health visitor see you at home in connection with your pregnancy before you had the baby? PROMPT AS NECESSARY (CODE AT MOST 2 ITEMS)

1 Midwife
2 Health visitor
3 Neither

81. HVLANG

IF MAIN LANGUAGE NOT ENGLISH AND NOT VERY WELL OR NOT AT ALL AT ENGUND

Did the health visitor speak to you mainly in English?

1 Yes
2 No

IF YES AT HVLANG

82. HVUND

Did you understand her.....

1 All of the time
2 Most of the time
3 Some of the time
4 Not at all
5 Or did someone interpret?

7

Page 9

97. TYPDLVRY

ALL

Thinking now of the birth itself, what type of delivery did you have?
PROMPT AS NECESSARY

1 Normal
2 Forceps
3 Vacuum extraction
4 Caesarean

98. WEIGHT

ALL

How much did your baby weigh when he/she was born?

1 Answer given in grams (Please specify at next question)
2 Answer given in pounds & ounces (Please specify at next question)

99. WTGRAMS

IF GRAMS AT WEIGHT

RECORD WEIGHT IN GRAMS

100. WTLBS

IF POUNDS AND OUNCES AT WEIGHT

RECORD WEIGHT IN POUNDS

101. WTOZ

IF POUNDS AND OUNCES AT WEIGHT

RECORD WEIGHT IN OUNCES

102. FIRSTHLD

About how long after your baby was born did you first hold him/her?
PROMPT AS NECESSARY

1 Immediately
2 Within an hour
3 More than 1 hr. up to 12 hrs
4 More than 12 hours later

103. OKABIRTH

After the birth was everything alright or was anything the matter with you?

1 Alright
2 Something the matter

104. AFFECTED

IF MATTER AT OKABIRTH

Did this problem affect your ability to feed your baby the way you wanted to?

1 Yes
2 No

105. SCAREM

ALL

Was your baby put into special care at all, or put under a lamp for jaundice? (CODE AT MOST 2 ITEMS)

1 Special Care
2 Put under lamp for jaundice
3 Neither

106. SCAREDYS

IF SPECIAL CARE OR LAMP AT SCAREM

For how long was your baby put into special care or put under a lamp?

1 1 day or less
2 2 or 3 days
3 4 days or more

107. SHOWFEED

ALL

The first time YOU fed your baby did anyone give you any help or show you what to do?

1 Yes
2 No

108. SHOWPM

IF YES AT SHOWFEED

Who was this? (CODE AT MOST 3 PERSONS)

1 Nurse/midwife
2 Doctor
3 Relative
4 Someone else (Please specify at next question)

108a. XSHOWPM

WRITE IN PERSON WHO GAVE ADVICE

109. MOSTSHOW

IF MORE THAN ONE PERSON GAVE ADVICE AT SHOWPM

Who gave you most advice?

1 Nurse/midwife
2 Doctor
3 Someone else

110. ADVHELP

Was the advice given by ...helpful?

1 Yes
2 No

111. ADVLIKE

IF NO AT SHOWFEED

Would you have liked any help or advice?

1 Yes
2 No

9

Page 10

112. TIMETOBR

IF BREASTED OR BREAST AND BOTTLE AT FEEDMODE OR YES AT BRSTEVER

How soon after the baby was born did you first put him/her to the breast?
PROMPT AS NECESSARY

1 Immediately
2 Within half an hour
3 More than 1/2 hr up to 1hr
4 More than 1 hr, up to 4 hrs
5 More than 4 hrs, up to 8 hrs
6 More than 8 hrs, up to 12 hrs
7 More than 12 hrs, up to 24 hrs
8 More than 24 hrs later

113. HOSPBO

IF HOSPITAL AT BIRTH AND BREAST AT FEEDMODE OR YES AT BRSTEVER

While you were in hospital did YOU give your baby a bottle of milk (apart from expressed breast milk) as well as being breast fed?

1 Yes
2 No

114. HOSBOFQ

IF YES AT HOSPBO

How often did you give your baby a bottle in hospital (while you were breast feeding as well)?

1 Once or twice only
2 Every feed
3 Just during night
4 Other arrangement (Please specify at next question)

114a. XHOSPBOF

WRITE IN HOW OFTEN BABY HAD A BOTTLE IN HOSPITAL

115. TIMETOBO

IF BOTTLE FED AT FEEDMODE AND NO AT BRSTEVER

How soon after he/she was born did you first give him/her a bottle?
PROMPT AS NECESSARY

1 Immediately
2 Within half an hour
3 More than 1/2 hr up to 1 hr
4 More than 1 hr, up to 4 hrs
5 More than 4 hrs, up to 8 hrs
6 More than 8 hrs, up to 12 hrs
7 More than 12 hrs, up to 24 hrs
8 More than 24 hrs later

116. BABYWMUM

IF HOSPITAL AT BIRTH

Did your baby stay beside you all the time you were in hospital?

1 Yes
2 No

117. ALWYSFED

IF NO AT BABYWMUM

Even though he/she was not always beside you, did you always feed your baby yourself or did the nurses ever feed him/her?

1 Always fed baby myself
2 Nurses sometimes fed baby

118. NURFEDM

IF NURSES AT ALWAYSFED

What did the nurses give your baby? (CODE AT MOST 3 ITEMS)

1 Expressed breast milk
2 Other baby milk
3 Dextrose or glucose
4 Water

119. FEEDPTN

IF HOSPITAL AT BIRTH

While you were in hospital did you feed your baby on demand or did you keep to set feeding times?

1 On demand
2 Set times
3 Only in hospital a few hours
4 Some other arrangement (Please specify at next question)

119a. XFEEDPTN

WRITE IN OTHER ARRANGEMENTS

120. PRFDHOSP

IF HOSPITAL AT BIRTH

Were there any problems feeding your baby while you were in hospital?

1 Yes
2 No

121. PRFDPM

IF YES AT PRFDHOSP

What problems were there?

122. PRFDHELP

IF HOSPITAL AT BIRTH AND YES AT PRFDHOSP

Did anyone give you any help or advice about this/these problems?

1 Yes
2 No

123. PRFDHM

IF YES AT PRFDHELP

Who helped or advised you? (CODE AT MOST 3 PERSONS)

1 Midwife
2 Nurse
3 Doctor
4 Someone else (Please specify at next question)

10

Page 12

140. VOADVICE

ALL

Have you got help or received advice from a voluntary organisation which helps new mothers?

(such as a local women's group, the National Childbirth Trust, La Leche League or the Association of Breast Feeding Mothers)

1 Yes
2 No

141. PRFDHOM1

IF HOSPITAL AT BIRTH

Since you left hospital have you had any problems with feeding your baby?

1 Yes
2 No

142. WHPRHOM

IF YES AT PRFDHOM1

What problems have you had?

143. PRFDHOM2

IF HOME AT BIRTH

Since your baby was born, have you had any problems feeding him/her?

1 Yes
2 No

144. WHPRHOM2

IF YES AT PRFDHOM2

What problems have you had?

145. PRFDHOHP

IF YES AT PRFDHOM1 OR PRFDHOM2

Did anyone give you any help or advice about this/these problems?

1 Yes
2 No

146. PRFDHPM

IF YES AT PRFDHOHP

Who helped or advised you?
(CODE AT MOST 4 PERSONS)

1 Midwife or nurse
2 Health visitor
3 Family doctor (GP)
4 Doctor at the child health clinic
5 Friend or relative
6 Someone else
(Please specify at next question)

146a. XPRFDHPM

WRITE IN OTHERS WHO HELPED OR ADVISED

---

147. BOOKS

ALL

During your pregnancy or since the birth of your baby were you given a copy of any of these books?
SHOW CARD A
(CODE AT MOST 2 ITEMS)

1 The pregnancy book
2 Birth to five
3 Neither of these

148. LEAFLETS

IF MAIN LANGUAGE NOT ENGLISH

Were you given any books, leaflets, magazines cassettes or videos in ...

1 when you were pregnant
2 after the birth of.......
3 or both during pregnancy and after the birth?
4 no

149. SMOKINFO

ALL

When you were pregnant did anyone give you any advice or information about smoking during pregnancy?

1 Yes
2 No

150. SMINFOM

IF YES AT SMOKINFO

Who gave you this advice?
(CODE AT MOST 5 PERSONS)

1 Doctor/GP
2 Health visitor
3 Midwife/nurse
4 Friend/relative
5 Someone else
(Please specify at next question)

150a. XSMINFM

WRITE IN WHO GAVE ADVICE

151. DRNKINFO

ALL

When you were pregnant did anyone give you any advice or information about drinking alcohol during pregnancy?

1 Yes
2 No

152. DRINFOM

IF YES AT DRINKINFO

Who gave you this advice?
(CODE AT MOST 5 PERSONS)

1 Doctor/GP
2 Health visitor
3 Midwife/nurse
4 Friend/relative
5 Someone else
(Please specify at next question)

12

Page 11

123a. XPRFDHM

WRITE IN OTHERS WHO HELPED OR ADVISED

124. HOSPHELP

IF HOSPITAL AT BIRTH

While you were in hospital were you always able to get help or advice when you needed it?

1 Always
2 Generally
3 No

125. FEEDMTHD

When you left hospital, were you ...

1 breast feeding completely
2 bottle feeding completely
3 giving both breast and bottle?

126. MDWFVIST

After you left hospital did a midwife come to visit you?

1 Yes
2 No

127. MDWFWHN

IF YES AT MDWFVIST

How soon after you left hospital did she come?

1 Same day
2 Next day
3 Two or more days later

128. FDHPHOSP

IF HOSPITAL AT BIRTH

After you left hospital, did you know how to get help with feeding your baby if you needed to?

1 Yes
2 No
3 Didn't need help

129. FDHPHOME

IF HOME AT BIRTH

After your baby was born, did you feel you knew how to get help with feeding him/her if you needed to?

1 Yes
2 No

130. HVSEEN

ALL

Since your baby was born has a health visitor been to see you?

1 Yes
2 No

131. HVDAYS

IF YES AT HVSEEN

How old was your baby when the health visitor first came?
SPECIFY ANSWER IN DAYS

---

132. HVOWNLGE

IF MAIN LANGUAGE NOT ENGLISH AND NOT VERY WELL OR NOT AT ALL AT ENGUND

Did the health visitor speak to you mainly in ...?

1 Yes
2 No

133. HVINTERP

IF NO AT HVOWNLGE

Did the health visitor use an interpreter?

1 Yes
2 No

134. DEVCH

ALL

Has your baby had a six week check-up yet?

1 Yes
2 No

135. DEVCHAT

IF YES AT DEVCH

Where did your baby have the development check-up?

1 At the child health clinic
2 At your family doctor's (GP)
3 Somewhere else
(Please specify at next question)

136. OTHCHAT

WRITE IN WHERE BABY HAD CHECK-UP

137. GPTALK

ALL

(Apart from check-ups) have you taken ..... to the doctor because he/she was unwell?

1 Yes
2 No

138. HOSPREF

Has ... ever been sent to a hospital?

1 Yes
2 No

139. ILLNESS

IF YES AT HOSPREF

What was the matter with...?

11

Panel (page 14)

168. SMOKEVER
ALL
Have you ever smoked cigarettes?
1 Yes
2 No

169. SMKNOW1
IF YES AT SMOKEVER
Do you smoke at all nowadays?
1 Yes
2 No

170. SMOK2YRS
IF NO AT SMKNOW1
Have you smoked at all in the past two years?
1 Yes
2 No

171. CIGSBEF
IF YES AT SMKNOW1 OR YES AT SMOK2YRS
About how many cigarettes a day were you smoking just before you became pregnant?

172. CIGSDUR
About how many cigarettes a day were you smoking while you were pregnant?

173. CIGSNOW1
IF YES AT SMKNOW1
About how many cigarettes a day are you smoking now?

174. DRINKEVER
ALL
Do you ever drink alcohol nowadays, including drinks you brew or make at home?
PLEASE EXCLUDE LOW OR NON ALCOHOLIC DRINKS
1 Yes
2 No

175. DRINK2YR
IF NO AT DRINKEVER
Have you drunk alcohol at all during the past two years?
1 Yes
2 No

176. DRUGEVR
IF INDIAN, PAKISTANI OR BANGLADESHI AT ETHNIC
Have you ever used shupari, paan, chown or shadda?
1 Yes
2 No

177. DRUGNOW
IF YES AT DRUGEVR
Do you use shupari, paan, chown or shadda now?
1 Yes
2 No

178. DRUGTYPE
IF YES AT DRUGNOW
What do you use?
(CODE AT MOST 4 ITEMS)
1 Shupari
2 Paan
3 Chown
4 Shadda

Now I would like to ask you a few questions about yourself

179. MUMEDEND
ALL
How old were you when you finished full-time education?
CODE 0 IF NO FULL-TIME EDUCATION

180. MUMEDST
IF OTHER THAN NO FULL-TIME EDUCATION AT MUMEDEND
How old were you when you started full-time education?
NOT NURSERY SCHOOL
CODE 0 IF NO FULL-TIME EDUCATION

181. PAIDEVR1
ALL
Have you ever had paid employment?
1 Yes
2 No

182. PAIDWRK1
IF YES AT PAIDEVR1
Are you doing .....
1 Any paid work at the moment including working at home
2 On paid maternity leave
3 On unpaid maternity leave
4 Not working or not on maternity leave?

183. WRKPLAN1
IF NO AT PAIDWRK1
Do you plan to start work again within the next two years?
1 Yes
2 No

14

Panel (page 13)

152a. XDRINFOM
WRITE IN WHO GAVE ADVICE

153. K1BFRED
IF NO AT FIRSTBBY
We would like to know how you fed your previous children.
Thinking of your ...child, was he/she breast fed at all?
1 Yes
2 No
3 Child no longer living

154. K1PERIOD
IF YES AT K1BFRED
If breast fed, how long did you continue breast feeding your ....child?
1 Answer given in days
(Please specify at next question)
2 Answer given in weeks
(Please specify at next question)
3 Answer given in months
(Please specify at next question)

155. K1DAYS
IF DAYS AT K1PERIOD
RECORD NUMBER OF DAYS

156. K1WEEKS
IF WEEKS AT K1PERIOD
RECORD NUMBER OF WEEKS

157. K1MONTHS
IF MONTHS AT K1PERIOD
RECORD NUMBER OF MONTHS

158. FEDIFF*
IF NOT ENGLAND OR ELSEWHERE IN GB AT RESPCOB
Thinking again about (....), if he/she had been born in.. would you have fed him/her differently?
1 Yes
2 No

159. WHATDIFF*
IF YES AT FEDIFF
What would you have done differently?
1 Breast fed mainly/entirely
2 Breast fed longer
3 Other

160. PRESBRBO
ALL
Now thinking again about this baby, did you feel you were under pressure to breast feed or bottle feed..?
1 Felt under pressure to breastfeed
2 Felt under pressure to bottle feed
3 Did not feel under pressure

161. BRAGAIN1
IF BREASTFED OR BREAST AND BOTTLE FED AT FEEDMODE OR YES AT BRSTEVER
If you had another baby would you (try to) breast feed again?
1 Yes
2 No
3 Not intending to have more children

162. BRLONG
IF BREASTFED OR BREAST AND BOTTLE FED AT FEEDMODE
How old do you think......will be when you stop breast feeding?
1 Answer given in weeks
(Please specify at next question)
2 Answer given in months
(Please specify at next question)

163. BRWEEKS
IF WEEKS AT BRLONG
RECORD NUMBER OF WEEKS

164. BRMON
IF MONTHS AT BRLONG
RECORD NUMBER OF MONTHS

165. CONTR
ALL
Now thinking about yourself, I would like to ask you a few questions about family planning.
SHOW CARD B OR ASK
Can I just check, since .... was born have you (or your husband/partner) started using any method of contraception?
1 Yes
2 No
3 Sterilised

166. CONTMETH
IF YES AT CONTR
What method have you used?
1 Pill
2 Other

167. CONTLONG
IF PILL AT CONTMETH
How long after .... was born did you start taking the pill?
PLEASE SPECIFY ANSWER IN WEEKS

13

Questionnaire page 16

193 HUSBEVER — IF OTHER THAN WAIT AT HUSBNOWK
(May I just check) Has he ever had a paid job, or done any paid work?
1 Yes
2 No

194. HUSBWK1 — IF YES AT HUSBWORK OR YES AT HUSBAWAY
What is your husband's/partner's job?

195. HUSBWK2 — IF WAIT AT HUSBNOWK AND NO AT HUSBWAIT
What is the job your husband/partner is waiting to take up?

196. HUSBWK3 — IF (WAIT AT HUSBNOWK AND YES AT HUSBWAIT) OR (YES AT HUSBEVER)
What was your husband's/partner's most recent job?

197. [REPEAT QUESTIONS 185a - 185c SOCNOW - SOCLS ABOVE FOR HUSBAND'S/PARTNER'S JOBS]

Now, thinking about your family,

198. HUSBCOB — IF MARRIED AT MARSTAT
In what country was your husband born?
1 England
2 Other GB
3 East Africa
4 India
5 Bangladesh
6 Pakistan
7 Other

199. MOTHCOB — ALL
In what country was your mother born?
1 England
2 Other GB
3 East Africa
4 India
5 Bangladesh
6 Pakistan
7 Other

200. FATHCOB — ALL
In what country was your father born?
1 England
2 Other GB
3 East Africa
4 India
5 Bangladesh
6 Pakistan
7 Other

201 MILCOB — IF MARRIED
In what country was your mother-in-law born?
1 England
2 Other GB
3 East Africa
4 India
5 Bangladesh
6 Pakistan
7 Other

202. FILCOB — In what country was your father-in-law born?
1 England
2 Other GB
3 East Africa
4 India
5 Bangladesh
6 Pakistan
7 Other

203. RELIGION — ALL
What is your religion?
1 No religion
2 Christian
3 Hinduism
4 Islam
5 Sikhism
6 Buddhism
7 Judaism
8 Other

203a. XRELIG — WRITE IN OTHER RELIGIONS

204. BEDROOMS — ALL
Now I would like to ask about your household's accommodation, not counting any rooms you may let or sublet. How many bedrooms do you have, including bedsitting rooms and spare bedrooms?

205. OTHROOMS — How many other rooms do you have, not counting kitchens, bathrooms and toilets?

Questionnaire page 15

184 FULLPART — IF YES AT WRKPLAN1
Do you plan to work full or part time?
1 full-time
2 part-time

185. SOCTEXT1 — What is your job?

185a. SOCNOW — OCCUPATION CODING [SOCNOW - SOCLS]
Is occupational coding to be done now or later?
1 Now
2 Later

185b. EMP — Are you working as ...
1 Employee
2 Self employed

185c. SUPMAN — Are you a manager or supervisor of any kind?
1 Manager
2 Foreman
3 Other Employee

185d. NEMPLEE — EMPLOYEE - SIZE OF ESTABLISHMENT
How many employees work(ed) in the establishment?
1 1 - 24
2 25 +

185e. NSLFEMP — SELF EMPLOYED - SIZE OF ESTABLISHMENT
How many employees?
0 None
1 1 - 24
2 25 +

185f. EMPSTAT — Employment status and Establishment size

185g. SOCCODE — Standard Classification of Occupation

185h. SEGRP — Socio-Economic Group

185i. SOCLS — Social Class

186. WRKHOME1 — IF PAIDWRK, PAIDMAT, UNPDMAT AT PAIDWRK1
Do you work mainly at home or do you go out to work?
1 Mainly at home
2 Go out to work

187. PREVSAME — IF PAIDWRK AT PAIDWRK1
Did you do the same or a different job before you had your baby?
1 Same
2 Different

188. PREVOCC — IF (YES AT PAIDEVR1) AND DIFFERENT AT PREVSAME OR NO AT PAIDWRK1
What was your last job before you had your baby?
REPEAT SOCNOW-SOCCLS ABOVE FOR PREVIOUS JOB

189 HUSBWORK — IF MARRIED OR COHABITING AND HUSBAND NOT ABROAD
Did your husband/partner do any paid work last week, that is in the seven days ending last Sunday, either as an employee or self-employed?
1 Yes
2 No

190. HUSBAWAY — IF NO AT HUSBWORK
Even though he was not working, did he have a job that he was away from last week?
1 Yes
2 No

191. HUSBNOWK — IF NO AT HUSBAWAY
Last week was he ....
1 Waiting to take up a job that he had already obtained
2 Looking for work
3 Intending to look for work but prevented by temporary sickness or injury
4 Going to school or college full-time
5 Permanently unable to work because of long-term sickness or disability
6 Retired
7 Looking after the home or family
8 Or was he doing something else

192. HUSBWAIT — IF WAIT AT HUSBNOWK
Apart from the job he is waiting to take up, has he ever had a paid job or done any paid work?
1 Yes
2 No

206. KITCHEN — Apart from the rooms you have mentioned, do you have the use of a kitchen, that is, a separate room in which you cook?
1 Yes
2 No
IF YES AT KITCHEN

207. KITSIZE — Is the narrowest side of the kitchen less than six and a half feet wide from wall to wall?
1 Less than six and a half feet
2 six and a half feet or more

208. SHAREKIT — Do you share the kitchen with any other household?
ASK OR RECORD
1 Yes
2 No
IF YES AT SHAREKIT

209. TAP — Do you share an indoor tap with any one other than people in your household?
1 Yes
2 No
ALL

210. REFRIG — Does your household have the use of a refrigerator in your (part of the) accommodation?
1 Yes
2 No

211. COOKER — Does your household have the use of a cooker in your (part of the) accommodation?
1 Yes
2 No

212. CAR — Is there a car or van normally available for use by you or any members of your household?
1 Yes
2 No

213. OWNRENT — Does your household own or rent this (HOUSE/FLAT/ROOM)? PROMPT IF NECESSARY
1 Owns with mortgage/loan
2 Owns outright
3 Rents LA/new town
4 Rents- Housing Association
5 Rents-Privately unfurnished
6 Rents-Privately furnished
7 Rents from employer
8 Rents- Other with payment
9 Rent free
10 Temporary accommmodation

214. FAMCRED — Can I just check are you (or your husband) currently receiving Family Credit?
1 Yes
2 No

215. INCSUP — And have you (or your husband) drawn Income Support at any time in the last 14 days?
1 Yes
2 No

216. INCOME — Could you look at this card and tell me which group represents your current GROSS income (and the income of your husband/partner)?
Please include income from all sources before any compulsary deductions such as income tax, national insurance and superannuation contributions
SHOW CARD C AND PROMPT AS NECESSARY
1 less than £50 per week
2 £50 less than £70 per week
3 £70 less than £100 per week
4 £100 less than £150 per week
5 £150 less than £200 per week
6 £200 less than £250 per week
7 £250 less than £300 per week
8 £300 less than £350 per week
9 £350 less than £400 per week
10 £400 less than £450 per week
11 £450 less than £500 per week
12 £500 or more per week
ALL

217. MHEIGHT — There is often a link between a child's height and the height of the natural parents. How tall are you?
1 Answer given in feet and inches
2 Answer given in centimetres
IF FEET/INCH AT MHEIGHT

218. FEETMOTH — Enter number of feet and follow with number of inches

219. INCHMOTH — Enter number of inches
IF CENTIMETRES AT MHEIGHT

220. CMSMOTH — Enter number of centimetres

17

ALL
221. FHEIGHT — How tall is the baby's father?
1 Answer given in feet and inches
2 Answer given in centimetres
IF FEET/INCH AT FHEIGHT

222. FEETFATH — Enter number of feet and follow with number of inches

223. INCHFATH — Enter number of inches
IF CENTIMETRES AT FHEIGHT

224. CMSFATH — Enter number of centimetres

BABY MEASUREMENTS
ALL
225. NOWLATER — Do you want to enter the measurements now or later?
1 Now
2 Later

226. DATEMEAS — Date weighed and measured

227. BABYWT — Baby's weight. Please give the weight in kilograms

228. WTREL — Was the baby's weight reliable?
1 Yes
2 No
IF BABY WEIGHED

229. WTATTEMP — PLEASE RECORD NUMBER OF ATTEMPTS AT MEASURING

230. WTAFCT — PLEASE RECORD ANY SPECIAL CIRCUMSTANCES THAT MIGHT HAVE AFFECTED WEIGHT
1 No special circumstances
2 Scales on uneven surface
3 Other (Please specify at next question)
IF OTHER AT WTAFCT

231. XWTFACT — WRITE IN OTHER CIRCUMSTANCES AFFECTING WEIGHT
ALL

232. HEADCIRC — Child's head circumference. Please give the circumference in centimetres

233. HEADREL — Was head circumference reliable?
1 Yes
2 No
IF HEAD CIRCUMFERENCE MEASURED

233. HDATTEMP — PLEASE RECORD NUMBER OF ATTEMPTS AT MEASURING

234. HDAFCT — PLEASE RECORD ANY SPECIAL CIRCUMSTANCES THAT MIGHT HAVE AFFECTED MEASUREMENT
1 No special circumstances
2 Did not keep still
3 Other (Please specify at next question)
IT OTHER AT HDAFCT

234a. XHDAFCT — WRITE IN OTHER CIRCUMSTANCES AFFECTING HEAD CIRCUMFERENCE MEASUREMENT
ALL

235. ARMCIRC — Child's mid upper arm circumference PLEASE RECORD THE CIRCUMFERENCE IN MILLIMETRES

236. ARMREL — Was arm circumference reliable?
1 Yes
2 No
IF ARM CIRCUMFERENCE MEASURED

237. ARATTEMP — PLEASE RECORD NUMBER OF ATTEMPTS AT MEASURING

238. ARAFCT — PLEASE RECORD ANY SPECIAL CIRCUMSTANCES THAT MIGHT HAVE AFFECTED MEASUREMENT
1 No special circumstances
2 Did not keep still
3 Other (Please specify at next question)
IF OTHER AT ARAFCT

238a. XARAFCT — WRITE IN OTHER CIRCUMSTANCES AFFECTING ARM CIRCUMFERENCE MEASUREMENT
ALL

239. LENGTH — Child's supine length. PLEASE GIVE THE LENGTH IN CENTIMETRES

18

INFANT FEEDING SURVEY
WAVE 2 QUESTIONNAIRE

Wave 1 variables carried forward to Wave 2 so that the appropriate Wave 2 questions could be asked.

1. NAME 1 — Baby's name
2. BIRTHDAT — Baby's date of birth
3. LANGUAG — Main language spoken at home?
4. ENGUND — Respondent's understanding of English
5. HUSBAND — Whether respondent has husband or partner in household
6. FEEDMODE — Method of feeding - breast or bottle fed
7. BOTTLE1 — Baby occasionally given milk in a bottle
8. SOLIDS1 — Baby eats solid foods
9. PAIDWRK1 — Mother doing paid work
10. HUSBPAID — Husband or partner doing paid work
11. NPERSONS — Number of people normally living in household
12. NADULTS — Number of people aged 16 or over normally living in household
13. NCHILD — Number of children aged under 16 normally living in household

Wave 2 Questions

14. NPERSON2 — I would like to begin by asking whether your household has changed since I/we last spoke to you. How many people are normally living in this household now?
15. NADULTS2 — How many people aged 16 or over are normally living in this household?
16. NCHILD2 — How many children aged under 16 are there normally living in this household?

17. HOUSEHOLD BOX (transferred from Wave 1) **The table contains the following 6 questions:**
17a. NAME — Baby's name
17b. SEX — 1 Male 2 Female
17c. AGE
17d. MARSTAT — Marital status
 1 Married
 2 Living together
 3 Single
 4 Widowed, divorced or separated
17e. RELTOMUM — Relationship of (....) to MOTHER
17f. STILLIN — (May I just check) is (.....) still living in the household?
 1 Yes
 2 No
18. NEWPPLE — Are there any people who normally live here now, but who were not living here when I/we last spoke to you?
 1 Yes
 2 No
19. HOUSEHOLD BOX - NEW PEOPLE **The table contains the following 6 questions about every new person in the household:**
19a. NAME
19b. SEX — 1 Male 2 Female
19c. AGE — Can I just check, what is (......) age now?
19d. MARSTAT — Is (......)
 1 Married
 2 Living together
 3 Single
 4 Widowed, divorced or separated

1

---

240. LTHREL — Was supine length reliable?
 1 Yes
 2 No

IF LENGTH MEASURED

241. LGATTEMP — PLEASE RECORD NUMBER OF ATTEMPTS AT MEASURING LENGTH

242. LGAFCT — PLEASE RECORD ANY SPECIAL CIRCUMSTANCES THAT MIGHT HAVE AFFECTED MEASUREMENT
 1 No special circumstances
 2 Could not straighten legs
 3 Could not lie flat
 4 Unable to lie still
 5 Uneven surface
 6 Other (Please specify at next question)

IF OTHER AT LGAFCT

242a. XLGAFCT — WRITE IN OTHER CIRCUMSTANCES WHICH MIGHT HAVE AFFECTED SUPINE LENGTH

ALL

243. FOLLOWUP — If we want to contact you about this survey in the future, will it be alright to call on you again?
 1 Yes, it would be alright (UNCONDITIONAL)
 2 No (UNCONDITIONAL)
 3 Yes (WITH CONDITIONS/ QUALIFICATIONS)

INTERVIEWER CODE

ALL

244. OTHPRES — Was another adult present at the interview?
 1 Yes
 2 No

IF YES AT OTHPRES

245. WHOELSE — Who else was present?
 1 Husband or partner
 2 Mother
 3 Mother-in-law
 4 Other female relative
 5 Other male relative
 6 Friend or neighbour
 7 Other (Please specify at next question)

246. XWHOELSE — WRITE IN WHO ELSE WAS PRESENT

IF MAIN LANGUAGE NOT ENGLISH

247. INTERP — Was an interpreter used?
 1 Yes
 2 No

IF YES AT INTERP

248. WHOINTRP — Who interpreted?
 1 Husband
 2 Other family member
 3 Friend/neigbour
 4 OPCS/Other govt.interpreter
 5 Professional interpreter
 6 Other (Please specify at next question)

248a. XWHOINTP — WRITE IN WHO INTERPRETED

IF YES AT INTERP

249. LGEINTRP — Which language?
 1 Gujarati
 2 Punjabi
 3 Bengali
 4 Hindi
 5 Urdu
 6 Others

250. WHTASIAN — Was the respondent an Asian in the White sample?
 1 Yes
 2 No

19

19e. RELTOMUM — What is the relationship of (....) to you?

19f. MOREPEOP — Are there any more new people who normally live in this household?
1 Yes
2 No

ALL

20. EARLY — First of all, can I just check, was (....) born at the right time or was he/she born early?

IF EARLY

21. WKSEARLY — How many weeks early was (...) born?

ALL
PLEASE ENTER NUMBER OF WEEKS

22. START — I would like to ask you some questions about how you feed (.......) now
1 CONTINUE

IF BREASTFED OR BREAST AND BOTTLE FED AT FEEDMODE

23. STILBRST — Are you still breast feeding (.......) at all?
1 Yes
2 No

IF YES AT STILBRST

24. NFEEDS — How many times a day do you breast feed him/her now?

25. BRDTIM2 — Do you breast feed him/her on demand or do you generally keep to set feeding times?
1 Demand
2 Set times
3 Depends

26. BRLONG2 — How old do you think he/she will be when you stop breast feeding?

TO ANSWER IN MONTHS, SELECT MONTHS AND RECORD NUMBER OF MONTHS AT NEXT QUESTION
1 Months
2 Will breast feed for as long as able
3 Will breast feed for as long as he/she wants

IF MONTHS AT BRLONG 2

27. BRMON2 — RECORD NUMBER OF MONTHS

IF YES AT STILBRST

28. BOTTLE2 — Do you give your baby milk in a bottle at present even if only occasionally? (apart from expressed breast milk)?
1 Yes (even if occasionally)
2 No

IF NO AT STILBRST

29. LBRW2 — How old was your baby when you last breast fed him/her?
PLEASE ENTER NUMBER OF WEEKS

30. LBRST2 — What were your reasons for stopping breast feeding? PROMPT AS NECESSARY
1 Insufficient milk
2 Painful breasts or nipples
3 Baby would not suck/rejected
4 Breastfeeding took too long/was tiring
5 Mother was ill
6 Baby was ill
7 Returned to work
8 Baby could not be fed by others
9 Inconvenient/no place to feed
10 Breastfed for as long as intended
11 Other

IF OTHER AT LBRST2

30a. XLBRST2 — WRITE IN OTHER REASON

31. LONGBR2 — Would you have liked to have continued breast feeding for longer?
1 Yes
2 No

IF (BOTTLE FED AT FEEDMODE OR (YES AT BOTTLE 2) OR (NO AT STILBRST)

32. MILKTYP2 — (When you bottle feed) Which kind of milk do you give your baby MOST of the time at the moment? ENTER 24 IF NOT IN LIST AND SPECIFY AT NEXT QUESTION
1 Cow & Gate Premium (powder)
2 Cow & Gate nutrition Premium (powder)
3 Cow & Gate Premium (ready-to-feed)
4 Cow & Gate Plus (powder)
5 Cow & Gate Nutrition Plus (powder)
6 Cow & Gate Plus (ready-to-feed)
7 Cow & Gate Formula S (powder)
8 Cow & Gate InfaSoy (powder)
9 Cow & Gate Step-up
10 SMA Gold Cap (powder)
11 SMA Gold Cap (readty-to-feed)
12 SMA White Cap (powder)
13 SMA White Cap (ready-to-feed)
14 SMA Wysoy (powder)
15 SMA Progress
16 Milupa Milumil (powder)
17 Milupa Aptamil (powder)
18 Milupa Prematil (powder)
19 Farley's Follow-on Milk
20 Farley's First Milk
21 Farley's OsterSoy
22 Boots Follow-on Milk (powder)
23 Boots Follow-on Milk (ready-to-feed)
24 Other kind of milk — Please specify at next question

IF OTHER AT MILKTYP2

32a. XMILKTY2 — WRITE IN NAME OF MILK — If liquid cow's milk please specify whether
(a) ordinary (whole) milk
(b) semi-skimmed
(c) skimmed milk

IF OTHER THAN NO AT BOTTLE2

33. STARTBOT — How old was (.....) when you started giving this kind of milk? SELECT WEEKS OR MONTHS AND RECORD AT NEXT QUESTION
1 Weeks
2 Months

IF WEEKS AT STARTBOT

34. WEEKST — RECORD NUMBER OF WEEKS

IF MONTHS AT STARTBOT

35. MONTHST — RECORD NUMBER OF MONTHS

IF OTHER THAN NO AT BOTTLE2

36. NBOTTLE — How many times a day do you give him/her a bottle of milk?

37. NOUNCE — How many fluid ounces of milk does he/she usually drink at each feed?
INTERVIEWER - IF AMOUNT IS VARIABLE WORK OUT AVERAGE

38. BOFDTIM2 — Do you bottle feed him/her on demand or do you generally keep to set feeding times?
1 on demand
2 set times
3 Depends

ALL

39. MTOKEN2 — Do you get milk tokens for free or reduced price milk?
1 Yes, Free milk
2 Yes, Reduced price milk
3 No, Neither

IF FREE OR REDUCED PRICE MILK AT MTOKEN2

40. MTOKEXC2 — Where do you exchange the tokens for milk?
1 Clinic
2 Milkman
3 Elsewhere — Please specify at next question

IF ELSEWHERE AT MTOKEXC2

40a. XTOKEXC2 — WRITE IN where milk tokens are exchanged.

IF MILKMAN OR OTHER AT MTOKEXC2

41. CHCMILK2 — Do you ever buy your baby's milk from the child health clinic?
1 Yes always
2 Sometimes
3 No

53. SOLREG2
IF YES AT SOLIDS1 OR SOLIDS2
At present, are you giving your baby cereal, rusks or any other solid food (soft weaning food) every day?
1 Yes
2 No

54. SOLR2M
IF YES AT SOLREG2
At which feeds do you regularly offer your baby solid (soft weaning) food at the moment?
1 Morning (before noon)
2 Afternoon (noon to before 6pm)
3 Evening (6pm to midnight)
4 Some other feed

54a. XSOLR2M
IF OTHER AT SOLR2M
WRITE IN THE NAMES OF OTHER FEEDS AT WHICH BABY IS OFFERED SOLID FOOD

55. SOLYEST2
Did you give your baby any cereal, rusks or solid food (soft weaning food) to eat yesterday?
1 Yes
2 No

56. SOLIDS TABLE
THE TABLE CONTAINS THE FOLLOWING 5 QUESTIONS:

56a. TYPEFOOD
What type of solid food did he/she eat?

56b. BABYFOOD
Was it baby food bought from a shop, homemade food or other food bought from a shop?
1 baby food bought from shop
2 homemade food
3 other food bought from a shop

56c. TIMEFEED
At which feed did he/she eat this solid food (soft weaning food)?
PROMPT AS NECESSARY
1 Morning (before noon)
2 Afternoon (noon to before 6pm)
3 Evening (6pm to midnight)
4 Some other feed

56d. AMOUNT
How many teaspoons of TYPEFOOD did he/she eat?
SHOW CARD E AND CONVERT TO TEASPOONS IF NECESSARY

56e. ANYMORE
Did you give your baby any more solid food yesterday?
1 Yes
2 No

---

57. MILKMIX
IF YES AT SOLREG2
Do you ever use milk to mix up his/her food?
1 Yes
2 No

58. TYPEMIX
IF YES AT MILKMIX
Do you use milk especially for babies, liquid cows milk, or something else?
1 Baby milk
2 Liquid cows milk
3 Something else
Please specify at next question

58a. XTYPEMIX
IF SOMETHING ELSE AT TYPEMIX
WRITE IN WHAT ELSE IS USED TO MIX UP FOOD

59. SOLIDOLD
IF MORE THAN 2 FEEDS SELECTED AT SOLR2M
How old was your baby when he/she regularly started having three meals of solid food a day?
SELECT WEEKS OR MONTHS AND RECORD AT NEXT QUESTION
1 Weeks
2 Months

60. SOLDWEEK
IF WEEKS AT SOLIDOLD
RECORD BABY'S AGE IN WEEKS

61. SOLDMON
IF MONTHS AT SOLIDOLD
RECORD BABY'S AGE IN MONTHS

62. FACTORS
What do you think is important when choosing what solid (soft weaning) food to give your baby?
1 Variety
2 Nutrition
3 Baby's preferences
4 Sugar content
5 Additives
6 Vitamins
7 Salt content
8 Home cooked
9 Ease of preparation
10 Price
11 Diet-halal, vegetarian, other special
12 Other

62a. XFACTORS
IF OTHER AT FACTORS
WRITE IN OTHER FACTORS

5

---

42. HOWSTER2
IF (BREASTFED AT FEEDMODE AND NO AT BOTTLE1 AND NO AT STILBRST) OR (YES AT BOTTLE2)
How do you USUALLY sterilise the bottles?
1 Sterilising tablets
2 Sterilising fluid
3 Bottle steamer
4 Hot Water
5 Microwave
6 Other method
Please specify at next question

42a. XHOWSTE2
IF OTHER AT HOWSTER2
WRITE IN OTHER METHOD OF STERILISING BOTTLES

43. WHOMAKE2
Who usually makes up the bottles?
1 Self
2 Husband or partner
3 Other children in the family
4 Other person
Please specify at next question

43a. XWHOMAK2
IF OTHER AT WHOMAKE2
Write in who else usually makes up the bottles

44. ADDMILK2
Do you ever add anything to the milk in the bottle?
1 Yes
2 No

45. WHATADD2
IF YES AT ADDMILK2
What do you add to the milk?
1 Sugar
2 Other
Please specify at next question

45a. XWHATAD2
IF OTHER AT WHATADD2
WRITE IN WHAT IS ADDED TO THE MILK

46. BOTMORE2
Do you ever make up more than one bottle at a time?
1 Yes
2 No

---

47. STORMAD2
IF YES AT BOTMORE2
Where do you USUALLY store the made up bottles?
1 Fridge
2 Cool Place
3 Kitchen work surface
4 Other
Please specify at next question

47a. XSTORE2
IF OTHER AT STORMAD2
WRITE IN where made up bottles stored

48. BOTLATE2
If your baby doesn't take all of its feed, do you ever keep it to use later?
1 Yes
2 No
3 Sometimes

49. SOLIDS2
IF NO AT SOLIDS1
Do you give your baby foods such as cereal, rusk or any other kind of solid food (soft weaning food), including any that you make yourself?
1 Yes
2 No

50. SOLAGE2
IF YES AT SOLIDS2
How old was your baby when he/she first had any food apart from milk?
PLEASE ENTER NUMBER OF WEEKS

51. SOLFRST2
What was the first food your baby had, apart from milk?
DESCRIBE NAME OF FOOD AND BRAND

52. SOLMEAL2
At which feed did you first offer your baby solid food (soft weaning food)?
1 Morning (before noon)
2 Afternoon (noon to before 6pm)
3 Evening (6pm to midnight)
4 Some other feed

52a. XSOLMEA2
IF OTHER AT SOLMEAL 2
WRITE IN NAME OF OTHER FEED WHEN BABY FIRST OFFERED SOLID (SOFT WEANING) FOOD

4

63. FAMDIET

ALL

(May I just check) Do most of the people living in this household eat only a vegetarian diet?

1 Yes
2 No

64. DRINK2

ALL

Apart from milk, do you give your baby water or anything else to drink at the moment?

1 Yes
2 No

65. WATER2

IF YES AT DRINK2

Does your baby USUALLY have plain water or some other type of drink? PROMPT IF NECESSARY

1 Plain Water
3 Water with sugar or honey added
2 Herbal drinks
4 Other

66. WATERTYP

IF PLAIN AT WATER2

Is that ....

1 water from the tap
2 water that you have boiled yourself
3 mineral water
4 purified water bought from a shop
5 or some other type of water?
Please specify at next question

66a. XWATERTY

IF OTHER AT WATERTYP

WRITE IN OTHER TYPE OF WATER

67. MINWATER

IF MINERAL AT WATERTYP

What brand of mineral water do you use?

1 Volvic
2 Malvern
3 Evian
4 Spa
5 Perrier
6 Other
Please specify at next question

67a. XMINWATER

IF OTHER AT MINWATER

WRITE IN OTHER BRAND OF MINERAL WATER

6

68. DRINKS TABLE

IF HERBAL DRINKS OR DRINKS OTHER THAN WATER AT WATER2

THE TABLE CONTAINS THE FOLLOWING 5 QUESTIONS:

68a. TYPDRINK — What other/herbal drink(s) do you gave your baby?

68b. BRAND — What is the name of the brand? PLEASE WRITE IN IF HOME MADE

68c. FLAVOUR — What is the flavour of the drink?

68d. BABYDRK — Is it a baby drink?
1 Yes
2 No

68e. ANYMORE — INTERVIEWER - ARE THERE ANY OTHER DRINKS
1 Yes
2 No

69. RDRINK2M — Why do you give your baby drinks? PROMPT AS NECESSARY

1 Because he/she is thirsty
2 Hungry between feeds
3 To give him/her extra vitamins
4 To help his/her digestion
5 To help his/her colic/wind
6 To help his/her constipation
7 Good for baby
8 Or for some other reason?

69a. XRDRNK2M

IF OTHER AT RDRINK2M

WRITE IN OTHER REASONS FOR GIVING BABY DRINKS

70. VIT2

ALL

Do you give your baby any extra vitamins at the moment (apart from any vitamin drinks you have already mentioned)?

1 Yes
2 No

71. VITDROP2

IF YES AT VIT2

Do you use Children's Vitamin Drops from the child health clinic or another brand?

1 Children's Vitamin Drops
2 Other Please specify at next question

71a. XVITDRP2

IF OTHER AT VITDROP2

WRITE IN NAME OF OTHER BRAND

72. VITBUY2

IF CHILDREN'S VITAMIN DROPS AT VITDROP2

Do you buy the vitamins or do you get them free from the clinic or on prescription?

1 Buy
2 Free
3 On Prescription

73. VITOTHER2

IF OTHER AT VITDROP2

Do you buy the vitamins or do you get them on prescription?

1 Buy
2 On Prescription

74. VITM2

ALL

Are you taking any extra vitamins or iron tablets yourself at the moment, either in tablet or powder form?

1 Yes
2 No

75. VITM2GET

IF YES AT VITM2

Where do you usually get the vitamins/iron tablets?

1 child health clinic
2 elsewhere

76. VITM2BUY

IF CHILD HEALTH CLINIC AT VITM2GET

Do you buy the vitamins/iron tablets or do you get them free from the clinic or on prescription?

1 Buy
2 Free
3 Prescription

77. VITM2OTH

IF ELSEWHERE AT VITM2GET

Do you buy the vitamins or do you get them on prescription?

1 Buy
2 On Prescription

78. CHECKUP2

ALL

I would like to ask you some questions about who gives you advice and helps you if you have any feeding problems. Do you take your baby anywhere for advice or regular check-ups?

1 Yes
2 No

79. WHERCHEC

IF YES AT CHECKUP2

Where do you take him/her?

1 Child health clinic
2 Family Doctor
3 Somewhere else Please specify at next question

80. OTHCHECK

IF OTHER AT WHERCHEC

WRITE IN WHERE BABY IS TAKEN FOR ADVICE OR CHECK-UPS

81. CLINOFT

IF CHILD HEALTH CLINIC AT WHERCHEC

How often do you take him/her to the child health clinic?

1 Once a week
2 Once a fortnight
3 Once a month
4 Less than once a month

82. DOCOFT

IF FAMILY DOCTOR AT WHERCHEC

How often do you take him/her to the doctor?

1 Once a week
2 Once a fortnight
3 Once a month
4 Less than once a month

83. OTHEROFT

IF OTHER AT WHERCHEC

How often do you take him/her to the (.......)?

1 Once a week
2 Once a fortnight
3 Once a month
4 Less than once a month

84. PROBFEED

ALL

Have you had any problems feeding or weaning your baby since I/we last spoke to you?

1 Yes
2 No

7

85. WHATPROB

IF YES AT PROBFEED

What problems have you had?......

1 Baby was hungry
2 Baby was ill
3 Baby didn't like breast milk
4 Baby didn't like bottled milk
5 Baby vomiting
6 Baby would not take solids
7 Baby would only take certain food
8 Baby was uninterested in food
9 Some other reason

85a. OTHPROB

IF OTHER AT WHATPROB

WRITE IN OTHER PROBLEMS WITH FEEDING BABY

86. GIVEHELP

IF YES AT PROBFEED

Did anyone give you help or advice about this/these problems?

1 Yes
2 No

87. OTHELP

IF NO AT PROBFEED

Has anyone given you help or advice on feeding or weaning since I/we last spoke to you?

1 Yes
2 No

88. WHOHELP

IF YES AT GIVEHELP OR OTHELP

Who helped or advised you?

1 Health visitor
2 Doctor at the child health clinic
3 Family doctor
4 Nurse at the doctors surgery
5 Friend or relative
6 Voluntary group for new mothers
7 Someone else
   Please specify at next question

88a. XWHOHELP

IF OTHER AT WHOHELP

WRITE IN WHO ELSE HELPED OR ADVISED YOU

89. HVLANG

IF (HEALTH VISITOR AT WHOHELP) AND (LANGUAGE OTHER THAN ENGLISH) AND (NOT VERY WELL OR NOT AT ALL AT ENGUND)

Which language did the health visitor speak?

1 English
2 Gujarati
3 Punjabi
4 Bengali
5 Hindi
6 Urdu
7 Other

90. HVUND

IF ENGLISH AT HVLANG

Did you understand the health visitor ...

1 all of the time
2 most of the time
3 some of the time
4 not at all
5 or did someone interpret?

91. CDOCLANG

IF (DOCTOR AT CHILD HEALTH CLINIC AT WHOHELP) AND (LANGUAGE OTHER THAN ENGLISH) AND (NOT VERY WELL OR NOT AT ALL AT ENGUND)

Which language did the doctor at the child health clinic speak?

1 English
2 Gujarati
3 Punjabi
4 Bengali
5 Hindi
6 Urdu
7 Other

92. CDOCUND

IF ENGLISH AT CDOCLANG

Did you understand the doctor ...

1 all of the time
2 most of the time
3 some of the time
4 not at all
5 or did someone interpret?

93. GPLANG

IF (FAMILY DOCTOR AT WHOHELP) AND (LANGUAGE OTHER THAN ENGLISH) AND (NOT VERY WELL OR NOT AT ALL AT ENGUND)

Which language did your family doctor speak?

1 English
2 Gujarati
3 Punjabi
4 Bengali
5 Hindi
6 Urdu
7 Other

94. GPUND

IF ENGLISH AT GPLANG

Did you understand the doctor ...

1 all of the time
2 most of the time
3 some of the time
4 not at all
5 or did someone interpret?

95. NURSLANG

IF (NURSE AT WHOHELP) AND (LANGUAGE OTHER THAN ENGLISH) AND (NOT VERY WELL OR NOT AT ALL AT ENGUND)

Which language did the nurse at the doctors surgery speak?

1 English
2 Gujarati
3 Punjabi
4 Bengali
5 Hindi
6 Urdu
7 Other

96. NURSUND

IF ENGLISH AT NURSLANG

Did you understand the nurse ...

1 all of the time
2 most of the time
3 some of the time
4 not at all
5 or did someone interpret?

97. WHICHGRP

IF VOLUNTARY GROUP AT WHOHELP

Which voluntary group helped or advised you?

1 a local womens group
2 the National Childbirth Trust
3 La Leche League
4 the Association of Breast Feeding Mothers some other voluntary group
5 Please specify at next question

97a. XGROUP

IF OTHER AT WHICHGRP

WRITE IN WHO RUNS THE OTHER VOLUNTARY GROUP

98. LEAFLET2

ALL

Since we last spoke to you, have you read any books, leaflets, or magazines, or watched any videos about looking after babies?

1 Yes
2 No

99. LEAFGET

IF YEST AT LEAFLET2

Where did you get it/them from?

1 Health visitor
2 Child health clinic
3 Doctor's surgery
4 Bought from a shop
5 Other Please specify at next question

99a. XLEAFGET

IF OTHER AT LEAFGET

WRITE IN WHERE GOT LEAFLETS ETC.

100. LEAFLANG

IF YES AT LEAFLET2 AND (LANGUAGE OTHER THAN ENGLISH) AND (NOT VERY WELL OR NOT AT ALL AT ENGUND)

What language were they in?

1 English
2 Gujarati
3 Punjabi
4 Bengali
5 Hindi
6 Urdu
7 Other

101. LOCGROUP

ALL

Do you go to any local groups for mothers with young babies?

1 Yes
2 No

102. GROUPORG

IF YES AT LOCGROUP

Who is the group organised by?

1 Child Health Clinic
2 Family doctor
3 Health Visitor
4 Religious organisation
5 Someone else
   Please specify at next question

Page 11 (right box)

111. SOCTEXT1
IF NOT SAME JOB AS BEFORE
What is your job?

111a. EMP
Are you working as ...
1 Employee
2 Self employed

111b. SUPMAN
Are you a manager or supervisor of any kind?
1 Manager
2 Supervisor
3 Other Employee

111c. NEMPLEE
EMPLOYEE - SIZE OF ESTABLISHMENT
How many employees work(ed) in the establishment?
1 1 - 24
2 25+

111d. NSLFEMP
SELF EMPLOYED - SIZE OF ESTABLISHMENT
How many employees
0 Self employed with no staff
1 Self employed with employees in estab with 1 - 24 employees
2 Self employed with employees in estab with 25+ employees

111e. SOCNOW
Is occupational coding to be done now or later?
1 Now
2 Later

111f. EMPSTAT
Employment status and Establishment size

111g. SOCCODE
1 Employee not elsewhere classified
2 Foreman or supervisor
3 Self Employed - no employees
4 Self Employed - Small establishment
5 Self Employed - Large establishment
6 Manager - Small establishment
7 Manager - Large establishment

111h. SEGRP
Socio-Economic Group

111i. SOCLS
Social Class

---

112. WRKHOME2
Do you work mainly at home or do you go out to work?
1 Mainly at home
2 Go out to work

IF PAID WORK AT PAIDWRK2

113. WHOMINDS
Who usually looks after the baby when you are working?
1 Self
2 Husband or partner
3 Mother
4 Mother-in-law
5 Other female relative
6 Child minder
7 Nursery or creche
8 Someone else
Please specify at next question

113a. XWHOMIND
IF OTHER AT WHOMINDS
WRITE IN WHO ELSE USUALLY LOOKS AFTER BABY WHEN WORKING

IF OTHER THAN SELF OR HUSBAND/PARTNER AT WHOMINDS

114. PAYMIND
Do you pay to have the baby looked after?
1 Yes
2 No

IF ON MATERNITY LEAVE OR NOT WORKING AT PAIDWRK2

115. WRKPLAN2
Do you plan to start work (again) in the next two years ..
1 Now
2 Later

IF YES AT WRKPLAN2

116. FULLPAR2
Do you plan to work full or part-time?
1 Full-time
2 Part-time

Page 10 (bottom box)

102a. XGRPORG
IF OTHER AT GROUPORG
WRITE IN WHO THE GROUP IS ORGANISED BY

103. GROUPLAN
IF YES AT LOCGROUP AND (LANGUAGE OTHER THAN ENGLISH) AND (NOT VERY WELL OR NOT AT ALL AT ENGUND)
What language do you speak with other mothers at the group(s)?
1 English
2 Gujarati
3 Punjabi
4 Bengali
5 Hindi
6 Urdu
7 Other

104. GROUPFED
IF YES AT LOCGROUP
Do you talk about feeding babies at this (these) group(s)?
1 Yes
2 No

ALL

105. PUBPLACE
Do you ever take your baby out to public places, for example, to a park or to the shops?
1 Yes, even if only occasionally
2 No, never

IF YEST AT PUBPLACE

106. PUBPROB
Have you ever had problems finding somewhere to feed your baby when you were out in public places?
1 Yes
2 No
3 Only go out between feeds

IF YES OR NO AT PUBPROB AND BREASTFED OR BREAST AND BOTTLE AT FEEDMODE

107. PUBBRFED
Have you ever breast fed your baby in a public place other than a hospital?
1 Yes
2 No

107a. PUBPREF
IF YES AT PUBBRFED
When you breastfeed in a public place do you ....
1 prefer to use a mother and baby room
2 prefer to breastfeed without going to any special place
3 have no preference where you breastfed

108. WHERFAC
IF YES AT PUBPLACE
Where do you think that it is important to have somewhere for feeding babies?
1 Shops / Shopping Centres
2 Restaurants
3 Public Toilets
4 Stations / Airports
5 Unimportant to have facilities
6 Other Please specify at next question

108a. XWHERFAC
IF OTHER AT WHERFAC
WRITE IN OTHER PLACES WHICH SHOULD HAVE FACILITIES

ALL

109. PAIDWRK2
I would like to ask some questions about yourself (and your husband/partner). At the moment are you ....
1 doing any paid work including working at home
2 on paid maternity leave
3 on unpaid maternity leave
4 not working or not on maternity leave?

IF HAS WORKED NOT WORKING OR NOT ON MATERNITY LEAVE AT WAVE 1 AND WORKING AT WAVE 2

110. MSAMEJOB
Was that the same job that you had before?
1 Yes
2 No

IF HUSBAND/PARTNER IN HOUSEHOLD

117. HUSBWOR2 — Did your husband/partner do any paid work last week that is in the seven days ending last Sunday, either as an employee or self-employed?
1 Yes
2 No

IF HUSBAND/PARTNER NOT WORKING LAST WEEK AT HUSBWOR2

118. HUSBAWA2 — Even though he was not working, did he have a job that he was away from last week?
1 Yes
2 No

IF HUSBAND/PARTNER WORKING LAST WEEK OR USUALLY WORKS BUT AWAY LAST WEEK

119. HSAMEJOB — Was that the same job that he had when we last spoke to you?
1 Yes
2 No

IF NO AT HSAMEJOB

120. HUSBNOW2 — Last week was he.....
1 Waiting to take up a job that he had already obtained
2 Looking for work
3 Intending to look for work but prevented by temporary sickness or injury
4 Going to school or college full time
5 Permanently unable to work because of long-term sickness or disability
6 Retired
7 Looking after the home or family
8 or was he doing something else?

IF WAITING AT HUSBNOW2

121. HUSBWK22 — What is the job your husband/partner is waiting to take up?

IF HUSBAND/PARTNER NOT WORKING AT WAVE 1 BUT WORKING AT WAVE 2 OR NEW TO HOUSEHOLD

122. HUSBWK12 — What is your husband's/partner's job?
[Repeat Questions 111-111i (EMP-SOCLS) above for husband]

ALL

123. SMKNOW2 — I would like to ask about smoking. Do you smoke cigarettes at all nowadays?
1 Yes
2 No

IF HUSBAND/PARTNER IN HOUSEHOLD

124. SMKHSNO2 — Does your husband/partner smoke cigarettes at all nowadays?
1 Yes
2 No

ALL

125. SAMEADD — (May I just check) Are you still living in the same house/flat as when I/we last spoke to you?
1 Yes
2 No

IF NO AT SAMEADD

126. BEDROOM2 — I would like to ask about your household's new accommodation, not counting any rooms you may let or sublet. How many bedrooms do you have, including bed sitting rooms and spare bedrooms?

127. OTHROOM2 — How many other rooms do you have, not counting kitchens, bathrooms and toilets?

128. KITCHEN2 — Apart from the rooms you have mentioned, do you have the use of a kitchen, that is, a separate room in which you cook?
1 Yes
2 No

IF YES AT KITCHEN2

129. KITSIZE2 — Is the narrowest side of the kitchen less than six and a half feet wide from wall to wall?
1 Less than six and a half feet
2 six and a half feet or more

130. SHAREKI2 — Do you share the kitchen with any other household? ASK OR RECORD
1 Yes
2 No

IF YES AT SHAREKI2

131. TAP2 — Do you share an indoor tap with anyone other than people in your household?
1 Yes
2 No

IF NO AT SAMEADD

132. REFRIG2 — (May I just check) Does your household have the use of a refrigerator in your (part of the) accommodation?
1 Yes
2 No

133. COOKER2 — Does your household have the use of a cooker in your (part of the) accommodation?
1 Yes
2 No

134. OWNRENT2 — Does your household own or rent this HOUSE/FLAT/ROOM. PROMPT IF NECESSARY
1 Owns with mortgage/loan
2 Owns outright
3 Rents LA/new town
4 Rents Housing Association
5 Rents privately unfurnished
6 Rents privately furnished
7 Rents from employer
8 Rents other with payment
9 Rent free
10 Temporary accommodation

ALL

135. CAR2 — (May I just check) Is there a car or van normally available for use by you or any members of your household?
1 Yes
2 No

136. FAMCRED2 — Can I just check are you (or your husband) currently receiving Family Credit?
1 Yes
2 No

137. INCSUP2 — And have you (or your husband) drawn Income Support at any time in the last 14 days?
1 Yes
2 No

138. INCOME2 — Could you look at this card and tell me which group represents your current GROSS income (and the income of your husband/partner). Please include income from all sources before any compulsory deductions such as income tax, national insurance and superannuation contributions?
SHOW CARD C AND PROMPT AS NECESSARY
1 Less than £50 per week
2 £50-less £70 per week
3 £70-less £100 per week
4 £100-less £150 per week
5 £150-less £200 per week
6 £200-less £250 per week
7 £250-less £300 per week
8 £300-less £350 per week
9 £350-less £400 per week
10 £400-less £450 per week
11 £450-less £500 per week
12 £500 or more per week

ALL

139. NOWLATER — Do you want to enter the measurements of the baby now or later?
1 Now
2 Later

140. DATEMEA2 — Date weighed and measured

IF BABY WEIGHED

141. BABYWT2 — Baby's weight (kilograms)

142. WTREL2 — Do you think the weight is reliable?
1 Yes
2 No

143. WTATTEM2 — NUMBER OF ATTEMPTS AT WEIGHING

INTERVIEWER CODE

ALL

159. OTHPRES2 — Was another adult present at the interview?
1 Yes
2 No

IF YES AT OTHPRES2
160. WHOELSE2 — Who else was present?
1 Interpreter
2 Husband or partner
3 Mother
4 Mother-in-law
5 Other female relative
6 Other male relative
7 Friend or neighbour
8 Other

IF OTHER AT WHOELSE2
160a. XWHOELS2 — WRITE IN Who else was present

IF MAIN LANGUAGE NOT ENGLISH
161. Interp2 — Was an interpreter used?
1 Yes
2 No

IF YES AT INTERP2
162. Whointr2 — Who interpreted?
1 Husband
2 Family
3 Friend
4 OPCS/other govt. interpreter
4 Professional interpreter
6 Other

IF OTHER AT WHOINTR2
162a. XWHOINT2 — WRITE IN WHO INTERPRETED

IF YES AT INTERP2
163. LGEINTR2 — Which language?
1 Gujarati
2 Punjabi
3 Bengali
4 Hindi
5 Urdu
6 Other

HC25/5 7/96
15

---

144. WTAFCT2 — SPECIAL CIRCUMSTANCES THAT MIGHT HAVE AFFECTED WEIGHT
1 No special circumstances
2 Scales on uneven surface
3 Other specify at next question

IF OTHER AT WTAFCT2
144a. XWTAFCT2 — WRITE IN other circumstances affecting weight

IF HEAD CIRCUMFERENCE MEASURED
145. HEADCIR2 — Head circumference (centimetres)

146. HEADREL2 — Do you think the measurement of head circumference is reliable?
1 Yes
2 No

147. HDATTEM2 — NUMBER OF ATTEMPTS AT MEASURING HEAD CIRCUMFERENCE

148. HDAFCT2 — SPECIAL CIRCUMSTANCES THAT MIGHT HAVE AFFECTED MEASUREMENT
1 No special circumstances
2 Did not keep still
3 Other please specify at next question

IF OTHER AT HDAFCT2
148a. XHDAFCT2 — WRITE IN other circumstances affecting head circumference measurement.

IF ARM CIRCUMFERENCE MEASURED
149. ARMCIRC2 — Mid upper arm circumference (centimetres)

150. ARMREL2 — Do you think the measurement of arm circumference is reliable?
1 Yes
2 No

151. ARATTEM2 — NUMBER OF ATTEMPTS AT MEASURING ARM CIRCUMFERENCE

152. ARAFCT2 — SPECIAL CIRCUMSTANCES THAT MIGHT HAVE AFFECTED MEASUREMENT
1 No special circumstances
2 Did not keep still
3 Other please specify at next question

IF OTHER AT ARAFCT2
152a. XARAFCT2 — WRITE IN other circumstances affecting arm circumference measurement

IF LENGTH MEASURED
153. LENGTH2 — Supine length (centimetres)

154. LTHREL2 — Do you think the supine length measurement is reliable
1 Yes
2 No

155. LGATTEM2 — NUMBER OF ATTEMPTS AT MEASURING LENGTH

156. LGAFCT2 — SPECIAL CIRCUMSTANCES THAT MIGHT HAVE AFFECTED MEASUREMENT
1 No special circumstances
2 Uneven surface
3 Did not lie still
4 Legs not straight
5 Did not lie flat
6 Other Please specify at next question

IF OTHER AT LGAFCT2
156a. XLGAFCT2 — WRITE IN other circumstances which might have affected supine length

157. MEASDON2 — Have you entered all measurements?
1 Yes
2 No

ALL
158. FOLLOWU2 — If we want to contact you about the survey in the future will it be alright to call on you again?
1 Yes, it would be alright
2 No, unconditional
3 Yes, with conditions, qualifications

14

INFANT FEEDING SURVEY
WAVE 3 QUESTIONNAIRE

Wave 1 Variables carried forward to Wave 3

No.	Variable	Question
1.	NAME1	Baby's name
2.	LANGUAG	Main language spoken at home
3.	ENGUND	Respondent's understanding of English
4.	RELIGION	Respondent's religion
5.	HUSBAND	Whether respondent has husband or partner in household
6.	BRSTEVER	Baby ever put to breast
7.	TIMETOBR	Length of time before started breastfeeding
8.	BIRTH	Was your baby born at home or in hospital
9.	SOLIDS1	Baby eats solid food

Wave 2 Variables carried forward to Wave 3

No.	Variable	Question
10.	PAIDWRK2	Mother doing paid work at Wave 2
11.	STILBRST	Are you still breastfeeding....at all?
12.	SOLIDS2	Do you give solid foods?
13.	SOLR2M	At which feeds do you regularly offer your baby solid (soft weaning) food at the moment?
14	HSAMEJOB	Husband's Wave 2 job same as Wave 1

Wave 3 Questions

No.	Variable	Question
15.	NPERSON3	Can I just check, how many people are normally living in this household now?
16.	NADULTS3	How many people aged 16 or over are normally living in this houshold?
17.	NCHILD3	How many children aged under 16 are there normally living in this household?

IF (STARTED BREASTFEEDING AFTER 24 HOURS AT TIMETOBR) AND (HOSPITAL AT BIRTH)

18. BRSTSTA3 — Thinking back to when ...... was born, did you first breastfeed before or after you left hospital?
1 Before
2 After

IF AFTER AT BRSTA3

19. AFTHOSP3 — Why did you not breastfeed until you got home?
1 Didn't have enough milk
2 Didn't want to feed colostrum
3 Didn't want to breastfeed in public
4 Not feeling relaxed in hospital
5 Other *Please specify at next question*

IF OTHER AT AFTHOSP3

20. AFTHOTH3 — WRITE IN why didn't breastfeed until left hospital

ALL

21. START3 — I would like to ask you some questions about how you feed ...... now

IF YES OR NO ANSWER AT STILBRST (WAVE 2)

22. STILBRS3 — Are you still breast feeding .... at all?
1 Yes
2 No

IF YES AT STILBRS3

23. NFEEDS3 — How many times a day do you breast feed him/her now?

24. BRFDTIM3 — Do you breast feed him/her on demand or do you generally keep to set feeding times?
1 On demand
2 Set times
3 Depends

1

---

25. BOTTLE3 — Do you give your baby milk from a bottle or cup at present even if only occasionally? (apart from expressed breast milk)?
1 Yes (even if occasionally)
2 No

IF NO AT STILBRS3

26. LBRW3 — How old was your baby when you last breast fed him/her?
PLEASE ENTER NUMBER OF MONTHS

27. LBRST3 — What were your reasons for stopping breast feeding? PROMPT AS NECESSARY
1 Insufficient milk
2 Baby still hungry
3 Baby not gaining / losing weight
4 Baby would not suck/rejected
5 Breastfeeding took too long/ was tiring
6 Mother was ill
7 Baby was ill
8 Returned to work
9 Baby could not be fed by others
10 Inconvenient/no place to feed
11 Breast fed for as long as intended
12 Other *Please specify at next question*

IF OTHER AT LBRST3

27a XLBRST3 — WRITE IN other reason

IF NO AT STILBRS3

28. LONGBR3 — Would you have liked to have continued breast feeding for longer?

IF OTHER THAN (STILL BREASTFEEDING AT STILBRS3 AND NO BOTTLE AT BOTTLE3)

29. MILKTYP3 — When you bottle feed) Which kind of milk do you give your baby MOST of the time at the moment?
1 Liquid cows milk - ordinary/full fat
2 Liquid cows milk - semi-skimmed
3 Liquid cows miik - skimmed
4 Cow and Gate Premium (powder)
5 Cow and Gate nutrilon Premium (powder)
6 Cow and Gate Premium (ready-to-feed)
7 Cow and Gate Plus (powder)
8 Cow and Gate Nutrilon Plus (powder)
9 Cow and Gate Plus (ready-to-feed)
10 Cow and Gate Formula S (powder)
11 Cow and Gate InfaSoy (powder)
12 Cow and Gate Step-up
13 SMA Gold Cap (powder)
14 SMA Gold Cap (ready-to-feed)
15 SMA White Cap (powder)
16 SMA White Cap (ready-to-feed)
17 SMA Wysoy (powder)
18 SMA Progress
19 Milupa Milumil (powder)
20 Milupa Aptamil (powder)
21 Milupa Prematil (powder)
22 Farley's Follow-on Milk
23 Farley's First Milk
24 Farley's OsterSoy
25 Boots Follow-on Milk (powder)
26 Boots Follow-on Milk (ready-to-feed)
27 Other kind of milk (*Please specify at next question*)

IF OTHER AT MILKTYP3

29a. XMILKTY3 — WRITE IN name of milk

IF OTHER THAN (STILL BREASTFEEDING AT STILBRS3 AND NO BOTTLE AT BOTTLE3)

30. STARTBO3 — How old was ...... when you started giving this milk?
RECORD NUMBER OF MONTHS - CODE 0 IF GIVEN FROM BIRTH

31. MILKTY3A — Do you ever give your baby any other kinds of milk?
1 Yes
2 No

2

Page 4

IF FREE OR REDUCED PRICE AT MTOKEN3

39. MTOKEXC3 — Where do you exchange the tokens for milk?
 1 Clinic,
 2 Milkman,
 3 Other (Please specify at next question)

IF OTHER AT MTOKEXC3

39a XTOKEXC3 — WRITE IN where milk tokens are exchanged

IF MILKMAN OR OTHER AT MTOKEXC3

40. CHCMILK3 — ASK OR RECORD
 Do you ever buy your baby's milk from the child health clinic
 1 Yes always
 2 Sometimes
 3 No

IF OTHER THAN (STILL BREASTFEEDING AT STILBRS3 AND NO BOTTLE AT BOTTLE3)

41. ADDMILK3 — Do you ever add anything to the milk in the bottle/cup?
 1 Yes
 2 No

IF YES AT ADDMILK3

42. WHATADD3 — What do you add to the milk?
 1 Sugar
 2 Honey
 3 Other (Please specify at next question)

IF OTHER AT WHATADD3

42a. XWHATAD3 — WRITE IN what is added to the milk

IF NO AT SOLIDS1 AND OTHER THAN YES AT SOLIDS2

43. SOLIDS3 — Do you give your baby such foods as cereal, rusk or any other kind of solid food (soft weaning food), including any that you make yourself?
 1 Yes
 2 No

IF YES AT SOLIDS3

44. SOLAGE3 — How old was your baby when he/she first had any food apart from milk?
 PLEASE ENTER NUMBER OF MONTHS

45. SOLFRST3 — What was the first food your baby had, apart from milk?
 DESCRIBE NAME OF FOOD AND BRAND

IF YES AT SOLIDS1 OR SOLIDS2 OR SOLIDS3

46. SOLREG3 — At present, are you giving your baby cereal, rusks or any other solid food (soft weaning food) every day?

47. SOLYEST3 — Did you give your baby any cereal, rusks or solid food (soft weaning food) to eat yesterday?
 1 Yes
 2 No

48. DIARY3 — Starting with when ...... woke up, I'd like you to tell me which solid foods you gave him/her yesterday, and how much he/she actually ate.

49. **SOLIDS TABLE**
 The table contains the following six questions:

49a. TIMEFEED — At which time of the day did he/she eat this solid food (soft weaning food)?
 PROMPT AS NECESSARY
 1 Between 6am and 10am
 2 Between 10am and 2pm
 3 Between 2pm and 6pm
 4 Between 6pm and 10pm
 5 Between 10pm and 6am

49b. TYPEFOOD — What type of solid food did he/she eat?

49c. AMOUNT — How many teaspoons did he/she eat?
 SHOW CARD AND CONVERT TO TEASPOONS WHERE NECESSARY

 Teaspoons - enter number at next question
 Rusk
 Banana (or other piece of fruit)
 Slice of bread (use for sandwiches)

Page 3

32. MILKTY3B — **IF YES AT MILKTY3A**
 Which other kinds of milk do you give your baby?
 1 Liquid cows milk - ordinary
 2 Liquid cows milk - semi-skimmed
 3 Liquid cows milk - skimmed
 4 Cow and Gate Premium (powder)
 5 Cow and Gate nutrition Premium (powder)
 6 Cow and Gate Premium (ready-to-feed)
 7 Cow and Gate Plus (powder)
 8 Cow and Gate Nutrition Plus (powder)
 9 Cow and Gate Plus (ready-to-feed)
 10 Cow and Gate Formula S (powder)
 11 Cow and Gate InfaSoy (powder)
 12 Cow and Gate Step-up
 13 SMA Gold Cap (powder)
 14 SMA Gold Cap (ready-to-feed)
 15 SMA White Cap (powder)
 16 SMA White Cap (ready-to-feed)
 17 SMA Wysoy (powder)
 18 SMA Progress
 19 Milupa Milumil (powder)
 20 Milupa Aptamil (powder)
 21 Milupa Prematil (powder)
 22 Farley's Follow-on Milk
 23 Farley's First Milk
 24 Farley's OsterSoy
 25 Boots Follow-on Milk (powder)
 26 Boots Follow-on Milk (ready-to-feed)
 27 Other kind of milk (Please specify at next question)

32a. XMILK3B — **IF OTHER AT MILKTY3B**
 WRITE IN name of milk

33. STARCOW3 — **IF (LIQUID COW'S MILK AT MILKTY3B) AND NOT (LIQUID COW'S MILK AT MILKTYP3)**
 How old was ...... when you started giving liquid cows milk?
 RECORD NUMBER OF MONTHS - CODE 0 IF GIVEN FROM BIRTH

IF OTHER THAN (STILL BREASTFEEDING AT STILBRS3 AND NO BOTTLE AT BOTTLE3)

34. CHOOSMLK — How do you choose which brand of formula milk to buy?
 1 Recommended by health professional (eg.health visitor)
 2 Recommended by family/friends
 3 Only one available from clinic
 4 Only one available from local shop
 5 Low price
 6 Baby allergic to other formulas
 7 Closest to breast milk
 8 Baby likes the taste
 9 Convenience/easy to make up
 10 Other (Please specify at next question)

IF OTHER AT CHOOSMLK

34a. XCHOOSML — WRITE IN how brand of formula milk is chosen

IF OTHER THAN (STILL BREASTFEEDING AT STILBRS3 AND NO BOTTLE AT BOTTLE3)

35. NBOTTLE3 — How many times a day do you give him/her a bottle of milk?

36. NOUNCE3 — How many fluid ounces of milk does he/she usually drink at each feed?
 INTERVIEWER - If amount is variable work out an average

37. BOFDTIM3 — Do you bottle feed him/her on demand or do you generally keep to set feeding times?
 1 On demand
 2 Set times
 3 Depends

ALL

38. MTOKEN3 — Do you get milk tokens for free or reduced price milk?
 1 Yes, Free milk
 2 Yes, Reduced price milk
 3 No, Neither

ALL

56. DRINK3 — Apart from milk, do you give your baby water or anything else to drink at the moment?
1 Yes
2 No
IF YES AT DRINK 3

57. DRINKS TABLE — The table contains the following four questions.

57a. TYPDRNK — What drinks do you give your baby?

57b. OTHDRNK3 — WRITE IN other drink (and/or brand where applicable)

57c. FREQU3 — How often do you usually give this to your baby?
SHOW CARD F OR PROMPT IF NECESSARY
1 More than once a day
2 Once a day
3 Less than once a day, but at least three times a week
4 Once or twice a week
5 Less than once a week

57d. ANYMORE — Do you give your baby any other drinks?
1 Yes
2 No
IF YES AT DRINK3

58. RDRINK3M — Why do you give your baby drinks?
SHOW CARD G OR PROMPT AS NECESSARY
1 Because he/she is thirsty
2 Hungry between feeds
4 To give him/her extra vitamins
5 To help his/her digestion
To help his/her colic/wind/hiccups
6 To help his/her constipation
7 Good for baby
8 Or for some other reason?
IF OTHER AT RDRINK3M

58a. XRDRNK3M — WRITE IN other reasons for giving baby drinks

ALL

59. FAMDIET3 — May I just check) Do most of the people living in this household eat meat or fish?
1 Yes
2 No
3 Equal number eat / don't eat meat and fish

6

IF (YES OR EQUAL AT FAMDIET3) AND (MUSLIM AT RELIGION)

60. HALAL3A — Do you (or other household members) eat Halal meat only?
1 Yes
2 No

IF (NO AT FAMDIET3) AND (MUSLIM AT RELIGION)

61. HALAL3B — Do you ever eat Halal meat?
1 Yes
2 No

ALL

62. WHOSHOP3 — Who does most of the shopping for food in this household?
1 Self
2 Husband / Partner
3 Parent (in-law)
4 Other adult
5 Child under 16
6 Other (Please specify at next question)
IF OTHER AT WHOSHOP3

62a. OTHSHOP3 — WRITE IN who does the shopping

ALL

63. BABYSHO3 — Where do you mainly buy food for the baby?
ENTER ONE CODE ONLY
1 Supermarket
2 Chemist (include Boots, Superdrug)
3 General food store
4 Clinic
5 Other (Please specify at next question)
IF OTHER AT BABYSHO3

63a. OTHBSHO3 — WRITE IN other place where baby food is bought

ALL

64. FAMSHO3 — Where do you mainly buy food for the family?
1 Supermarket
2 General food store
3 Market
4 Other (Please specify at next question)

IF AMOUNT = TEASPOON

49d. TEASP — RECORD NUMBER OF TEASPOONS

IF AMOUNT OTHER THAN TEASPOON

49e. FRACTN — RECORD HOW MUCH WAS EATEN
Half a rusk/banana/slice of bread
One
Oneplus
Two

49f. ANYMORE — Did you give your baby any more solid food yesterday?
1 Yes
2 No
IF YES AT SOLREG3

50. MILKMIX3 — Do you ever use milk to mix up his/her food?
1 Yes
2 No
IF YES AT MILKMIX3

51. TYPEMIX3 — Do you use milk especially for babies, liquid cows milk, or something else?
1 Baby milk
2 Liquid cows milk
3 Something else
Please specify at next question
IF SOMETHING ELSE AT TYPEMIX3

51a. XTYPEMI3 — WRITE IN what else is used to mix up food
IF LIQUID COW'S MILK AT TYPEMIX3

52. LIQCOWOL — How old was your baby when you first used liquid cows milk to mix up his/her food?
PLEASE ENTER NUMBER OF MONTHS
IF YES AT SOLREG3

53. SOLR3M — At which times of the day do you regularly offer your baby solid (soft weaning) food at the moment?
1 Between 6am and 10am
2 Between 10am and 12pm
3 Between 12pm and 2pm
4 Between 2pm and 6pm
5 Between 6pm and 10pm
6 Between 10pm and 6am

IF THREE OR MORE MEALS A DAY AT SOLR3M AND NOT THREE OR MORE MEALS A DAY AT SOLR2M

54. SOLIDOL3 — How old was your baby when he/she regularly started having three meals of solid food a day?
PLEASE ANSWER IN MONTHS
IF YES AT SOLIDS1 OR SOLIDS2 OR SOLIDS3

55. FDINTRO3 — I am going to ask you how often you give your baby different types of foods
FOOD FREQUENCY TABLE
ASK FoodTy3 to FComme3 FOR EACH OF THE FOLLOWING TYPES OF FOOD
meat
fish
cereal or rusk
bread or chapati
rice or pasta
potatoes
peas, beans, lentils or chickpeas
egg
fruit
other vegetables
yoghurt or cheese
chocolate or sweets

55a. FFREQU3 — How often do you usually give your baby ......?
SHOW CARD F OR PROMPT IF NECESSARY
1 More than once a day
2 Once a day
3 Most days
4 At least once a week
5 Less than once a week
6 Never
IF FFREQU3 OTHER THAN NEVER

55b. FCOMME3 — ASK OR RECORD
When you give your baby ......, is it usually part of a baby meal bought from a shop, fresh food or part of a homemade meal or neither?
1 Baby food bought from a shop
2 Fresh / homemade meal
3 Neither

5

64a. OTHFSHO3
IF OTHER AT FAMSHO3
WRITE IN other place where family food is bought

ALL

65. WHOCOOK3
Who does most of the cooking in this household?
1 Self
2 Husband / Partner
3 Parent (in-law)
4 Other adult
5 Child under 16
6 Other (Please specify at next question)

65A. OTHCOOK3
IF OTHER AT WHOCOOK3
WRITE IN who does the cooking

ALL

66. MEALTIM3
Does ...... usually eat at the same time as the rest of the family?
1 Yes
2 No
3 Eats at the same time as other children

67. SAMEFOO3
IF YES AT SOLIDS1 OR SOLIDS2 OR SOLIDS3
Do you ever give ...... the same food as the rest of the family
1 Yes
2 No

68. ALTER3
IF YES AT SAMEFOO3
Do you ever alter it before you give it to the baby?
1 Yes
2 No

69. HOWALT3
IF YES AT ALTER3
How do you alter it?
1 Leave out ingredients
2 Mash or mince it
3 Sieve, blend or liquidise it into a puree
4 Cook the food for longer/to soften it
5 Other (Please specify at next question)

69a. OTHALT3
IF OTHER AT HOWALT3
WRITE IN how food is altered

ALL

70. CUP3
Has your baby ever drunk from a cup or beaker with a spout, or been given liquid from a spoon?
1 Cup
2 Beaker with a spout
3 Spoon
3 None of these

71. CUPUS3
IF CUP OR BEAKER AT CUP3
Does ...... usually drink from a cup or beaker?
1 Yes
2 No

72. FINGER3
IF YES AT SOLIDS1 OR SOLIDS2 OR SOLIDS3
Has your baby ever fed him/herself using a spoon or using his/her fingers?
1 Fingers
2 Spoon
3 Neither

73. FINGUS3
IF FINGERS OR SPOON AT FINGER3
Does s/he usually feed him/herself?
1 Yes
2 No

74. FACTORS3
IF THREE OR MORE MEALS A DAY AT SOLR3M
What do you look for when choosing which solid (soft weaning) foods to give your baby?
1 Variety
2 Nutrition generally eg 'balanced diet'
3 Baby's preferences
4 Additives
5 Vitamins
6 Sugar content
7 Salt content
8 Home cooked
9 Ease of preparation
10 Price
11 Family has halal, vegetarian or other specialised diet
12 Other (Please specify at next question)

74a. XFACTOR3
IF OTHER AT FACTORS3
WRITE IN other factors

7

ALL

75. AVOIDIN3
ASK OR RECORD
(You've already told me that you don't give the baby meat or fish).
Do you avoid giving your baby (other) foods containing particular ingredients?
1 Yes
2 No

76. WHATAVD3
IF YES AT AVOIDIN3
What ingredients do you avoid?
1 Sugar
2 Salt
3 Spices
4 Additives
5 Colouring
6 Preservatives
7 Fat
8 Specific foods (Please code at next question)
9 Other (Please specify at next question)

77. SPECAVD3
IF SPECIFIC FOOD AT WHATAVD3
CODE Food avoided
1 Baked beans
2 Bananas
3 Milk products
4 Cheese
5 Spices
6 Egg / Egg White
7 Other Please specify at next question

77a. SPECOTH3
IF OTHER AT SPECAVD3
WRITE IN other food avoided

78. OTHING3
IF OTHER AT WHATAVD3
WRITE IN what else is avoided

79. WHYAVD3
IF YES AT AVOIDIN3
Why do you avoid this(these) ingredients?
1 Not beneficial
2 Harmful
3 Allergies
4 Baby doesn't like them
5 Will develop a sweet tooth
6 Bad for teeth
7 Religious reasons
8 Publicity / Media / Advice
9 Other (Please specify at next question)

79a. OTHAVD3
IF OTHER AT WHYAVD3
WRITE IN other reason for avoiding particular ingredients

ALL

80. PROBWEAN
Has your baby been difficult to wean onto solid food?
1 Yes
2 No

81. WHATWEAN
IF YES AT PROBWEAN
In what way has it been difficult?
1 Baby would not take solids
2 Baby would only take certain solids
3 Baby was disinterested in food
4 Baby vomiting
5 Some other reason (Please specify at next question)

81a. OTHWEAN
IF OTHER AT WHATWEAN
WRITE IN other problems with feeding baby

82. WFAMHEL3
IF YES AT PROBWEAN
Did any family or friends give you help or advice about this/these problems?
1 Yes
2 No

83. WFAMWHO3
IF YES AT WFAMHEL3
Who helped or advised you?
1 Mother or mother-in-law
2 Sister or sister-in-law
3 Husband
4 Other relative
5 Friend or neighbour

84. WOTHHEL3
IF YES AT WFAMHEL3
Did anyone else give you help or advice about this/these problems?
1 Yes
2 No

85. WEANHEL
IF YES AT WOTHHEL3
Who else helped or advised you?
1 Health visitor
2 Doctor at the child health clinic
3 Family doctor
4 Nurse at the doctors surgery
5 Voluntary group for new mothers
6 Someone else (Please specify at next question)

8

IF OTHER AT WEANHEL3

85a. XWEAN3 — WRITE IN who else helped or advised

ALL

86. PROBFEE3 — Have you had any (other) difficulties feeding your baby since I/we last spoke to you?
1 Yes
2 No

IF YES AT PROBFEE3

87. WHATPRO3 — What problems have you had?
1 Baby was hungry
2 Baby was ill
3 Baby didn't like breast milk
4 Baby didn't like bottled milk
5 Baby vomiting
6 Baby was disinterested in food
7 Some other reason (Please specify at next question)

IF OTHER AT WHATPRO3

88. OTHPROB3 — WRITE IN other problems with feeding baby

IF YES AT PROBFEE3

89. PFAMHEL3 — Did any family or friends give you help or advice about this/these problems?
1 Yes
2 No

IF YES AT PFAMHEL3

90. PFAMWHO3 — Who helped or advised you?
1 Mother or mother-in-law
2 Sister or sister-in-law
3 Husband
4 Other relative
5 Friend or neighbour

IF YES AT PROBFEE2

91. POTHHEL3 — Did anyone else give you help or advice with this/these problems?
1 Yes
2 No

IF (NO AT PROBWEAN) AND (NO AT PROBFEE3)

92. OTHELP3 — Has anyone given you help or advice on feeding or weaning since I/we last spoke to you?
1 Yes
2 No

IF (YES AT POTHHEL3) OR (YES AT OTHELP3)

93. WHOHELP3 — Who (else) helped or advised you?
1 Health visitor
2 Doctor at the child health clinic
3 Family doctor
4 Nurse at the doctors surgery
5 Voluntary group for new mothers
6 Someone else (Please specify at next question)

IF OTHER AT WHOHELP3

93a. XWHOHEL3 — WRITE IN who else helped or advised you

IF VOLUNTARY GROUP AT WHOHELP3 OR WEANHEL3

94. WHICHGR3 — Which voluntary group helped or advised you?
1 Local womens group
2 National Childbirth Trust
3 La Leche League
4 Association of Breast Feeding Mothers
5 Some other voluntary group (Please specify at next question)

IF OTHER AT WHICHGR3

94a. XGROUP3 — WRITE IN who runs the other voluntary group

IF (HEALTH VISITOR AT WHOHELP3 OR WEANHEL3) AND (NOT ENGLISH AT LANGUAG) AND (NOT WELL AT ENGUND)

95. HVLAN3 — When you spoke with the Health visitor, which language did she or he speak?
1 English
2 Gujarati
3 Punjabi
4 Bengali
5 Hindi
6 Urdu
7 Other

9

IF (DOCTOR AT CHILD HEALTH CLINIC AT WHOHELP3 OR WEANHEL3) AND (NOT ENGLISH AT LANGUAG) AND (NOT WELL AT ENGUND)

96. CDOCLAN3 — When you spoke with the doctor at the child health clinic, which language did the she or he speak?
1 English
2 Gujarati
3 Punjabi
4 Bengali
5 Urdu
6 Hindi
7 Other

IF (GP AT WHOHELP3 OR WEANHEL3) AND (NOT ENGLISH AT LANGUAG) AND (NOT WELL AT ENGUND)

97. GPLAN3 — When you spoke with the doctor, which language did she or he speak?
1 English
2 Gujarati
3 Punjabi
4 Bengali
5 Hindi
6 Urdu
7 Other

IF (NURSE AT WHOHELP3 OR WEANHEL3) AND (NOT ENGLISH AT LANGUAG) AND (NOT WELL AT ENGUND)

98. NURSLAN3 — When you spoke with the doctor, which language did she or he speak?
1 English
2 Gujarati
3 Punjabi
4 Bengali
5 Hindi
6 Urdu
7 Other

IF ENGLISH AT HVLAN3

99. HVUND3 — Did you understand the health visitor ...
1 All of the time
2 Most of the time
3 Some of the time
4 Not at all
5 or did someone interpret?

IF ENGLISH AT CDOCLAN3

100. CDOCUND3 — Did you understand the doctor ...
1 All of the time
2 Most of the time
3 Some of the time
4 Not at all
5 or did someone interpret?

IF ENGLISH AT GPLAN3

101. GPUND3 — Did you understand the doctor ...
1 All of the time
2 Most of the time
3 Some of the time
4 Not at all
5 or did someone interpret?

IF ENGLISH AT NURSUND3

102. NURSUND3 — Did you understand the nurse ...
1 All of the time
2 Most of the time
3 Some of the time
4 Not at all
5 or did someone interpret?

ALL

103. LEAFLET3 — Since we last spoke to you, have you read any books, leaflets, or magazines, or watched any videos about looking after babies?
1 Yes
2 No

IF YES AT LEAFLET3

104. LEAFGET3 — Where did you get it/them from?
1 Health visitor
2 Child health clinic
3 Doctor's surgery
4 Bought from a shop
5 Other (Please specify at next question)

IF OTHER AT LEAFGET3

104a. XLEAFGE3 — WRITE IN WHERE GOT LEAFLETS ETC

IF (YES AT LEAFLET3) AND (NOT ENGLISH AT LANGUAG) AND (NOT WELL AT ENGUND)

105. LEAFLAN3 — What language were they in?
1 English
2 Gujarati
3 Punjabi
4 Bengali
5 Hindi
6 Urdu
7 Other

10

Top panel

5 Other female relative
6 Child minder
7 Nursery or creche
8 Someone else
(Please specify at next question)

OFFUPATION CODING (SOCNOW-SOCLS)

119. SOCNOW — Is occupational coding to be done now or later?

119a. EMP — Are you working as..
1 Employee
2 Self employed

119b. SUPMAN — Are you a manager or supervisor of any kind?
1 Manager
2 Supervisor
3 Other employee

119c. NEMPLEE — How many employees work(ed) in the establishment?
1 1-24
2 25+

119d. NSLFEMP — How many employees
0 None
1 1-24
2 25+

119e. EMPSTAT — Employment status and establishment size

119f. SOCODE — Standard Occupation
1 Employee not elsewhere classified
2 Foreman or supervisor
3 Self Employed - no employees
4 Self Employed - Small establishment
5 Self Employed - Large establishment
6 Manager - Small establishment
7 Manager - Large establishment

119g. SEGRP — Socio-Economic Group

119h. SOCLS — Social Class

120. WRKHOME3 — **IF PAIDWORK AT PAIDWRK3**
Do you work mainly at home or do you go out to work?
1 Mainly at home
2 Go out to work

121. WHOMIND3 — Who usually looks after the baby when you are working?
1 Self
2 Husband or partner
3 Mother
4 Mother-in-law

121a. XWHOMIN3 — **IF OTHER AT WHOMIND3**
WRITE IN WHO ELSE USUALLY LOOKS AFTER BABY WHEN WORKING

122. PAYMIND3 — **IF NOT (SELF OR HUSBAND/PARTNER) AT WHOMIND3**
Do you pay to have the baby looked after?
1 Yes
2 No

123. HUSBLIV3 — **IF NOT SINGLE AT HUSBAND**
ASK OR RECORD (May I just check) Is your husband/partner living in this household at the moment?
1 Yes
2 No

124. HUSBWOR3 — **IF YES AT HUSBLIV3**
Did your husband/partner do any paid work last week that is in the seven days ending last Sunday, either as an employee or self-employed?
1 Yes
2 No

125. HUSBAWA3 — **IF NO AT HUSBWOR3**
Even though he was not working, did he have a job that he was away from last week?
1 Yes
2 No

126. HSAMEJO3 — **IF (YES AT HUSBWOR3 OR YES AT HUSBAWA3) AND (YES AT HSAMEJOB)**
Was that the same job that he had when we last spoke to you?
1 Yes
2 No

12

Bottom panel

106. VIT3 — **ALL**
Do you give your baby any extra vitamins at the moment (apart from any vitamin drinks you have already mentioned)?
1 Yes
2 No

107. VITDROP3 — **IF YES AT VIT3**
Do you use Children's Vitamin Drops from the child health clinic or another brand?
1 Children's Vitamin Drops
2 Other (Please specify at next question)

107a XVITDRP3 — **IF OTHER AT VITDROP3**
WRITE IN name of other brand

108. VITBUY3 — **IF CHILDREN'S VITAMIN DROPS AT VITDROP 3**
Do you buy the vitamins or do you get them free from the clinic or on prescription?
1 Buy
2 Free
3 On Prescription

109. VITOTHER3 — **IF OTHER AT VITDROP3**
Do you buy the vitamins or do you get them on prescription?
1 Buy
2 On Prescription

110. VITM3 — **ALL**
Are you taking any extra vitamins or iron tablets yourself at the moment, either in tablet or powder form?
1 Yes
2 No

111. VITM3GET — **IF YES AT VITM3**
Where do you usually get the vitamins/iron tablets?
1 Child health clinic
2 Elsewhere

112. VITM3BUY — **IF CHILD HEALTH CLINIC AT VITM3GET**
Do you buy the vitamins/iron tablets or do you get them free from the clinic or on prescription?
1 Buy
2 Free
3 Prescription

113. VITM3OTH — **IF ELSEWHERE AT VITM3GET**
Do you buy the vitamins or do you get them on prescription?
1 Buy
2 On Prescription

114. PAIDWRK3 — **ALL**
I would like to ask some questions about yourself (and your husband/partner).
At the moment are you ...
1 doing any paid work including working at home
2 on paid maternity leave
3 on unpaid maternity leave
4 not working or not on maternity leave

115. MSAMEJO3 — **IF (WORKING OR ON MATERNITY LEAVE AT PAIDWRK2) AND (WORKING AT PAIDWRK 3)**
Was that the same job that you had before you had your baby?
1 Yes
2 No

116. WRKPLAN3 — **IF NOT WORKING AT PAIDWRK3**
Do you plan to start work (again) in the next two years?
1 Yes
2 No

117. FULLPAR3 — **IF YES AT WORKPLAN3**
Do you plan to work full or part-time?
1 Full-time
2 Part-time

118. SOCTEXT1 — **IF (NO AT MSAMEJOB) OR (WORKING AT PAIDWRK3)**
What is your job?

11

142. HDAFCT3 — Special circumstances that might have affected measurement
1 No special circumstances
2 Did not keep still
3 Other circumstances (Please specify at next question)

IF OTHER AT HDAFCT3

142a. XHDAFCT3 — WRITE IN other circumstances affecting head circumference measurement

143. ARMCIRC3 — Mid upper arm circumference (centimetres)

144. ARMREL3 — Do you think the measurement of arm circumference is reliable?
1 Yes
2 No

IF ARM CIRCUMFERENCE MEASURED

145. ARATTEM3 — Number of attempts at measuring arm circumference

146. ARAFCT3 — Special circumstances that might have affected measurement
1 No special circumstances
2 Did not keep still
3 Other circumstances (Please specify at next question)

IF OTHER AT ARAFCT3

146a. XARAFCT3 — WRITE IN other circumstances affecting arm circumference measurement

147. LENGTH3 — Supine length (centimetres)

148. LTHREL3 — Do you think the supine length measurement is reliable?
1 Yes
2 No

IF LENGTH MEASURED

149. LGATTEM3 — Number of attempts at measuring length

150. LGAFCT3 — Special circumstances that might have affected length
1 No special circumstances
2 Uneven surface
3 Did not lie still
4 Legs not straight
5 Did not lie flat
6 Head slipped down
7 Wearing clothes/nappy
8 Other

IF OTHER AT LGAFCT3

150a. XLGAFCT3 — WRITE IN Other circumstances which might have affected supine length

ALL

151. MEASDON3 — Have you entered all measurements?
1 Yes
2 No

152. FOLLOWU3 — Will it be alright to call on you once more, in about 6 months time?
1 Yes, it would be alright (Unconditional)
2 No, (Unconditional)
3 Yes (With conditions/ qualifications)

153. OTHPRES3 — INTERVIEWER CODE Was another adult present at the interview?
1 Yes
2 No

IF YES AT OTHPRES3

154. WHOELSE3 — Who else was present?
1 Interpreter
2 Husband or partner
3 Mother
4 Mother-in-law
5 Other female relative
6 Other male relative
7 Friend or neighbour
8 Other

IF OTHER AT WHOELSE3

154a. XWHOELS3 — WRITE IN Who else was present?

IF NOT ENGLISH AT LANGUAG

155. INTERP3 — INTERVIEWER CODE Was an interpreter used, or did you do the interview in another language?
1 Yes
2 No

14

IF NO AT HUSBAWA3

127. HUSBNOW3 — Last week was he.....
1 Waiting to take up a job that he had already obtained
2 Looking for work
3 Intending to look for work but prevented by temporary sickness or injury
4 Going to school or college full time
5 Permanently unable to work because of long-term sickness or disability.
6 Retired
7 Looking after the home or family or was he doing something else?

IF (YES AT HUSBWOR3 OR HUSBAWA3) AND (NO AT HSAMEJO3)

128. HUSBWK13 — What is your husband's/partner's job?

IF WAITING AT HUSBNOW3

129. HUSBWK23 — What is the job your husband/ partner is waiting to take up?

[Repeat Questions 119a-119h (Emp-Socls) above for husband]

ALL

130. INCOME3 — Could you look at this card and tell me which group represents your current GROSS income (and the income of your husband-partner). Please include income from all sources before any compulsory deductions such as income tax, national insurance and superannuation contributions? SHOW CARD C AND PROMPT AS NECESSARY
1 less than £50 per week
2 £50 - less £70 per week
3 £70 - less £100 per week
4 £100 - less £150 per week
5 £150 - less £200 per week
6 £200 - less £250 per week
7 £250 - less £300 per week
8 £300 - less £350 per week
9 £350 - less £400 per week
10 £400 - less £450 per week
11 £450 - less £500 per week
12 £500 or more per week

131. FAMCRED3 — Can I just check are you (or your husband) currently receiving Family Credit?
1 Yes
2 No

132. INCSUP3 — And have you (or your husband) drawn Income Support at any time in the last 14 days?
1 Yes
2 No

133. NOWLATER — INTERVIEWER Do you want to enter the measurements of the baby now or later?
1 Now
2 Later

134. DATEMEA3 — Date weighed and measured

135. BABYWT3 — Baby's weight (in kilograms)

136. WTREL3 — Do you think the weight is reliable?
1 Yes
2 No

IF BABY WEIGHED

137. WTATTEM3 — NUMBER OF ATTEMPTS AT WEIGHING

138. WTAFCT3 — Special circumstances that might have affected weight
1 No special circumstances
2 Scales on uneven surface
3 Wearing clothes/nappy
4 Other circumstances (Please specify at next question)

IF OTHER AT WTAFCT3

138a. XWTAFCT3 — WRITE IN other circumstances affecting weight

139. HEADCIR3 — Head circumference (centimetres)

140. HEADREL3 — Do you think the measurement of head circumference is reliable?
1 Yes
2 No

IF HEAD CIRCUMFERENCE MEASURED

141. HDATTEM3 — Number of attempts at measuring head circumference

13

INFANT FEEDING SURVEY
WAVE 4 QUESTIONNAIRE

Wave 1 variables carried forward to Wave 4

1.	NAME1	Baby's name
2.	LANGUAG	Main language spoken at home
3.	ENGUND	Respondent understands English
4.	HUSBAND	Whether respondent has husband or partner in household
5.	SOLIDS1	Baby eats solid food

Wave 2 variables carried forward to Wave 4

6.	PAIDWRK2	Mother doing paid work at Wave 2
7.	STILBRST	Are you still breastfeeding 'Name' at all?
8.	SOLIDS2	Do you give solid foods?
9.	SOLR2M	At which feeds do you regularly offer your baby solid (soft weaning) food at the moment?
10.	HUSBWOR2	Whether husband working at Wave 2

Wave 3 variables carried forward to Wave 4

11.	PAIDWRK3	Mother doing paid work at Wave 3
12.	STILBRS3	Are you still breastfeeding 'Name' at all?
13.	SOLIDS3	Do you give solid foods?
14.	SOLR3M	At which times of the day do you regularly offer your baby solid (soft weaning) food at the moment?
15.	W3COW	Whether baby had been given cow's milk at Wave 3
16.	HUSBWOR3	Whether husband working at Wave 3

Number of interviews achieved with mother in Waves 1 to 3

17.	NUMBINTS	1 Waves 1 to 3
		2 Wave 2 missing
		3 Wave 3 missing

Wave 4 Questions

		ALL
18.	START4	I would like to start by asking you some questions about how you feed 'Name' now
		IF (YES AT STILBRS3) OR (YES AT STILBRST AND NO INTERVIEW AT WAVE 3)
19.	STILBRS4	Are you still breast feeding 'Name' at all?
		1 Yes
		2 No
		IF YES AT STILBRS4
20.	NFEEDS4	How many times a day do you breast feed him/her now?
21.	BRFDTIM4	Do you breast feed him/her on demand or do you generally keep to set feeding times?
		1 On demand
		2 Set times
		3 Depends
22.	BRLONG4	How old do you think s/he will be when you stop breastfeeding? TO ANSWER IN MONTHS, SELECT MONTHS AND RECORD AT NEXT QUESTION
		1 Months
		2 Will breastfeed for as long as able
		3 Will breastfeed for as long as wants
		IF MONTHS AT BRLONG4
23.	BRMON4	RECORD NUMBER OF MONTHS
		IF NO AT STILBRS4
24.	LBRW4	How old was your child when you last breast fed him/her? PLEASE ENTER NUMBER OF MONTHS THIS SHOULD ONLY BE BELOW 9 MONTHS IF RESPONDENT WAS NOT INTERVIEWED AT WAVE 3

1

		IF YES AT INTERP3
156.	WHOINTR3	Who interpreted?
		1 Husband
		2 Other family member
		3 Friend/ neighbour
		4 OPCS/Other Govt. Interpreter
		5 Professional Interpreter
		6 Interviewer used another language
		7 Other
		IF OTHER AT WHOINTR3
156a.	XWHOINT3	WRITE IN who interpreted
		IF YES AT INTERP3
157.	LGEINTR3	Which language?
		1 Gujarati
		2 Punjabi
		3 Bengali
		4 Hindi
		5 Urdu
		6 Other
		ALL
158.	FINISH	"End of interview"

15

25. LBRST4 — What were your reasons for stopping breast feeding?
PROMPT AS NECESSARY
Up to 5 answers from
1 Insufficient milk
2 Breast fed for as long as intended
3 Returning to work
4 Child teething, biting
5 Mother pregnant
6 Child still hungry
7 Child would not suck/rejected
8 Breastfeeding took too long/was tiring
9 Mother was ill
10 Child was ill
11 Inconvenient/no place to feed
12 Other (Please specify at next question)

IF OTHER AT LBRST4
25a. XLBRST4 — WRITE IN other reason

ALL
26. BOTTLE4 — Do you give your child milk from a bottle at present even if only occasionally?
(apart from expressed breast milk)?
1 Yes
2 No

IF YES AT BOTTLE4
27. CUP4 — Do you give him/her milk from a cup, glass or beaker at present, even if only occasionally?
1 Yes (even if occasionally)
2 No

IF YES AT BOTTLE4
28. NBOTTLE4 — How many bottles of milk does s/he drink each day?
IF LESS THAN ONE A DAY, PLEASE ENTER '0'

IF YES AT CUP4
29. NCUP4 — How many cups of milk does s/he drink each day?
IF LESS THAN ONE A DAY, PLEASE ENTER '0'

30. MILKTYP4 — IF YES AT BOTTLE4 OR YES AT CUP4
Which kind of milk do you give your child MOST of the time at the moment?
DO NOT INCLUDE BREAST MILK
1 Liquid cows milk - ordinary/full fat
2 Liquid cows milk - semi-skimmed
3 Liquid cows milk - skimmed
4 Cow and Gate Premium (powder)
5 Cow and Gate Nutrilon Premium (powder)
6 Cow and Gate Premium (ready-to-feed)
7 Cow and Gate Plus (powder)
8 Cow and Gate Nutrilon Plus (powder)
9 Cow and Gate Plus (ready-to-feed)
10 Cow and Gate Formula S (powder)
11 Cow and Gate InfaSoy (powder)
12 Cow and Gate Step-up
13 SMA Gold Cap (powder)
14 SMA Gold Cap (ready-to-feed)
15 SMA White Cap (powder)
16 SMA White Cap (ready-to-feed)
17 SMA Wysoy (powder)
18 SMA Progress
19 Milupa Milumil (powder)
20 Milupa Aptamil (powder)
21 Milupa Prematil (powder)
22 Farley's Follow-on Milk
23 Farley's First Milk
24 Farley's Second Milk
25 Farley's OsterSoy
26 Boots Follow-on Milk (powder)
27 Boots Follow-on Milk (ready-to-feed)
28 Other kind of milk Please specify at next question

IF OTHER AT MILKTYP4
30a. XMILKTY4 — WRITE IN name of milk

31. STARTBO4 — IF (LIQUID COW'S MILK AT MILKTYA) AND (MILK NOT AS DRINK AT W3COW OR NO INTERVIEW AT WAVE3)
How old was 'Name' when you started giving this milk as a drink?
RECORD NUMBER OF MONTHS

2

32. MILKTY4A — IF YES AT BOTTLE4 OR YES AT CUP4
Do you ever give your child any other kinds of milk to drink?
1 Yes
2 No

IF YES AT MILKTY4A
33. MILKTY4B — Which other kinds of milk do you give your child?
DO NOT INCLUDE BREAST MILK
Up to 3 answers from
1 Liquid cows milk - ordinary/full fat
2 Liquid cows milk - semi-skimmed
3 Liquid cows milk - skimmed
4 Cow and Gate Premium (powder)
5 Cow and Gate Nutrilon Premium (powder)
6 Cow and Gate Premium (ready-to-feed)
7 Cow and Gate Plus (powder)
8 Cow and Gate Nutrilon Plus (powder)
9 Cow and Gate Plus (ready-to-feed)
10 Cow and Gate Formula S (powder)
11 Cow and Gate InfaSoy (powder)
12 Cow and Gate Step-up
13 SMA Gold Cap (powder)
14 SMA Gold Cap (ready-to-feed)
15 SMA White Cap (powder)
16 SMA White Cap (ready-to-feed)
17 SMA Wysoy (powder)
18 SMA Progress
19 Milupa Milumil (powder)
20 Milupa Aptamil (powder)
21 Milupa Prematil (powder)
22 Farley's Follow-on Milk
23 Farley's First Milk
24 Farley's Second Milk
25 Farley's OsterSoy
26 Boots Follow-on Milk (powder)
27 Boots Follow-on Milk (ready-to-feed)
28 Other kind of milk Please specify at next question

IF OTHER AT MILKTY4B
33a. XMILK4B — WRITE IN name of milk

34. STARCOW4 — IF (LIQUID COW'S MILK AT MILKTY4B) AND (MILK NOT AS DRINK AT W3COW OR NO INTERVIEW AT WAVE3) AND (NOT LIQUID COW'S MILK AT MILKTY4)
How old was 'Name' when you started giving liquid cows milk?
RECORD NUMBER OF MONTHS

35. ADDMILK4 — IF YES AT BOTTLE4 OR YES AT CUP4
Do you ever add anything to the milk in the bottle/cup?
1 Yes
2 No

IF YES AT ADDMILK4
36. WHATADD4 — What do you add to the milk?
1 Sugar
2 Honey
3 Other (Please specify at next question)

IF OTHER AT WHATADD4
36a. XWHATAD4 — WRITE IN what is added to the milk

ALL
37. DRINK4 — Do you give your child water or any drinks other than milk?
1 Yes
2 No

Drinks Diary

IF YES AT DRINK4
38. DDIARY4 — Starting with when 'Name' woke up, I'd like you to tell me all the drinks you gave him/her yesterday, other than milk.

38a. TIMDRNK4 — At which time of the day did he/she (first) have a drink?
PROMPT AS NECESSARY
1 Between 6am and 10am
2 Between 10am and 2pm
3 Between 2pm and 6pm
4 Between 6pm and 10pm
5 Between 10pm and 6am

38b. TYPDRNK4 — What type of drink did he/she have?

3

Bottom panel (questions 36c–43a)

36c. OTHDRNK4 — WRITE IN other drink (and/or brand where applicable

38d. ANYMORE — Did you give your child any other drinks yesterday?

1 Yes
2 No

Drinks Diary - Coding frame

1 Baby Ribena
2 Ribena (not baby)
3 Fruit juice/drinks (not teas)
31 Pure / Fresh (ready to drink, no added sugar)
311 Baby drink
312 Other pure/fresh juice
32 Concentrated baby fruit drink
33 Fruit squash (other concentrated) - no added sugar
34 Fruit squash (other concentrated) - added sugar
4 Herbal
41 Homemade
411 Fennel
412 Camomile
413 Clove
414 Cardamum
415 Aniseed
416 Mixed
417 Other homemade herbal
42 Commercial baby drink
421 Fennel
422 Orange and clove
423 Camomile
424 Lemon, barley and camomile
425 Peach and herb
426 Hibiscus, apple & rosehip
427 Other commercial herbal
5 Water / Gripe water
51 Water from the tap
52 Boiled tap water
53 Water with sugar/honey added
54 Mineral water
55 Purified water bought from a shop
56 Gripe water
57 Other water drink
6 Tea / Coffee / Fruit tea
61 Milk, no sugar
62 Milk and sugar
63 Sugar, no milk
64 Neither milk or sugar
65 Fruit tea
7 Fizzy drinks eg cola, lemonade
8 Other milk-based drinks
81 Chocolate / cocoa
82 Malt drink
83 Other milk-based drinks
9 Other drink (Please specify at next question)

IF YES AT DRINK4

39. BOTTCUP4 — Do you usually give these drinks in a bottle or in a cup or glass?

1 Bottle
2 Cup or glass
3 Uses both

40. HOLD4 — Does s/he hold the bottles or cups him/herself? PROMPT IF NECESSARY

1 Usually
2 Sometimes
3 Never

41. DKMEAL4 — Does s/he have fruit or vitamin drinks with his/her meals? PROMPT IF NECESSARY

1 Usually
2 Sometimes
3 Never

42. BEDRINK4 — Does s/he usually have a drink before going to bed?

1 Yes
2 No

IF YES AT BEDRINK4

43. BEDWHAT4 — What drink(s) does s/he usually have? Up to 4 answers from

1 Milk
2 Malt drink such as horlicks, ovaltine
3 Hot chocolate or cocoa
4 Water
5 Tea (not herbal) or coffee
6 Herbal drink, including herbal tea
7 Fruit drink
8 Other (Please specify at next question)

IF OTHER AT BEDWHAT4

43a. XBEDWHA4 — WRITE IN other drink given before bed

Top panel (questions 44–50)

IF YES AT DRINK4

44. BOTTBED4 — Does s/he take a bottle to bed? PROMPT IF NECESSARY

1 Usually
2 Sometimes
3 Never

Drink Frequencies Table

IF YES AT DRINK4

45. DKINTRO4 — I am going to ask you how often 'Name' has different types of drinks

DFREQU4 — How often does she/he drink

1 water, including fizzy water
2 pure or fresh fruit juice
3 herbal drinks
4 tea or coffee
5 fizzy drinks such as lemonade

SHOW CARD F OR PROMPT IF NECESSARY FOR EACH OF THE ABOVE

1 More than once a day
2 Once a day
3 Three or more times a week
4 At least once a week
5 Less than once a week
6 Never

IF NO SOLID FOOD GIVEN AT SOLIDS1 OR SOLIDS2 OR SOLIDS3

46. SOLIDS4 — Do you give your child foods such as cereal, rusk or any other kind of solid food (soft weaning food), including any that you make yourself?

1 Yes
2 No

IF YES AT SOLIDS4

47. SOLAGE4 — How old was your child when s/he first had any food apart from milk? PLEASE ENTER NUMBER OF MONTHS

IF YES AT SOLIDS1 OR SOLIDS2 OR SOLIDS3 OR SOLIDS4

48. SOLR4M — Do you regularly feed him/her at least three times a day?

1 Yes
2 No

49. SOLYEST4 — Did your child eat any solid food yesterday?

1 Yes
2 No

Solid food Diary

IF YES AT SOLYEST4

50. DIARY4 — Starting with when 'Name' woke up, I'd like you to tell me all the food you gave him/her yesterday, including any sweets, snacks or small pieces of food.

50a. Timefeed — At which time of the day did s/he eat this food?

1 Between 6am and 10am
2 Between 10am and 2pm
3 Between 2pm and 6pm
4 Between 6pm and 10pm
5 Between 10pm and 6am

50b. Typefood — What type of food did s/he eat?

50c. Othfood — PLEASE WRITE IN other food

50d. Amount — Did s/he eat just one or two mouthfuls of this, or more than that?

1 One or two mouthfuls
2 More than one or two mouthfuls

50e. Anymore — Did you give your child any more food yesterday?

1 Yes
2 No

Food Diary - Coding frame

1 Asian food
11 Chapati
111 Chapati only
112 Chapati dipped in curry / sauce
12 Dahl or other pulse dish
121 Dahl / pulse dish only
122 Dahl / pulse dish with rice
13 Vegetable (potato) dish / curry
131 Vegetable dish only
132 Vegetable dish with rice
14 Meat dish / curry
141 Meat dish only
142 Meat dish with rice (+vegetables)
15 Fish or seafood dish / curry
151 Fish dish only
152 Fish dish with rice (+vegetables)
16 Dairy food dish (eg. Paneer)
161 Dairy dish only
162 Dairy dish with rice (+vegetables)

Page 6

- 17 Other savoury
- 171 Other savoury food only
- 172 Other savoury food with rice (+veg)
- 18 Dessert / sweets
- 19 Other Asian

- 2 Commercial baby food
- 21 Baby rice / Cereals
- 211 Plain baby rice
- 212 Flavoured baby rice
- 213 Porridge
- 214 Cereal with fruit
- 215 Other cereal
- 22 Rusk
- 221 Plain
- 222 Flavoured
- 223 Plain, low sugar
- 224 Flavoured, low sugar
- 23 Meat (and vegetables/rice/pasta)
- 231 Beef
- 232 Chicken / Turkey
- 233 Lamb
- 234 Pork
- 235 Bacon
- 236 Other / mixed
- 24 Fish (and vegetables/rice/pasta)
- 25 Vegetables / rice / pasta
- 251 Mixed vegetables
- 252 Vegetables and rice
- 253 Vegetables and pasta
- 254 Cheese and vegetables
- 255 Cheese and pasta (and vegetables)
- 26 Puddings / desserts / fruit
- 261 Pure fruit / fruit salad
- 262 Rice pudding / semolina
- 263 Chocolate pudding
- 264 Yoghurt / fromage frais
- 265 Other fruit pudding
- 266 Egg custard (with rice)
- 267 Creme caramel
- 27 Baby sauces
- 271 White
- 272 Cheese
- 273 Tomato
- 274 Other sauce

- 3 Other cereal / bread
- 31 Porridge
- 32 Other cereal
- 33 Bread / sandwiches / toast
- 331 Slice of bread / toast
- 332 Cheese sandwich / toast
- 333 Egg sandwich / toast
- 334 Meat sandwich / toast
- 335 Vegetable sandwich / toast
- 336 Jam / sweet spread / toast
- 337 Other sandwich / toast
- 34 Rice only
- 35 Pasta only

- 4 Meat or Fish dish
- 41 Meat or fish only
- 411 Beef
- 412 Chicken/Turkey
- 413 Lamb
- 414 Pork
- 415 Bacon/ham
- 416 Fish
- 417 Other or mixed meat or fish
- 42 With vegetables
- 421 Beef
- 422 Chicken/Turkey
- 423 Lamb
- 424 Pork
- 425 Bacon/ham
- 426 Fish
- 427 Other or mixed meat/fish
- 43 With rice or pasta
- 431 Beef
- 432 Chicken/Turkey
- 433 Lamb
- 434 Pork
- 435 Bacon/ham
- 436 Fish
- 437 Other or mixed meat/fish
- 44 With vegetables and rice/pasta
- 441 Beef
- 442 Chicken / Turkey
- 443 Lamb
- 444 Pork
- 445 Bacon
- 446 Fish (including tuna)
- 447 Other or mixed meat/fish
- 45 With chips
- 451 Beef
- 452 Chicken / Turkey
- 453 Lamb
- 454 Pork
- 455 Bacon
- 456 Fish (including tuna)
- 457 Other or mixed meat/fish
- 46 With chips and vegetables
- 461 Beef
- 462 Chicken / Turkey
- 463 Lamb
- 464 Pork

Page 7

- 465 Bacon
- 466 Fish (including tuna)
- 467 Other or mixed meat/fish

- 5 Vegetable, potato or pulse dish
- 51 Fresh vegetables / potatoes
- 52 Baked potato
- 521 Baked potato only
- 522 Baked potato with cheese
- 523 Baked potato with meat
- 524 Baked potato with fish (eg. tuna)
- 525 Baked potato with beans / vegetables
- 53 Other potato products (eg. chips)
- 54 Processed vegetables - frozen, tinned, baked beans etc
- 55 Fresh, with rice/pasta
- 56 Processed, with rice/pasta

- 6 Dairy or Egg
- 61 Egg
- 611 Egg only
- 612 Egg and cheese (+vegetables) eg. omelette
- 613 Egg and meat (+vegetables)
- 614 Egg and vegetables
- 62 Egg yolk only
- 63 Cheese
- 64 Yoghurt, fromage frais

- 7 Fruit or nuts
- 71 Fresh fruit
- 72 Processed fruit eg. tinned
- 73 Nuts
- 74 Dried fruit and nuts

- 8 Desserts / confectionery / biscuits
- 81 Biscuits
- 82 Cakes / pastries
- 83 Pies / puddings eg. egg custard
- 84 Sweets / chocolate
- 85 Icecream / sorbet
- 86 Other desserts or confectionery

- 9 Miscellaneous
- 91 Pizza
- 92 Crisps / savoury snacks
- 94 Vegetable protein / vegetable sausages
- 95 Other miscellaneous

52. MILKMIX4

IF YES AT SOLIDS1 OR SOLIDS2 OR SOLIDS3 OR SOLIDS4

Do you ever use milk to mix up his/her food?

1 Yes
2 No

53. TYPEMIX4

IF YES AT MILKMIX4

Do you use milk especially for babies, liquid cows milk, or something else?
Up to 3 answers from

1 Baby milk
2 Liquid cows milk, or combination of baby milk and liquid cows milk
3 Something else (Please specify at next question)

53a. XTYPEMI4

IF OTHER AT TYPEMIXR

WRITE IN what else is used to mix up food

Food Frequencies Table

54. FdIntro4

IF YES AT SOLIDS1 OR SOLIDS2 OR SOLIDS3 OR SOLIDS4

I am going to ask you how often you give your child different types of foods

FFrequ4

How often do you usually give your child

1 meat or fish
2 cereal, rusk, bread or chapati
3 rice, pasta or potatoes
4 eggs, yoghurt, and cheese
5 fresh or dried vegetables
6 fresh fruit
7 puddings and desserts
8 sweets and chocolate

SHOW CARD F OR PROMPT IF NECESSARY FOR EACH OF THE ABOVE

1 More than once a day
2 Once a day
3 Three or more times a week
4 At least once a week
5 Less than once a week
6 Never

IF YES AT SOLR4M AND NOT THREE MEALS A DAY AT SOLR2M AND SOLR3M

51. SOLIDOL4

How old was your child when he/she regularly started having three meals of solid food a day?
PLEASE ANSWER IN MONTHS

67a. XNOTEAT4 — IF OTHER AT NOTEAT4
WRITE IN other food not eaten by child

68. VIT4 — ALL
Do you give your child any extra vitamins at the moment (apart from any vitamin drinks you have already mentioned)?
1 Yes
2 No

69. VITDROP4 — IF YES AT VIT4
Do you use Children's Vitamin Drops from the child health clinic or another brand?
1 Children's Vitamin Drops
2 Other (Please specify at next question)

69a. XVITDRP4 — IF OTHER AT VITDROP4
WRITE IN name of other brand

70. VITBUY4 — IF CHILDREN'S VITAMIN DROPS AT VITDROP4
Do you buy the vitamins or do you get them free or at reduced price from the clinic or on prescription?
1 Buy
2 Free
3 Buy at reduced price
4 On prescription

71. VITOTHER4 — IF OTHER AT VITDROP4
Do you buy the vitamins or do you get them on prescription?
1 Buy
2 On Prescription

72. PROBWEA4 — ALL
Have you had any difficulty feeding 'Name' solid foods since I/we last spoke to you?
1 Yes
2 No

73. PROBFEE4 — ALL
Have you had any (other) problems feeding him/her since I/we last spoke to you?"
1 Yes
2 No

62a. XOTHAVD4 — IF OTHER AT WHYAVD4
WRITE IN other reason for avoiding particular ingredients

63. EASYFEE4 — ALL
Compared to other children of the same age, how easy or difficult do you find 'Name' to feed? PROMPT IF NECESSARY
1 Very Easy
2 Easy
3 About average
4 Difficult
5 Very difficult

64. APPETIT4 — ALL
Does 'Name' have a good appetite, an average appetite or a poor appetite?
1 Good
2 Average
3 Poor

65. VARIETY4 — ALL
Does 'Name' eat a variety of foods, or would you say s/he is fussy about what s/he will eat?
1 Eats a variety of foods
2 Is fussy about eating

66. WONTEAT4 — ALL
Are there any foods which s/he will not eat because s/he does not like them?
1 Yes
2 No

67. NOTEAT4 — IF YES AT WONTEAT4
What foods won't s/he eat? PLEASE CODE TYPE OF FOOD eg. raw carrot = fresh vegetable Up to 5 answers from
1 Meat
2 Curry or other spicy foods
3 Fish
4 Rice or pasta
5 Bread or chapati
6 Fresh vegetables
7 Other vegetables
8 Fruit
9 Puddings
10 Other (Please specify at next question)

---

55. SPOON4 — IF YES AT SOLIDS1 OR SOLIDS2 OR SOLIDS3 OR SOLIDS4
Does 'Name' usually ...
1 Feed him/herself with his/her fingers
2 Feed him/herself with a spoon or fork
3 Or does someone feed him/her
DO NOT PROMPT - Uses both fingers and spoon
4

56. SAMEFOO4 — Does 'Name'?
1 Always eat the same food as the family
2 Usually eat the same food
3 Occasionally eat the same food or does s/he never eat the same food as the rest of the family
4

57. ALTER4 — IF OTHER THAN NEVER AT SAMEFOO4
Do you ever change the food in any way (for instance, wash the spices off) before you give it to the child?
1 Yes
2 No

58. HOWALT4 — IF YES AT ALTER4
How do you change it? Up to 4 answers from
1 Leave out ingredients
2 Mash or mince it
3 Sieve, blend or liquidise it into a puree
4 Cook the food for longer/to soften it
5 Remove spices or chillis, wash food
6 Add liquid, sauce or yoghurt
7 Other (Please specify at next question)

58a. OTHALT4 — IF OTHER AT HOWALT4
WRITE IN how food is altered

59. FACTORS4 — IF YES AT SOLR4M
How do you choose which solid foods to give to your child? Up to 5 answers from
1 Variety
2 Nutrition generally eg 'balanced diet', 'healthy/fresh food'
3 What the child likes
4 Sugar content
5 No additives
6 Vitamins, iron or minerals
7 Salt content
8 Home cooked
9 Ease of preparation
10 Price
11 Same food as rest of the family
12 Family has halal, vegetarian or other specialised diet
13 Other (Please specify at next question)

59a. XFACTOR4 — IF OTHER AT FACTORS4
WRITE IN other factors

60. AVOIDIN4 — ALL
Are there any foods or ingredients, such as spices, which you don't give your child?
1 Yes
2 No

61. WHATAVD4 — IF YES AT AVOIDIN4
What foods or ingredients do you avoid? Up to 8 answers from
1 Sugar
2 Salt
3 Spices, chillis
4 Additives, colouring, preservatives, E numbers
5 Meat and animal products eg. non-halal meat, animal fat
6 Fish
7 Eggs, milk, cheese and other dairy products
8 Sweets, chocolate and puddings
9 Other (Please specify at next question)

61a. XOTHING4 — IF OTHER AT WHATAVD4
WRITE IN what else is avoided

62. WHYAVD4 — IF YES AT AVOIDIN4
Why do you avoid this(these) food(s) or ingredient(s)? Up to 8 answers from
1 Not beneficial
2 Harmful
3 Allergies, make child ill
4 Child doesn't like them
5 Will develop a sweet tooth
6 Bad for teeth
7 Too strong or hot for child, child too young to digest certain food
8 Religious or traditional reasons, Halal or vegetarian diet
9 Publicity / Media / Advice
10 Other (Please specify at next question)

82. WHYCHEC4 — IF YES AT CHECKUP4

Why did you take him/her there?
Up to 3 answers from

1 Checkup
2 Child was ill (minor illness eg cold)
3 Child has a medical condition (eg hip or heart problem)
4 Concern over child's growth, weight, or diet
5 Child had an accident
6 Other (Please specify at next question)

82a. XWHYCHE4 — IF OTHER AT WHYCHEC4

WRITE IN other reason for taking child for advice or checkup

83. MOSTADV4 — ALL

Since 'Name' was born, who has given you most help or advice about feeding him/her?
Up to 2 answers from

1 Health visitor or midwife
2 Family doctor or staff at the health clinic or hospital
3 Mother or mother-in-law
4 Other relative
5 Friend
6 Voluntary group
7 Haven't needed any help or advice
8 Other (Please specify at next question)

83a. XOTHADV4 — IF OTHER AT MOSTADV4

WRITE IN who else has given most advice

84. MOREADV4 — ALL

Would you have liked more help or advice about feeding your child?

1 Yes
2 No

85. WHATADV4 — IF YES AT MOREADV4

What would you have liked more help or advice about?
PLEASE ANSWER FOR FEEDING ISSUES ONLY
Up to 5 answers from

1 Breastfeeding
2 Bottle feeding
3 Giving solid foods
4 Healthy diet for child
5 Other (Please specify at next question)

85a. XWHATEL4 — IF OTHER AT WHATADV4

WRITE IN what other help or advice mother would have liked

86. LEAFLET4 — ALL

Since we last spoke to you, have you read any books, leaflets, or magazines, or watched any videos about looking after babies?

1 Yes
2 No

87. LEAFGET4 — IF YES AT LEAFLET4

Where did you get it/them from? IF PART OF A BOUNTY PACK, STATE WHO BOUNTY PACK IS FROM
Up to 3 answers from

1 Health visitor/midwife
2 Child health clinic
3 Doctor's surgery
4 Commercial food/baby organisation eg. Boots, baby food company etc
5 Hospital
6 TV programmes
7 Family and friends
8 Library
9 Other (Please specify at next question)

87a. XLEAFGE4 — IF OTHER AT LEAFGET4

WRITE IN where GOT LEAFLETS ETC

88. LEAFLAN4 — IF NOT ENGLISH AT LANGUAG AND NOT WELL AT ENGUND

What language were they in?
Up to 3 answers from

1 English
2 Gujarati
3 Punjabi
4 Bengali
5 Hindi
6 Urdu
7 Other

---

74. WHATPRO4 — IF YES AT PROBWEA4 OR YES AT PROBFEE4

What difficulties or problems have you had (with feeding solid foods)?
Up to 5 answers from

1 Child would not take certain solid foods or drinks
2 Child would not take milk - bottle or breast
3 Child was disinterested in food, or preferred milk
4 Child is sick a lot
5 Child was ill
6 Child would not eat from spoon
7 Child teething
8 Child would only eat small amounts
9 Child is allergic to some foods
10 Some other reason (Please specify at next question)

74a. XOTHPRO4 — IF OTHER AT WHATPRO4

WRITE IN other problems with feeding child

75. PFAMHEL4 — IF YES AT PROBWEA4 OR YES AT PROBFEE4

Did any family or friends give you help or advice about this/these problems?

1 Yes
2 No

76. PFAMWHO4 — IF YES AT PFAMHEL4

Who helped or advised you?
Up to 4 answers from

1 Mother or mother-in-law
2 Sister or sister-in-law
3 Husband
4 Other relative
5 Friend or neighbour

77. POTHHEL4 — IF YES AT PROBWEA4 OR YES AT PROBFEE4

Did anyone else give you help or advice with this/these problems?

1 Yes
2 No

78. WHOHELP4 — IF YES AT POTHHEL4

Who helped or advised you?
Up to 4 answers from

1 Health visitor
2 Doctor at the child health clinic
3 Family doctor
4 Nurse at the doctors surgery
5 Voluntary group for new mothers
6 Someone else (Please specify at next question)

78a. XWHOHEL4 — IF OTHER AT WHOHELP4

WRITE IN who else helped or advised you

79. WHICHGR4 — IF VOLUNTARY GROUP AT WHOHELP4

Which voluntary group helped or advised you

1 a local womens group
2 the National Childbirth Trust
3 La Leche League
4 the Association of Breast Feeding Mothers
5 some other voluntary group?

80. CHECKUP4 — ALL

Have you taken your child anywhere for advice or a checkup in the last six months?

1 Yes
2 No

81. WHERCHE4 — IF YES AT CHECKUP4

Where have you taken him/her? SHOW CARD I
Up to 2 answers from

1 Child health clinic (or health visitor at clinic)
2 Family doctor, clinic at the surgery, other health centre, home visit by doctor
3 Hospital
4 Health visitor
5 Dietician
6 Other (Please specify at next question)

81a. XOTHCHE4 — IF OTHER AT WHERCHE4

WRITE IN where child taken for advice or checkup

IF NO AT HUSBWOR4

101. HUSBAWA4 — Even though he was not working, did he have a job that he was away from last week?
1 Yes
2 No

IF (YES AT HUSBWOR4 OR YES AT HUSBAWA4) AND EITHER [(YES AT HUSBWOR3) OR (YES AT HUSBWOR2 AND NO INTERVIEW AT WAVE 3)]

102. HSAMEJO4 — Was that the same job that he had when we last spoke to you six months ago?
1 Yes
2 No

IF NO AT HUSBAWA4

103. HUSBNOW4 — Last week was he.....
1 Waiting to take up a job that he had already obtained
2 Looking for work
3 Intending to look for work but prevented by temporary sickness or injury
4 Going to school or college full time
5 Permanently unable to work because of long-term sickness or disability
6 Retired
7 Looking after the home or family
8 or was he doing something else?

IF YES AT HUSBWOR4 OR YES AT HUSBAWA4 AND NO/ EMPTY AT HSAMJO4

104. HUSBWK14 — What is your husband's/partner's job?

IF WAITING AT HUSBNOW4

105. HUSBWK24 — What is the job your husband/partner is waiting to take up?

ALL

106. INCOME4 — Could you look at this card and tell me which group represents your current GROSS income (and the income of your husband/partner).
Please include income from all sources before any compulsory deductions such as income tax, national insurance and superannuation contributions?
SHOW CARD C AND PROMPT AS NECESSARY
1 less than £50 per week
2 £50 - less £70 per week
3 £70 - less £100 per week
4 £100 - less £150 per week
5 £150 - less £200 per week
6 £200 - less £250 per week
7 £250 - less £300 per week
8 £300 - less £350 per week
9 £350 - less £400 per week
10 £400 - less £450 per week
11 £450 - less £500 per week
12 £500 or more per week

107. FAMCRED4 — Can I just check are you (or your husband) currently receiving Family Credit?
1 Yes
2 No

108. INCSUP4 — And have you (or your husband) drawn Income Support at any time in the last 14 days?
1 Yes
2 No

109. NEWBAB4A — ASK OR RECORD Have you had another baby since 'Name', or are you pregnant at the moment?
1 Yes, had another baby
2 Yes, pregnant
3 No

IF NO AT NEWBAB4A

110. NEWBAB4B — Do you plan to become pregnant in the next year?
1 Yes
2 No

IF OTHER THAN NO AT NEWBAB4A

111. NEWFEED4 — Do you plan to feed (are you feeding) the new (next) baby in the same way, or differently?
1 Same
2 Differently

13

ALL

89. PAIDWRK4 — I would like to ask some questions about yourself (and your husband/partner). At the moment are you ....
1 doing any paid work, including working at home
2 on paid maternity leave
3 on unpaid maternity leave
4 not working or not on maternity leave?

IF (PAID WORK AT PAIDWRK4) AND [(EITHER PAIDWORK/ MATERNITY LEAVE AT PAIDWRK3) OR (PAIDWORK/ MATERNITY LEAVE AT PAIDWRK2 AND NO INTERVIEW AT WAVE 3)]

90. MSAMEJO4 — Was that the same job that you had as last time / before you had your baby?
1 Yes
2 No

IF ON PAID OR UNPAID MATERNITY LEAVE OR NOT WORKING AT PAIDWRK4

91. WRKPLAN4 — Do you plan to start work (again) in the next two years ....
1 Yes
2 No

IF YES AT WRKPLAN4

92. FULLPAR4 — Do you plan to work full or part-time?
1 Full-time
2 Part-time

IF (PAID WORK AT PAIDRK4) AND [(NO AT MSAMEJO4) OR (NOT WORKING AT PAIDWRK3) OR (NOT WORKING OR NOT ON MATERNITY LEAVE AT PAIDWRK2 AND NO INTERVIEW AT WAVE 3)]

93. SOCTEXT1 — What is your job?

94. WRKHOME4 — Do you work mainly at home or do you go out to work?
1 Mainly at home
2 Go out to work

IF PAID WORK AT PAIDWRK4

95. WHOMIND4 — Who usually looks after the child when you are working? Up to 4 answers from
1 Self
2 Husband or partner
3 Mother
4 Mother-in-law
5 Other female relative
6 Child minder
7 Nursery or creche
8 Someone else (Please specify at next question)

IF OTHER AT WHOMIND4

95a. XWHOMIN4 — WRITE IN WHO ELSE USUALLY LOOKS AFTER CHILD WHEN WORKING

IF OTHER THAN SELF OR HUSBAND AT WHOMIND4

96. PAYMIND4 — Do you pay to have the child looked after?
1 Yes
2 No

IF OTHER THAN SELF AT WHOMIND4

97. MINDFEE4 — Does 'Whoever looks after child' feed the child when you are at work?
1 Yes
2 No

IF YES AT MINDEFEE4

98. DECIDFE4 — Who decides what food to give the child when you are at work?
1 Self
2 Person(s) looking after child

IF NOT SINGLE AT HUSBAND

99. HUSBLIV4 — ASK OR RECORD(May I just check) Is your husband/partner living in this household at the moment?
1 Yes
2 No

IF YES AT HUSBLIV4

100. HUSBWOR4 — Did your husband/partner do any paid work last week that is in the seven days ending last Sunday, either as an employee or self-employed?
1 Yes
2 No

12

IF LENGTH MEASURED

129. LGATTEM4 — Number of attempts at measuring length

130. LGAFCT4 — Special circumstances that might have affected length. Up to 6 answers from
1 No special circumstances
2 Uneven or cramped surface or carpet
3 Did not lie still
4 Legs not straight, one leg only, ankles extended
5 Did not lie flat
6 Head slipped down, not high enough
7 Wearing clothes/nappy
8 Child upset, unwell
9 Child too long for rollametre
10 Other PLEASE WRITE IN AT NEXT QUESTION

IF OTHER AT LGAFCT4

130a. XLGAFCT4 — WRITE IN other circumstances which might have affected supine length

ALL

131. MEASDON4 — Have you entered all measurements?
1 Yes
2 No

ALL

132. FOLLOWU4 — This is the last interview we have planned, but if we wanted to call on you in the future, would it be alright?
1 Yes, it would be alright (Unconditional)
2 No, (Unconditional)
3 Yes (With conditions/ qualifications)

133. OTHPRES4 — INTERVIEWER CODE / Was another adult present at the interview?
1 Yes
2 No

IF YES AT OTHPRES4

134. WHOELSE4 — Who else was present? Up to 4 answers from
1 Interpreter
2 Husband or partner
3 Mother
4 Mother-in-law
5 Other female relative
6 Other male relative
7 Friend or neighbour
8 Other

IF OTHER AT WHOELSE4

134a. XWHOELS4 — WRITE IN Who else was present?

135. INTERP4 — IF NOT ENGLISH AT LANGUAGE / INTERVIEWER CODE / Was an interpreter used, or did you do the interview in another language?
1 Yes
2 No

IF YES AT INTERP4

136. WHOINT4 — Who interpreted?
1 Husband
2 Other family member
3 Friend/ neighbour
4 OPCS/Other Govt. Interpreter
5 Professional Interpreter
6 Interviewer used another language
7 Other

IF OTHER AT WHOINTR4

136a. XWHOINT4 — WRITE IN who interpreted

IF YES AT INTERP4

137. LGEINTR4 — Which language?
1 Gujarati
2 Punjabi
3 Bengali
4 Hindi
5 Urdu
6 Other

ALL

138. NAME4 — CHECK WITH MOTHER Is 'Name' spelt right?
1 Yes
2 No

IF NO AT NAME4

138a. XNAME4 — WRITE IN correct spelling

IF DIFFERENT AT NEWFEED4

112. WHATNEW4 — What will you do (are you doing) differently? Up to 4 answers from
1 Breastfeed instead of bottle feed
2 Bottle feed instead of breastfeed
3 Breastfeed for longer
4 Breastfeed for less time
5 Give different type of milk or food
6 Start feeding solids earlier
7 Start feeding solids later
8 Other (Please specify at next question)

IF OTHER AT WHATNEW4

112a. OTHNEW4 — WRITE IN what mother will do differently

ALL

113. NOWLATER — INTERVIEWER / Do you want to enter the measurements of the child now or later?
1 Now
2 Later

114. DATEMEA4 — Date weighed and measured

115. BABYWT4 — Child's weight (in kilograms)

116. WTREL4 — Do you think the weight is reliable?
1 Yes
2 No

IF BABY WEIGHED

117. WTATTEM4 — NUMBER OF ATTEMPTS AT WEIGHING

118. WTAFCT4 — Special circumstances that might have affected weight. Up to 3 answers from
1 No special circumstances
2 Scales on uneven surface or carpet
3 Wearing clothes/nappy
4 Scales not working properly
5 Child upset, did not keep still or not put on scales properly
6 Child ill
7 Other circumstances (Please specify at next question)

IF OTHER AT WTAFCT4

118a. XWTAFCT4 — WRITE IN other circumstances affecting weight

119. HEADCIR4 — Head circumference (centimetres)

120. HEADREL4 — Do you think the measurement of head circumference is reliable?
1 Yes
2 No

IF HEAD CIRCUMFERENCE MEASURED

121. HDATTEM4 — Number of attempts at measuring head circumference

122. HDAFCT4 — Special circumstances that might have affected measurement. Up to 3 answers from
1 No special circumstances
2 Did not keep still
3 Other circumstances (Please specify at next question)

IF OTHER AT HDAFCT4

122a. XHDAFCT4 — WRITE IN Other circumstances affecting head circumference measurement

123. ARMCIRC4 — Mid upper arm circumference (centimetres)

124. ARMREL4 — Do you think the measurement of arm circumference is reliable?
1 Yes
2 No

IF ARM CIRCUMFERENCE MEASURED

125. ARATTEM4 — Number of attempts at measuring arm circumference

126. ARAFCT4 — Special circumstances that might have affected measurement. Up to 3 answers from
1 No special circumstances
2 Did not keep still
3 Other circumstances (Please specify at next question)

IF OTHER AT ARAFCT4

126a. XARAFCT4 — WRITE IN Other circumstances affecting arm circumference measurement

127. LENGTH4 — Supine length (centimetres)

128. LTHREL4 — Do you think the supine length measurement is reliable?
1 Yes
2 No

List of figures and tables

Chapter 1

Chapter 2

Figures

Tables

Chapter 3

Figures

Tables

Chapter 6

Figures

Tables

Chapter 7

Appendix A

Appendix B

Appendix C

Appendix D

Tables

Appendix E

Tables

Printed in the United Kingdom for the Stationery Office
Dd 0303523   2/97   65536   04/37419